The Heart Healthy Cookbook for Beginners

1500 Days of Easy Recipes to Approach a New Lifestyle with AHA Recommendations and Nutrition Facts.

Have Fun with Easy-to-Make Low Sodium and Low-Fat Recipes to Approach Step-by-Step, a New Lifestyle, Lower Your Blood Pressure and Cholesterol Levels.

4-Week Meal Plan and **10 Handy Tips**

to Easily Keep Your Heart Healthy Included.

Katherine Mason

© **Copyright 2023 - All rights reserved.**

The content contained within this book may not be reproduced, duplicated, or transmitted without direct written permission from the author or the publisher.
Under no circumstances will any blame or legal responsibility be held against the publisher, or author, for any damages, reparation, or monetary loss due to the information contained within this book. Either directly or indirectly.

Legal Notice:
This book is copyright protected. This book is only for personal use. You cannot amend, distribute, sell, use, quote, or paraphrase any part, or the content within this book, without the consent of the author or publisher.

Disclaimer Notice:
Please note the information contained within this document is for educational and entertainment purposes only. All effort has been executed to present accurate, up-to-date, reliable, and complete information. No warranties of any kind are declared or implied. Readers acknowledge that the author is not engaging in the rendering of legal, financial, medical, or professional advice. The content within this book derives from various sources. Please consult a licensed professional before attempting any techniques outlined in this book.

By reading this document, the reader agrees that under no circumstances is the author responsible for any losses, direct or indirect, which are incurred as a result of the use of the information contained within this document, including, but not limited to, — errors, omissions, or inaccuracies.

About the Author

Welcome! Nice to meet you, Katherine here! It means a lot to me!

I've never had heart problems or other cardiovascular diseases until 32. After a culinary vacation with friends in Provence, France, I felt dizzy, sweaty, and had chest pain. I was lucky enough that a friend of mine was a paramedic and helped me lay down till the ambulance arrived and I went to the ER. Long story short: I **risked severe stroke damage,** and even though I've always been a foodie, I've to make drastic changes in my daily habits. I quit smoking. After my nine-to-five job, I began going for long evening walks 3-4 times a week (never been very athletic).

As I said, **I'm a foodie,** and it has been a real challenge to switch my habits and have a more plant-based and fat-free diet. However, I ended up enjoying this new lifestyle more than my old one, as I was able to **lose weight** (I've lost 22 pounds in a year) and **lower my cholesterol level.** So right now, I feel much more energized, in a good mood, and focused!

For this reason, I've gathered some valuable **tips** to give you helpful directions, a short **glossary**, a **28-Days-Meal-Plan,** and many easy and very healthy **recipes** to satisfy every taste so you can share them with your friends and family. Changing habits can be hard at first, but with these delicious options, you won't even remember what you used to eat.

I hope you enjoy these recipes as much as I do every day!

Lots of love,

Katherine

Table Of Content

10 Steps to prevent the risks of heart disease	**22**
Let's go Grocery Shopping!	**25**
4 Tips to make your recipes last longer:	26
Conversion Charts	**27**
Cooking Glossary	**29**
Recipes Alphabetical Index	**14**
Recipes abbreviations	32
Breakfast and Snacks	**33**
1) *Banana Oat Muffins*	34
2) *Raisin Oats with berries*	34
3) *Porridge*	35
4) *Porridge with banana and strawberries*	35
5) *Dark chocolate cookies*	36
6) *Crunchy cereal cookies*	36
7) *Blueberry Soufflé*	37
8) *Vegan chocolate porridge*	37
9) *Blackberries pancakes*	38
10) *Cereal with apples and pears*	38
11) *Ricotta cheese with caramelized apples*	39
12) *Bananas and honey bars*	39
13) *Berries cake*	40
14) *Berries salad*	40
15) *Chocolate porridge*	41
16) *Mango porridge*	41
17) *Greek yoghurt granola*	42
18) *Melon salad with berries*	42
19) *Fruit tortillas*	43
20) *Cottage cheese with granola*	43
21) *Raisins couscous*	44
22) *Granola with cranberries*	44
23) *Blueberry porridge with banana*	45

24)	Muffins with pumpkin	45
25)	Mustard sandwich	46
26)	Couscous with peaches	46
27)	Quinoa chocolate snack	47
28)	Apple sauce with cinnamon	47
29)	Whole-wheat bread	48
30)	Oatmeal blackberry waffle	48
31)	Chickpea bread roll	49
32)	Sommer rice pudding	49
33)	Flaxseeds rye bread	50
34)	Yoghurt and apricots pancakes	50
35)	Pumpkin pancakes	51
36)	Papaya salad	51
37)	Antioxidants salad	52
38)	Orange oatmeal	52
39)	Cinnamon pancakes	53
40)	Vanilla soufflé	53
41)	Rice pudding	54
42)	Blueberry bagel	54
43)	Banana bread	55
44)	Sourdough Bread	55
45)	Tomato bread	56
46)	Buckwheat bread	56
47)	Cornbread	57
48)	Gluten-free buns	57
49)	Raisin bread	58
50)	Caramel overnight oats	58
51)	Red smoothie	59
52)	Coconut smoothie	59
53)	Pudding with spinach	60
54)	Strawberry smoothie	60
55)	Green smoothie	61
56)	Blue smoothie	61
57)	Coconut shake	62
58)	Walnut shake	62
59)	Yellow smoothie	63
60)	Cinnamon mix cream	63

61)	Mango smoothie	64
62)	Dates smoothie	64
63)	Peach smoothie	65
64)	Peanut butter shake	65
65)	Summer smoothie	66
66)	Kale smoothie	66
67)	Fried bananas	67
68)	Sweet potatoes fries	67
69)	Spiced veggie rolls	68
70)	Veggie sticks with mustard	68
71)	Tumeric latte with honey	69
72)	Ginger muffins	69

Lunch — 70

73)	Stuffed peppers	71
74)	Sautéed artichokes	71
75)	Hummus wraps with avocado	72
76)	Vegetable quiche	72
77)	Pasta with tuna and broccoli	73
78)	Bean soup with chicken	73
79)	Chickpea salad	74
80)	Black beans salad	74
81)	Chicken with herbs and pumpkin	75
82)	Tacos mix	75
83)	Spinach quiche with sweet potato	76
84)	Mexican salad	76
85)	Stuffed tomatoes with salmon	77
86)	Cauliflower rice with salmon	77
87)	Chicken rice with broccoli	78
88)	Chicken veggie mix	78
89)	Stuffed chicken with spinach	79
90)	Sweet potatoes with avocado	79
91)	Chicken curry and rice	80
92)	Spiced roasted chicken with potatoes	80
93)	Chickpea curry and rice	81

94)	Chickpea salad with dressing	81
95)	Spinach and potato pie	82
96)	Cucumber mixed salad	82
97)	Chicken tortillas	83
98)	Ground beef chili	83
99)	Vegetable chili	84
101)	Stuffed potatoes with vegetables	85
102)	Greens chicken quinoa	85
103)	Crispy nuggets with greens	86
104)	Paella with peas	86
105)	Greens-stuffed mushrooms	87
106)	Chicken with snap peas	87
107)	Veggie ratatouille	88
108)	Spinach pizza	88
109)	Mango mix sandwich	89
110)	Cauliflower greens rice	89
111)	Cucumber wraps	90
112)	Rice with beets	90
113)	Curry loin rice	91
114)	Chicken fricassee with peas	91
115)	Fish & chips with greens	92
116)	Multigrain turkey sandwich	92
117)	Beef rice	93
118)	Cod salad	93
119)	Melon-chicken salad	94
120)	Roasted greens risotto	94
121)	Lentil Sloppy Joe	95
122)	Chicken fruit skewers	95
123)	Turmeric chicken risotto	96
124)	Stuffed pumpkins	96
125)	Asian spicy chicken	97
126)	Rice salad with beets	97
127)	Boston baked beans (quick version)	98
128)	Colorful Thanksgiving	98
129)	Black beans burger	99
130)	Kidney beans gumbo	99
131)	Orange salad	100

132)	*Shrimps risotto*	100
133)	*Spinach pasta*	101
134)	*Rye pasta with spinach*	101
135)	*Greens casserole*	102
136)	*Greens muffins*	102
137)	*Roasted salmon with roasted greens*	103
138)	*Fried fish with spinach*	103
139)	*Scrambled eggs with ricotta*	104
140)	*Tomato omelet*	104
141)	*Couscous soup*	105
142)	*Classic olive salad*	105
143)	*Millet with greens*	106
144)	*Coconut curry with rice*	106
145)	*Roasted chickpeas with avocado*	107
146)	*Quick avocado toast with tomatoes*	107
147)	*Creamy mushrooms*	108
148)	*Eggplant -potato mix*	108
149)	*Summer bruschetta*	109
150)	*Leek with eggplants*	109
151)	*Colorful crusted salmon*	110
152)	*Honey walnut shrimps mix*	110
153)	*Quiche with kale and pumpkin*	111
154)	*Taleggio bowl with cranberries*	111
155)	*Kale mixed salad*	112
156)	*Mexican cheesy nachos*	112
157)	*Summer skewers*	113
158)	*Shrimps mixed salad*	113
159)	*Spinach quesadilla*	114
160)	*Spinach mixed eggs*	114
161)	*Lemon pasta*	115
162)	*Yellow rice salad*	115
163)	*Rice noodles with tomatoes*	116
164)	*Whole grain rice with string beans*	116
165)	*Thyme pasta with walnuts*	117
166)	*Green mix noodles*	117
167)	*Roasted Brussel sprouts mix*	118
168)	*Griddled beef (Italian version)*	118

169)	*Griddled beef quinoa*	119
170)	*Greens tartlets*	119
171)	*Sweetly spiced chips*	120
172)	*Greens quick fritters*	120
173)	*Spinach and ricotta tart*	121
174)	*Italian classic rice*	121

Dinner 122

175)	*Cauliflower sweet soup*	123
176)	*Mediterranean red soup*	123
177)	*Couscous greens soup*	124
178)	*Italian minestrone*	124
179)	*Yellow turmeric soup*	125
180)	*Sweet ginger soup*	125
181)	*Leek – lentil soup*	126
182)	*Summer corn soup*	126
183)	*Fresh shrimps - cuttlefish soup*	127
184)	*Green broccoli pureed soup*	127
185)	*Classic goulash*	128
186)	*Veggie Goulash*	128
187)	*Mexican pozole mix*	129
188)	*Cashew salad mix*	129
189)	*Easy vegan nuggets*	130
190)	*Creamy greens roll-up*	130
191)	*Easy roasted potatoes dish*	131
192)	*Cheesy potato soup*	131
193)	*Chicken mix soup*	132
194)	*Yellow greens soup*	132
195)	*Peppers creamy soup*	133
196)	*Julienne zucchini soup*	133
197)	*Green soup*	134
198)	*Pumpkin stew*	134
199)	*Creamy curry-cumin soup*	135
200)	*Cold greens & fish soup*	135
201)	*Old west soup*	136

202)	*Spanish gazpacho*	136
203)	*Fresh cucumber finger food*	137
204)	*Red skewers*	137
205)	*Quick avocado-mustard rolls*	138
206)	*Healthy tostones*	138
207)	*Italian ravioli pan*	139
208)	*Lentil dahl*	139
209)	*Classic gnocchi with sauce*	140
210)	*Chestnut gnocchi with champignons*	140
211)	*Lemon tagliatelle*	141
212)	*Whole grain rigatoni with pesto*	141
213)	*Noodle soup with kale*	142
214)	*Gado-gado Asian salad*	142
215)	*Asian spring rolls*	143
216)	*Cilantro -shrimps rice*	143
217)	*Thai curry chicken*	144
218)	*Healthy thai salad*	144
219)	*Asian quinoa salad*	145
220)	*Spicy shrimps salad*	145
221)	*Healthy peanut bowl*	146
222)	*Vegan avocado sushi*	146
223)	*Sweet walnuts casserole*	147
224)	*Healthy veg. Mac & Cheese*	147
225)	*Brussels sprouts spaghetti*	148
226)	*Shepherd's Pie*	148
227)	*Healthy burger plate*	149
228)	*Salmon burger*	149
229)	*Green steak*	150
230)	*Easy and quick bagel*	150
231)	*Caesar summer Pasta*	151
232)	*Mixed jalapeño toasts*	151
233)	*Parmesan crackers*	152
234)	*Savory snacks*	152
235)	*Shrimps couscous*	153
236)	*Burger mixed salad*	153
237)	*Flatbread*	154
238)	*Classic focaccia*	154

239)	Chicken quesadillas	155
240)	Sweet potato quesadillas	155
241)	Horseradish shrimps	156
242)	Hash muffins	156
243)	Creamy dip	157
244)	Corn salad	157
245)	Lemon cream	158
246)	Mexican casserole	158
247)	Vegan gratin	159
248)	Delicious turkey treats	159
249)	Cauliflower healthy gnocchi	160
250)	Arrowroot -apple fritters	160
251)	Corn fritters with ricotta	161
252)	Kale tortillas	161
253)	Whole-grain salmon pasta	162
254)	Choco-chickpeas	162
255)	Eggplant-shrimps skewers	163
256)	Grapefruit salmon	163
257)	Herbs chicken	164
258)	Grilled chicken & green sauce	164
259)	Summer greens spaghetti	165
260)	Hazelnuts salad	165
261)	Summer mango snacks	166
262)	Pomegranate pralines	166
263)	Crunchy cookies	167
264)	Delicious pecan bars	167
265)	Classic roasted almond	168
266)	Choco-banana ice cream	168
267)	Choco-pumpkin cookies	169
268)	Healthy granola bars	169
269)	Mulberries cup	170
270)	Healthy blueberry pie	170
271)	Classic berries cake	171
272)	Berries tostadas	171
273)	Berry sherbet	172
274)	Strawberries pie	172
275)	French brioche	173

276)	*Salty French croissants*	173
277)	*Choco mousse*	174
278)	*Dipped pineapple with ricotta*	174
279)	*Easy dipped apples*	175
280)	*Quick blackberry smoothie*	175
281)	*Caribbean skewers*	176
282)	*Mixed fruits skewers*	176
283)	*Choco-dipped apples*	177
284)	*Summer popsicles*	177
285)	*Apple-cinnamon crumble*	178
286)	*Oatmeal little sweets*	178
287)	*Orange sauce pancakes*	179
288)	*Healthy pink ice cream*	179
289)	*Healthy lemon cake*	180
290)	*Coconut little sweets*	180
291)	*Coco-choco cupcakes*	181
292)	*Little blue cake*	181
293)	*Fresh roll-ups*	182
294)	*Easy chip cookies*	182
295)	*Cranberry muffins*	183
296)	*Little cheesecake*	183
297)	*Classic choco berries*	184
298)	*Berries summer shortcake*	184
299)	*Berries chia pudding*	185
300)	*Red skewers with choco drizzle*	185

4-Weeks-Meal-Plan **187**

Recipes Alphabetical Index

Number	Breakfast and Snacks	Page
37)	Antioxidants salad	52
28)	Apple sauce with cinnamon	47
43)	Banana bread	55
1)	Banana Oat Muffins	34
12)	Bananas and honey bars	39
13)	Berries cake	40
14)	Berries salad	40
9)	Blackberries pancakes	38
56)	Blue smoothie	61
42)	Blueberry bagel	54
23)	Blueberry porridge with banana	45
7)	Blueberry Soufflé	37
46)	Buckwheat bread	56
50)	Caramel overnight oats	58
10)	Cereal with apples and pears	38
31)	Chickpea bread roll	49
15)	Chocolate porridge	41
60)	Cinnamon mix cream	63
39)	Cinnamon pancakes	53
57)	Coconut shake	62
52)	Coconut smoothie	59
47)	Cornbread	57
20)	Cottage cheese with granola	43
26)	Couscous with peaches	46
6)	Crunchy cereal cookies	36
5)	Dark chocolate cookies	36
62)	Dates smoothie	64
33)	Flaxseeds rye bread	50
67)	Fried bananas	67
19)	Fruit tortillas	43
72)	Ginger muffins	69
48)	Gluten-free buns	57
22)	Granola with cranberries	44
17)	Greek yoghurt granola	42
55)	Green smoothie	61
66)	Kale smoothie	66

16)	Mango porridge	41
61)	Mango smoothie	64
18)	Melon salad with berries	42
24)	Muffins with pumpkin	45
25)	Mustard sandwich	46
30)	Oatmeal blackberry waffle	48
38)	Orange oatmeal	52
36)	Papaya salad	51
63)	Peach smoothie	65
64)	Peanut butter shake	65
3)	Porridge	35
4)	Porridge with banana and strawberries	35
53)	Pudding with spinach	60
35)	Pumpkin pancakes	51
27)	Quinoa chocolate snack	47
49)	Raisin bread	58
2)	Raisin Oats with berries	34
21)	Raisins couscous	44
51)	Red smoothie	59
41)	Rice pudding	54
11)	Ricotta cheese with caramelized apples	39
32)	Sommer rice pudding	49
44)	Sourdough Bread	55
69)	Spiced veggie rolls	68
54)	Strawberry smoothie	60
65)	Summer smoothie	66
68)	Sweet potatoes fries	67
45)	Tomato bread	56
71)	Tumeric latte with honey	69
40)	Vanilla soufflé	53
8)	Vegan chocolate porridge	37
70)	Veggie sticks with mustard	68
58)	Walnut shake	62
29)	Whole-wheat bread	48
59)	Yellow smoothie	63
34)	Yoghurt and apricots pancakes	50

Number	Lunch	Page
125)	Asian spicy chicken	97
78)	Bean soup with chicken	73
117)	Beef rice	93
129)	Black beans burger	99
80)	Black beans salad	74
127)	Boston baked beans (quick version)	98
110)	Cauliflower greens rice	89
86)	Cauliflower rice with salmon	77
91)	Chicken curry and rice	80
114)	Chicken fricassee with peas	91
122)	Chicken fruit skewers	95
87)	Chicken rice with broccoli	78
97)	Chicken tortillas	83
88)	Chicken veggie mix	78
81)	Chicken with herbs and pumpkin	75
106)	Chicken with snap peas	87
93)	Chickpea curry and rice	81
79)	Chickpea salad	74
94)	Chickpea salad with dressing	81
142)	Classic olive salad	105
144)	Coconut curry with rice	106
118)	Cod salad	93
151)	Colorful crusted salmon	110
128)	Colorful Thanksgiving	98
141)	Couscous soup	105
147)	Creamy mushrooms	108
103)	Crispy nuggets with greens	86
96)	Cucumber mixed salad	82
111)	Cucumber wraps	90
113)	Curry loin rice	91
148)	Eggplant -potato mix	108
115)	Fish & chips with greens	92
138)	Fried fish with spinach	103
166)	Green mix noodles	117
135)	Greens casserole	102
102)	Greens chicken quinoa	85
136)	Greens muffins	102
172)	Greens quick fritters	120
170)	Greens tartlets	119
105)	Greens-stuffed mushrooms	87
168)	Griddled beef (Italian version)	118
169)	Griddled beef quinoa	119
98)	Ground beef chili	83
152)	Honey walnut shrimps mix	110
75)	Hummus wraps with avocado	72
174)	Italian classic rice	121
155)	Kale mixed salad	112

130)	Kidney beans gumbo	99
150)	Leek with eggplants	109
161)	Lemon pasta	115
121)	Lentil Sloppy Joe	95
109)	Mango mix sandwich	89
119)	Melon-chicken salad	94
156)	Mexican cheesy nachos	112
84)	Mexican salad	76
143)	Millet with greens	106
116)	Multigrain turkey sandwich	92
131)	Orange salad	100
104)	Paella with peas	86
77)	Pasta with tuna and broccoli	73
153)	Quiche with kale and pumpkin	111
146)	Quick avocado toast with tomatoes	107
163)	Rice noodles with tomatoes	116
126)	Rice salad with beets	97
112)	Rice with beets	90
167)	Roasted Brussel sprouts mix	118
145)	Roasted chickpeas with avocado	107
120)	Roasted greens risotto	94
137)	Roasted salmon with roasted greens	103
134)	Rye pasta with spinach	101
74)	Sautéed artichokes	71
139)	Scrambled eggs with ricotta	104
158)	Shrimps mixed salad	113
132)	Shrimps risotto	100
92)	Spiced roasted chicken with potatoes	80
95)	Spinach and potato pie	82
173)	Spinach and ricotta tart	121
160)	Spinach mixed eggs	114
133)	Spinach pasta	101
108)	Spinach pizza	88
159)	Spinach quesadilla	114
83)	Spinach quiche with sweet potato	76
89)	Stuffed chicken with spinach	79
73)	Stuffed peppers	71
101)	Stuffed potatoes with vegetables	85
124)	Stuffed pumpkins	96
85)	Stuffed tomatoes with salmon	77
149)	Summer bruschetta	109
157)	Summer skewers	113
90)	Sweet potatoes with avocado	79
171)	Sweetly spiced chips	120
82)	Tacos mix	75
154)	Taleggio bowl with cranberries	111
165)	Thyme pasta with walnuts	117

140)	Tomato omelet	104
123)	Turmeric chicken risotto	96
99)	Vegetable chili	84
76)	Vegetable quiche	72
107)	Veggie ratatouille	88
164)	Whole grain rice with string beans	116
162)	Yellow rice salad	115

Number	Dinner	Page
250)	Arrowroot -apple fritters	160
219)	Asian quinoa salad	145
215)	Asian spring rolls	143
225)	Brussels sprouts spaghetti	148
236)	Burger mixed salad	153
231)	Caesar summer Pasta	151
188)	Cashew salad mix	129
249)	Cauliflower healthy gnocchi	160
175)	Cauliflower sweet soup	123
192)	Cheesy potato soup	131
210)	Chestnut gnocchi with champignons	140
193)	Chicken mix soup	132
239)	Chicken quesadillas	155
254)	Choco-chickpeas	162
216)	Cilantro -shrimps rice	143
238)	Classic focaccia	154
209)	Classic gnocchi with sauce	140
185)	Classic goulash	128
200)	Cold greens & fish soup	135
251)	Corn fritters with ricotta	161
244)	Corn salad	157
177)	Couscous greens soup	124
199)	Creamy curry-cumin soup	135
243)	Creamy dip	157
190)	Creamy greens roll-up	130
248)	Delicious turkey treats	159
230)	Easy and quick bagel	150
191)	Easy roasted potatoes dish	131
189)	Easy vegan nuggets	130
255)	Eggplant-shrimps skewers	163
237)	Flatbread	154
203)	Fresh cucumber finger food	137
183)	Fresh shrimps - cuttlefish soup	127
214)	Gado-gado Asian salad	142
256)	Grapefruit salmon	163
184)	Green broccoli pureed soup	127
197)	Green soup	134
229)	Green steak	150
258)	Grilled chicken & green sauce	164
242)	Hash muffins	156
260)	Hazelnuts salad	165
227)	Healthy burger plate	149
221)	Healthy peanut bowl	146
218)	Healthy thai salad	144
206)	Healthy tostones	138

224)	Healthy veg. Mac & Cheese	147
257)	Herbs chicken	164
241)	Horseradish shrimps	156
178)	Italian minestrone	124
207)	Italian ravioli pan	139
196)	Julienne zucchini soup	133
252)	Kale tortillas	161
181)	Leek – lentil soup	126
245)	Lemon cream	158
211)	Lemon tagliatelle	141
208)	Lentil dahl	139
176)	Mediterranean red soup	123
246)	Mexican casserole	158
187)	Mexican pozole mix	129
232)	Mixed jalapeño toasts	151
213)	Noodle soup with kale	142
201)	Old west soup	136
233)	Parmesan crackers	152
195)	Peppers creamy soup	133
198)	Pumpkin stew	134
205)	Quick avocado-mustard rolls	138
204)	Red skewers	137
228)	Salmon burger	149
234)	Savory snacks	152
226)	Shepherd's Pie	148
235)	Shrimps couscous	153
202)	Spanish gazpacho	136
220)	Spicy shrimps salad	145
182)	Summer corn soup	126
259)	Summer greens spaghetti	165
180)	Sweet ginger soup	125
240)	Sweet potato quesadillas	155
223)	Sweet walnuts casserole	147
217)	Thai curry chicken	144
222)	Vegan avocado sushi	146
247)	Vegan gratin	159
186)	Veggie Goulash	128
212)	Whole grain rigatoni with pesto	141
253)	Whole-grain salmon pasta	162
194)	Yellow greens soup	132
179)	Yellow turmeric soup	125

Number	Sweets	Page
285)	Apple-cinnamon crumble	178
299)	Berries chia pudding	185
298)	Berries summer shortcake	184
272)	Berries tostadas	171
273)	Berry sherbet	172
281)	Caribbean skewers	176
283)	Choco-dipped apples	177
277)	Choco mousse	174
266)	Choco-banana ice cream	168
267)	Choco-pumpkin cookies	169
271)	Classic berries cake	171
297)	Classic choco berries	184
265)	Classic roasted almond	168
291)	Coco-choco cupcakes	181
290)	Coconut little sweets	180
295)	Cranberry muffins	183
263)	Crunchy cookies	167
264)	Delicious pecan bars	167
278)	Dipped pineapple with ricotta	174
294)	Easy chip cookies	182
279)	Easy dipped apples	175
275)	French brioche	173
293)	Fresh roll-ups	182
270)	Healthy blueberry pie	170
268)	Healthy granola bars	169
289)	Healthy lemon cake	180
288)	Healthy pink ice cream	179
292)	Little blue cake	181
296)	Little cheesecake	183
282)	Mixed fruits skewers	176
269)	Mulberries cup	170
286)	Oatmeal little sweets	178
287)	Orange sauce pancakes	179
262)	Pomegranate pralines	166
280)	Quick blackberry smoothie	175
300)	Red skewers with choco drizzle	185
276)	Salty French croissants	173
274)	Strawberries pie	172
261)	Summer mango snacks	166
284)	Summer popsicles	177

10 Steps to prevent the risks of heart disease

As I said, I had to change my lifestyle habits, and I'd like to begin this book by explaining to you these changes. I invite you to take these tips as generic guidelines and always ask your doctor for specific recommendations. With this being remarked, I find it helpful to write this down for you[1]:

1) Eat more vegetables and fruits

It sounds obvious, but it could be a real challenge when you're not so used to that. Eating more greens helps you reduce the consumption of high-calorie foods like snacks, meat, or cheese. They're not only very precious sources of vitamins and minerals but also low in calories and rich in dietary fibers, which is excellent for many reasons! Avoid fresh or frozen fruits and vegetables, low-sodium canned products or canned food with water or juice instead of fried or breaded vegetables, canned products packed with sauces, added sugar, or heavy syrups.

2) Whole grains

This food contains many fiber and nutrients that are useful for regulating your blood pressure. From my experience, choosing whole-grain foods is more accessible than eating lots of fruit and vegetables since you find many alternatives to replace refined grain products. Some great options are whole-wheat flour, whole-grain bread, whole-grain farro, quinoa, brown rice, barley, or oatmeal. Avoid pies, cakes, doughnuts, cornbread, frozen waffles, muffins, white bread, buttered products, high-fat snacks, etc.

3) Limit fat

The Western diet is usually affluent in saturated and trans fat, however, try and be committed to reducing them. As time flies, trans fats produce plaque in the arteries (atherosclerosis), leading to stroke or heart attack. The AHA (American Heart Association) suggests altogether avoiding trans fat and limiting the saturated fats to 6% of your daily intake of calories. If you're asking yourself how you can do that, it's pretty easy. For instance, I've found it very useful to choose lean meat and stop using margarine or butter (try to reduce them at first if you're used to eating them a lot).

---

[1] References: https://www.mayoclinic.org/diseases-conditions/heart-disease/in-depth/heart-healthy-diet/art-20047702

Pay attention to the labels, as trans fat can be listed as partially hydrogenated oil. A few suggestions I've followed: <u>choose</u> flaxseeds (rich in omega 3), olive oil, vegetable or nut oil, avocados, or margarine with low cholesterol levels, for example; <u>limit</u> fats you find in lard, gravy, bacon, hydrogenated margarine, sauces, creamers or palm oil. Sometimes you can't avoid saturated or polyunsaturated fats. For this reason, I believe **awareness and moderation are two key factors**. Always keep that in mind.

4) Low-fat protein sources

Fish is rich in omega-three, which helps you reduce your triglycerides levels and inflammations. In this case, there are lots of healthy options. Wild Alaskan salmon (Sockeye), cold-water fish, herrings, mackerel, sardine, soybeans, flaxseeds, walnuts, and legumes are excellent omega-3 fatty acids. Other alternatives could be low-fat dairy products, poultry, eggs, or, as already said, lean meat.

5) Limit sodium (salt)

The AHA recommendations explain that healthy adults should not exceed the daily intake of 2.300 mg of salt (about a teaspoon), whereas most adults have no more than 1.500 mg daily. From my point of view, it's important to highlight that even though it's recommended to reduce the salt used while cooking, you find the majority of sodium in processed, frozen, or canned foods and condiments. For this reason, it's helpful to read the labels and be aware of the ingredients. Here are a few low-sodium options: salt-free seasoning blends, herbs, reduced-salt soy sauce or ketchup, spices, or meals with no salt added.

6) Weekly meal-plan

Use these suggestions to plan your daily menus. Preparing your meals lets you focus on your meals and ingredients for a short period. You don't have to worry about eating healthy and have the suitable options ready at home as you've already done the grocery shopping and know what you'll eat that day. For this reason, I've created a four-week meal plan in this book with many options selected from the various recipes here. You can have fun following my hints and tips or replacing a recipe with another.

7) Reduce the portions

Sometimes we eat more than what we need. I've found it helpful to track the number of servings, use a smaller plate, and avoid high calories and junk food. Try to control and reduce the portions, and your heart will thank you.

There are other lifestyle suggestions I want to share with you. to me, it wasn't easy to adopt a more active lifestyle, but the benefits are so great I wouldn't come back[2].

8) Quit smoking and drinking

Smoking can be a tough habit to break nicotine, one of the most addictive substances you find out there. Try to change your routine and prefer an electronic cigarette instead. I've done this personally, and after a few months, I also tried to stop the electronic one. Keep in mind that smoking is very mental. Therefore, you have to understand the psychological roots of this problem and replace this type of negative escape valve with something positive. It is the same thing with drinking. Avoid alcoholic and energy drinks. It makes a lot of difference.

9) Keep a healthy weight

A healthy weight should be the outcome of everything said until now. The combination of healthy food, choosing the proper nutrients, being active, and quitting bad habits like smoking should lead you to keep your weight under control.

10) Sport

Physical activity is beneficial in preventing a wide variety of diseases. A few examples are stroke, diabetes, control stress, high blood pressure, helping you to keep your weight under control, improving the quality of your sleep, osteoporosis, boosting your cardiovascular system, and having lots of fun. Sadly, I've never been very sporty, but I began to do long walks three times a week, which helped me lose weight and activate my metabolism.

---

[2] References: https://www.hsph.harvard.edu/nutritionsource/disease-prevention/cardiovascular-disease/preventing-cvd/#:~:text=The%20best%20diet%20for%20preventing,sodium%2C%20and%20foods%20with%20trans

Let's go Grocery Shopping!

Here is a handy food list to summarize the main categories of what's best and what's better to limit or avoid[3] :

BEST OPTIONS	LIMIT / AVOID
Grain	
Amaranth	Cereals with refined grains
Barley	Every product with refined grains
Brown rice	
Buckwheat	Grain-based desserts and cereal
Farro	White pasta, bread, rice
Kamut	
Oats and oatmeal	
Quinoa	
Whole-grain bread or pasta	
Whole-grain cereals	
Proteins	
Beans, peas	Bacon
Eggs	Hot dogs
Lean meat	Red meat
Lentils, almonds	Salami
Nuts and seeds	Sausage (and other processed meats)
Poultry (without skin)	
Salmon, sardines, mackerel	
Shellfish	
Tofu and tempeh	
Dairy	
Flavorful cheese (ex. Parmesan, Cheddar, blue cheese)	Butter
	Heavy cream
Low-sodium cheese	Sweetened yoghurt /dairy alternatives
Plain low-fat / fat-free milk and yoghurt	

---

[3] References: https://www.eatingwell.com/article/7872995/complete-list-of-heart-healthy-foods/
https://health.gov/myhealthfinder/topics/health-conditions/heart-health/heart-healthy-foods-shopping-list
https://www.healthline.com/nutrition/heart-healthy-foods#TOC_TITLE_HDR_4

BEST OPTIONS   **LIMIT / AVOID**

Sauces, spices and condiments	
Natural butters without added sugars/ hydrogenated oils	(Sweet) sauces with also heavy cream
	Bottled salad dressing
Plant-based oils (ex. Olive, canola, nuts/seed)	Coconut oil
	Jellies and jams
Spices and dried herbs	Sauces high in salt (sodium)
Vinegar	Spice blends with salt

Snacks	
Dehydrated fruit and veggies	Chips and similar
Dried bean snacks	High-sugar snack options
Nuts and seeds	Salty snacks
Snacks made using dried fruit / nuts / seeds	Snacks with refined grains / sugar
Whole-grain snacks	

Frozen foods	
Bean-and vegetable based burgers (or similar)	Breaded and fried options
	Frozen dinners and desserts
Berries (ex. Blueberries, blackberries, raspberries etc.)	
Fruits and vegetables (fresh / frozen: ex. spinach, kale, cabbage, carrots, tomatoes, broccoli, cauliflower, bananas, oranges, pears, peaches)	
Plain frozen fish	
Whole grains options	
Whole-wheat bread and other options	

Drinks	
Unsweetened tea, coffee, juices	Alcohol
Water	Drinks with creams / sugar of syrups
	Sugary beverages

4 Tips to make your recipes last longer:

1) Double the quantity: you already spend time meal prepping, so double the ingredients, and you'll have more meals ready!
2) Combine leftovers: you'll be amazed by the results!
3) Difference recipes with the same ingredients
4) Cooking the main dish with a side dish simultaneously: oven filled, time saved!

Conversion Charts

Have you ever struggled with recipe directions? I worked a lot when I was a newbie at cooking. I've decided to add a conversion chart with helpful information about temperature and conversions.

Celsius (C°)	Fahrenheit (F°)
0°	32°
5°	41°
10°	50°
15°	59°
20°	68°
25°	77°
30°	86°
40°	104°
50°	122°
60°	140°
70°	158°
80°	176°
90°	194°
100°	212°
150°	302°
180°	356°
200°	392°
250°	482°
300°	572°

$$F° = C° \times (9/5) + 32$$

CONVERSIONS

CUPS	OZ	GRAMS	TBSP	TSP	ML
1	8	225	16	48	250
3/4	6	170	12	36	175
2/3	5	140	11	32	150
1/2	4	115	8	24	125
1/3	3	70	5	16	70
1/4	2	60	4	12	60
1/8	1	30	2	6	30
1/16	1/2	15	1	3	15

1 Pound = 16 oz = 454 g
1 Ounce = 28.35 grams
1 Tbsp = 14.78 ml = 0.015 L = 15 g (1 tbsp of water only)

1 TBSP	GRAMS
of water	15
of butter	14
of cocoa	7.5
of whole-grain flour	9
of icecream	14
of milk	15
of mascarpone cheese	14
of honey	20
of oil	14
of breadcrumbs	9.5
of cooked rice	5
of raw rice	9
of maple syrup	20
of yoghurt	15
of sugar	12.5
of sugar cane	14

1 CUP	GRAMS
of four	125
of whole-grain flour	120
of sugar cane	220
of caster sugar	220
of cocoa	82
of milk	240
of cream	250
of water	240
of olive oil	215
of butter	227
of peanut butter	250
of honey	350
of yoghurt	250
of oatmeal	85
of puffed rice	25
of starch	140

Cooking Glossary

Here we are, with another exciting and valuable section. When you're a newbie, recipes with detailed descriptions and precise vocabulary can make you feel overwhelmed and frustrated because you don't understand the meaning of the words and what you need to do just to cook a simple meal. For this reason, you'll find the glossary below very helpful in every situation[4].

B

Bake	to cook usually in the oven, slowly with gentle heat.
Basting	to brush liquid (like water) during roasting in order to add flavor and to prevent drying out.
Beat	stirring a mixture up with a spoon, fork, wire shisk, electric mixer etc.
Blanch	to boil briefly
Blend	to mix two or more ingredients
Boil	to cook food in heated water
Braise	to cook slowly using the heat from an oven and a bit of water or broth.

C

Chop	to cut into irregular pieces
Coat	to evenly cover food with crumbs, flour or a batter
Caramelization	to brown foods and add flavor; it occurs when sugar is heated.

---

[4] References: https://www.heart.org/en/healthy-living/healthy-eating/cooking-skills/cooking/common-terminology-for-healthy-cooking / https://www.heart.org/en/healthy-living/healthy-eating/cooking-skills/cooking/common-terminology-the-science-of-food

D

Dash	a measure of 1/16 teaspoon
Denaturation	it's the process of changing part of the protein's natural structure by a chemical / physical reaction.
Dice	to cut into cubes or square shapes

E

Emulsification	when two liquids that usually don't dissolve together (ex. water and oil) are combined together.

M

Marinate	to coat or immerse foods in a liquid or dry rub, to add flavor before cooking
Mash	to beat or press to remove lumps
Mince	to cut food into tiny pieces
Mix	to beat or stir two or more foods together until they're combined

P

Puree	to mash or sieve food into a thick liquid

R

Roast	to cook uncovered in the oven

S

Season	to enhance the flavor of foods by adding ingredients like pepper, herbs or spices etc.
Shred	to cut or tear into long narrow strips
Simmer	a low boil that cook food in a liquid so that small bubbles begin to break the surface and around the edge of the pot.
Steam	to cook over boiling water in a covered pan
Stir-Fry	cooking with a very high heat with continual and rapid stirring

V - W - Z

Vinaigrette	any sauce made with vinegar, seasonings and oil
Whisk	to mix of fluff by beating
Zest	the act of removing the outer part of citrus fruits using a knife

Recipes abbreviations

△ Servings   ⏰ overall time

Nutrition Facts

Noun	Abbreviations
Calories	Cal.
Protein	Prot.
Carbs:	
Dietary Fiber	Diet. Fiber
Total Sugars	Tot. Sugars
Fats:	
Saturated Fats	Sat. Fat
Monounsaturated Fat	Mon. Fat
Polyunsaturated Fat	Poly. Fat
Cholesterol	Cholest.
Sodium	Sodium
Salt	Salt

!!! The values in the nutrition section are intended for the number of servings written near every title.

Tips for enjoying the book:

- ✓ The ideas and ingredients are countless, so remember that you can replace one or more components as you prefer (better with even healthier new options in the market).

- ✓ It's understood that the ingredients you find in the recipes are always considered the healthiest option, even if it's not always specified. You should always consider the option with the lowest amount of sodium, sugar, etc.

- ✓ You can read a few recipes where a pinch of salt is used. The most important thing is to keep a balance and adopt a different lifestyle in every aspect of your life.

Breakfast and Snacks

1) *Banana Oat Muffins* 👤 2 ⏰ 30 Min.

Ingredients:

20 g Rolled Oats

1 small Banana

25 g. Eggs

1 tsp. Honey

1/6 tsp. Baking powder

10 ml. Rice milk (unsweetened)

Instructions:

1) Fill half a cup with the oats, while finely chop the other half with a processor. **2)** Mash the banana with a fork, add the chopped oats, rice milk, eggs, honey and the baking powder all together. *(If you prefer, season it with a bit of salt or others).* **3)** Add the remaining oat flakes and divide the mixture evenly among the muffins' cups. **4)** Bake the muffins in the oven at 350 °F (175 °C) about 20 minutes.

Nutrition Facts:

Cal. 161	**Carbs**: 25 g	**Fat**: 3.5 g	Sat.Fat 0.9 g	Cholest. 92 mg
Protein 5.6 g	Diet. Fiber 2.5 g		Mon.Fat 1.3 g	Sodium 114 mg
	Tot. Sugars 13.4 g		Poly.Fat 0.8 g	Salt -

༄༅

2) *Raisin Oats with berries* 👤 2 ⏰ 20 Min.

Ingredients:

100 g. Oatmeal flakes

1 Apple

15 g. Raisins

15 g. Walnuts

100 g. Frozen berries

200 g. Yogurt (nonfat)

Instructions:

1) Grate the apple and mix it with your favourite yogurt. **2)** Add the oatmeal flakes and fronzen berries to the yoghurt. **3)** Let everything soak for approx. 20 minutes. **4)** Break into small pieces the walnuts and sprinkle them over the oatmeal.

Nutrition Facts:

Cal. 659	**Carbs**: 101	**Fat**: 12.6 g	Sat.Fat 1.7 g	Cholest. -
Protein 23.9 g	Diet. Fiber 15.7 g		Mon.Fat 5.4 g	Sodium 121 mg
	Tot. Sugars 40.3 g		Poly.Fat 3.5 g	Salt 0.3 g

3) *Porridge*   👤 2   ⏰ 5 Min.

Ingredients:

100 g. Rolled oats

500 ml. Almond milk (unsweetened)

20 g. Honey

Cinnamon (to taste)

Instructions:

1) Take one pot and bring together the oatmeal and water. Let them boil. **2)** Remove the pot from the heat, cover it and let everything soak for approx. 5 minutes. **3)** Garnish everything with honey and cinnamon.

Nutrition Facts:

Cal. 434	**Carbs**: 74.6	**Fat**: 6.7 g Sat.Fat 1.1 g	Cholest. -
Protein 13.3 g	Diet. Fiber 9.7 g	Mon.Fat 2.2 g	Sodium 2 mg
	Tot. Sugars 15.5 g	Poly.Fat 2.2 g	Salt -

༅༃

4) *Porridge with banana and strawberries*   👤 2   ⏰ 10 Min

Ingredients:

170 ml. Almond milk (to taste, unsweetened)

130 ml. Water

100 g. Strawberries

100 g. Rolled oats

1 medium Banana

Chia seeds (to taste)

Instructions:

1) Mash ¾ of the banana with a fork. Add the oatmeal flakes, water and the unsweetened milk. Season to taste. **2)** Heat the porridge in the microwave on medium heat for approx. 2 minutes, stir it and than heat the porridge again for another 40 sec. **3)** Cut the strawberries in small pieces and use them with the remaining banana and chia seeds to garnish the porridge.

Nutrition Facts:

Cal. 745	**Carbs**: 123.7 g	**Fat**: 14.9 g Sat.Fat 1.9 g	Cholest. -
Protein 19.3 g	Diet. Fiber 23.5 g	Mon.Fat 2.9 g	Sodium 12 mg
	Tot. Sugars 59.3	Poly.Fat 7.5 g	Salt -

5) *Dark chocolate cookies* 👤 4 ⏰ 20 Min.

Ingredients:

5 g. Dark chocolate

15 g. Whole-wheat flour

20 g. Rolled oats

2/5 tbsp. Peanut butter (or other alternatives your prefer)

½ Banana

Instructions:

1) Firstly preheat the oven to 350 °F (150 °C) and secondly, mash the banana with a fork and finely chop the dark chocolate. **2)** Use a mixer to combine and blend all the ingredients together. **3)** Create small balls, with baking paper cover a baking sheet and use it to place the dough balls. **4)** Bake the cookies for approx. 12 minutes until they turn golden-brown.

Nutrition Facts:

Cal. 224	**Carbs**: 26 g	**Fat**: 5.9 g	Sat.Fat 1.6 g	Cholest. 2 mg
Protein 14.5 g	Diet. Fiber 3.9 g		Mon.Fat 2.5 g	Sodium 32 mg
	Tot. Sugars 12.7 g		Poly.Fat 1.4 g	Salt -

৶চ

6) *Crunchy cereal cookies* 👤 2 ⏰ 15 Min.

Ingredients:

1 tbsp. Oliven oil

340 ml. Rice or almond milk (unsweetened)

20 g. Blueberries

120 g. Rolled oats flakes

1 ripe Banana

30 ml. Agave nectar

Instructions:

1) Mash the banana with a fork and then add the olive oil, agave nectar and oat flakes. Mix everything until it has a pasty consistency. **2)** Cover a baking sheet wit appropriate paper and spread the mixture. Bake it in the oven at 350 °F (175 °C) for approx. 10 minutes. **3)** Let everything cool down and break the cereals into small pieces. **4)** Serve with rice / almond milk (or others) and blueberries.

Nutrition Facts:

Cal. 826	**Carbs**: 143.5 g	**Fat**: 17 g	Sat.Fat 8 g.	Cholest. -
Protein 18.3 g	Diet. Fiber 14.6 g		Mon.Fat 1.4 g	Sodium 25 mg
	Tot. Sugars 61 g		Poly.Fat 1.5 g	Salt -

7) *Blueberry Soufflé*   👤 3   ⏰ 65 Min.

Ingredients:

2 Eggs + Agave nectar (to taste)

40 g. Pudding Mix. (unsweetened / organic)

250 ml. Almond milk (unsweetened)

80 g. Blueberries

500 g. Yoghurt (unsweetened, low-fat)

Instructions:

1) Beat the yoghurt, eggs, almond milk and pudding mix with a hand mixer until its consistency is uniform. **2)** Add the blueberries (*keep a few of them aside as garnish*); sweeten the mixture to taste and pour it into a soufflé dish. **3)** Bake the soufflé in the oven at 320 °F (160 °C) for approx. 60 minutes. Let the soufflé cool down and garnish it with the remaining blueberries.

Nutrition Facts:

Cal. 899	**Carbs**: 69.4 g	**Fat**: 23.9 g	Sat.Fat 10.6 g	Cholest. 582 mg
Protein 93.2 g	Diet. Fiber 3.9 g		Mon.Fat 8 g	Sodium 637 mg
	Tot. Sugars 43.4 g		Poly.Fat 2.8 g	Salt 1.6 g

☙❧

8) *Vegan chocolate porridge*   👤 2   ⏰ 10 Min.

Ingredients:

250 ml. Almond milk (unsweetened)

2 tbsp. Dark cocoa

60 g. Strawberries

60 g. Blackberries

1 medium Banana

80 g. Rolled oats

Instructions:

1) Mash the banana with a fork and heat together with the oatmeal flakes, almond milk and dark baking cocoa in one pot. **2)** Cook everything for 3-4 minutes and keep on stirring until the oat flakes have absorbed the milk. **3)** Wash and cut the strawberries and blackberries, use them as a garnish and serve the porridge in a bowl.

Nutrition Facts:

Cal. 778	**Carbs**: 121.1 g	**Fat**: 15.9 g	Sat.Fat 5.1 g	Cholest. -
Protein 23.3 g	Diet. Fiber 24.7 g		Mon.Fat 4.8 g	Sodium 98 mg
	Tot. Sugars 64.4 g		Poly.Fat 3.3 g	Salt 0.2 g

9) *Blackberries pancakes* 👤 2   ⏰ 25 Min.

Ingredients:

12 Egg whites

2 tbsp. Whole-wheat flour and olive oil

250 ml. Rice or almond milk and 450 ml. Apple sauce (unsweetened)

130 g. Blackberries

80 g. Rolled oats

Instructions:

1) Put the egg whites, oat flakes, whole-wheat flour and unsweetened milk in a blender. Sweeten the mixture to taste and blend it until the mixture obtain a smooth consistency. **2)** Take a pan and heat the olive oil, add the dough and bake it on both sides until it's golden brown. **3)** Garnish the pancakes with the blackberries and apple sauce.

Nutrition Facts:

Cal. 979	**Carbs:** 114.7 g	**Fat:** 25.1 g	Sat.Fat 14.3 g	Cholest. -
Protein 61.2 g	Diet. Fiber 22.2 g		Mon.Fat 3 g	Sodium 1671 mg
	Tot. Sugars 59.4 g		Poly.Fat 3.5 g	Salt 4.2 g

ॐ☪

10) *Cereal with apples and pears* 👤 2   ⏰ 15 Min.

Ingredients:

2 Pears

2 Apple

80 ml. Water

10 ml. Agave nectar

350 g. Yoghurt (nonfat, unsweetened)

80 g. Rolled oats

Instructions:

1) Peel the pears and apples into small pieces and mix them in a pot adding the water. Cook everything for approx. 10 minutes. **2)** As the water evaporates remove the pot from the heat and add the agave nectar to the fruits. **3)** Put the yoghurt in a bowl and garnish it with hot fruits and oatmeal flakes.

Nutrition Facts:

Cal. 760	**Carbs:** 125 g	**Fat:** 12.2 g	Sat.Fat 1.7 g	Cholest. -
Protein 26.6 g	Diet. Fiber 20.1 g		Mon.Fat 5.2 g	Sodium 205 mg
	Tot. Sugars 69.3 g		Poly.Fat 3.3 g	Salt 0.5 g

11) *Ricotta cheese with caramelized apples* 👤 2 ⏰ 5 Min

Ingredients:

2 Apples

2 tbsp. Honey (to taste)

400 g. Ricotta cheese

Walnuts (to taste)

Instructions:

1) Peel the apples and chop them into small pieces. Place the apples pieces in a non-stick pan and light caramelize them with the honey. **2)** Divide the ricotta cheese in two bowls, add the caramelized apples and if you like season them a bit with cinnamon. Garnish them with pieces of walnuts.

Nutrition Facts:

Cal. 593	**Carbs**: 53 g	**Fat**: 17.8 g	Sat.Fat 10.1 g	Cholest. 44 mg
Protein 50.2 g	Diet. Fiber 5.6 g		Mon.Fat 5.7 g	Sodium 924 mg
	Tot. Sugars 48.8 g		Poly.Fat 0,9 g	Salt 2.3 g

༺༻

12) *Bananas and honey bars* 👤 2 ⏰ 20 Min.

Ingredients:

35 g. Rolled oats

20 ml. Almond milk (unsweetened)

0.18 tbsp. Honey

½ Banana

Instructions:

1) Firstly preheat your oven to 320 °F (160 °C), secondly peel the banana and mash it with a fork. **2)** Use a hand mixer to combine all the ingredients and place them in a casserole covered with baking paper. **3)** Bake the mixture on the middle rack for approx. 15 minutes. **4)** Let everything cool down and then cut the granola into small bars.

Nutrition Facts:

Cal. 235	**Carbs**: 34.5 g	**Fat**: 6.1 g	Sat.Fat 1.1 g	Cholest. -
Protein 7.3 g	Diet. Fiber 5.1 g		Mon.Fat 2.6 g	Sodium 3 mg
	Tot. Sugars 11.6 g		Poly.Fat 1.8 g	Salt <0.1 g

13) *Berries cake* 👤 4   ⏰ 50 Min.

Ingredients:

25 g. Eggs

70 g. Blueberries

70 g. Blackberries

80 g. Whole-wheat flour

60 ml. Buttermilk

1 ripe Banana

Honey (to taste)

Instructions:

1) Firstly preheat the oven to 350 °F (175 °C), secondly mesh the banana and using a mixer add the eggs and honey. **2)** Mix both types of berries with 2 tbsp. of flour. **3)** Add the remaining flour and buttermilk to the banana to keep the cake very soft. Mix everything until you have a creamy batter. **4)** Gently pour the berries in the mixture and then into a cake form. **5)** Bake everything on the middle rack for approx. 40 minutes.

Nutrition Facts:

Cal. 405	**Carbs**: 66.3 g **Fat**: 5 g	Sat.Fat 1.2 g	Cholest. 93 mg
Protein 15.6 g	Diet. Fiber 12.5 g	Mon.Fat 1.3 g	Sodium 465 mg
	Tot. Sugars 14 g	Poly.Fat 1.6 g	Salt 1.2 g

෴

14) *Berries salad* 👤 2   ⏰ 10 Min.

Ingredients:

60 g. Quinoa

100 g. Strawberries, Blueberries and blackberries

1 Banana

1 tbsp. Lemon juice and honey

Mint and/or pumpkin seeds (to taste)

Instructions:

1) Prepare the quinoa according to the instructions. Wash and cut into pieces the strawberries, blueberries and blackberries. **2)** Put the fruits into a bowl together with the lemon juice and honey. **3)** Once is ready, add the cooked quinoa and garnish with mint and/ or pumpkin seeds according to your taste.

Nutrition Facts:

Cal. 464	**Carbs**: 83 g **Fat**: 5.7 g	Sat.Fat 0.5 g	Cholest. -
Protein 10.5 g	Diet. Fiber 14.2 g	Mon.Fat 1.2 g	Sodium 11 mg
	Tot. Sugars 44.1 g	Poly.Fat 2.7 g	Salt < 0.1 mg

15) *Chocolate porridge* 👤 2   ⏰ 10 Min.

Ingredients:

430 ml. Almond milk (unsweetened)

2 medium Bananas

Honey (to taste)

2 tbsp. Sesame seeds

15 g. Dark cocoa powder (unsweetened)

60 g. Raspberries

Instructions:

1) Use a mixer in order to blend the almond milk, the two bananas and cocoa powder. **2)** Add the honey or other sweetener. **3)** Let everything boil and simmer until the mixture thickens. **4)** Serve the porridge in two bowls and garnish it with sesame seeds and raspberries.

Nutrition Facts:

Cal. 544   **Carbs**: 93.6 g   **Fat**: 9.2 g   Sat.Fat 1.9 g   Cholest. -
Protein 13.9 g   Diet. Fiber 15 g   Mon.Fat 2.2 g   Sodium 41 mg
                 Tot. Sugars 44.8 g   Poly.Fat 2 g   Salt   0.1 g

⊰⊱

16) *Mango porridge* 👤 2   ⏰ 10 Min.

Ingredients:

1 Mango

300 ml. Almond milk (unsweetened)

2 ripe Bananas

80 g. Bulgur

2 tbsp. Coconut flakes

Instructions:

1) Bring the milk and bulgur to boil and let everything swell. With a fork mash the bananas after peeling them. **2)** Peel the mango and cut it into pieces. **3)** Add the fruits to the bulgur and mix them. **4)** Garnish everything with the coconut powder.

Nutrition Facts:

Cal. 982   **Carbs**: 163 g   **Fat**: 18.4 g   Sat.Fat 1.9 g   Cholest. -
Protein 26.7 g   Diet. Fiber 22.2 g   Mon.Fat 7.9 g   Sodium 172 mg
                 Tot. Sugars 93.2 g   Poly.Fat 5.8 g   Salt   0.4 g

17) *Greek yogurt granola* 👤 2 ⏰ 5 Min.

Ingredients:

1 ½ Apples

350 g. Greek yoghurt

50 g. Granola cereal

Honey (to taste)

2 tbsp. Coconut flakes

Instructions:

1) Pell the apples and cut them into small pieces. **2)** Fill 1/2 of a glass with yoghurt and layer it on some apple pieces and crispy cereals and sweeten with a bit of honey. **3)** Garnish everything with a bit of coconut powder.

Nutrition Facts:

Cal. 679	**Carbs**: 63.5 g	**Fat**: 38.4 g	Sat.Fat 22.3 g	Cholest. 130 mg
Protein 14.8 g	Diet. Fiber 6.5 g		Mon.Fat 12 g	Sodium 221 mg
	Tot. Sugars 45.6 g		Poly.Fat 1.9 g	Salt 0.6 g

☼☋

18) *Melon salad with berries* 👤 2 ⏰ 10 Min.

Ingredients:

1 small Melon

100 g. Blueberries

100 g. Raspberries

2 Pears

Honey (to taste)

Instructions:

1) Dice the melon's pulp, peel the two pears and cut everything into pieces. **2)** Wash the berries and pour everything in a bowl with the melon and a bit of honey (as you prefer).

Nutrition Facts:

Cal. 315	**Carbs**: 58 g	**Fat**: 4.6 g	Sat.Fat 3.3 g	Cholest. -
Protein 4.3 g	Diet. Fiber 10.5 g		Mon.Fat 0.4 g	Sodium 36 mg
	Tot. Sugars 53.3 g		Poly.Fat 0.7 g	Salt < 0.1 g

19) *Fruit tortillas* 👤 2   ⏰ 10 Min.

Ingredients:

130 g. Strawberries

2 Tortillas

80 g. Cream cheese (low fat and sodium)

4 tbsp. Oatmeal flakes

2 tbsp. Pumpkin seeds and honey (to taste)

Instructions:

1) Wash and slice the strawberries. **2)** Spread the tortillas with you favourite cream cheese and slices the strawberries. **3)** Garnish with oatmeal flakes, pumpikin seeds and a bit of honey. **4)** Roll up the tortillas.

Nutrition Facts:

Cal. 595	**Carbs**: 86.7 g	**Fat**: 16 g	Sat.Fat 7.5 g	Cholest. 3 mg
Protein 20.4 g	Diet. Fiber 6.6 g		Mon.Fat 3.5 g	Sodium 532 mg
	Tot. Sugars 26.1 g		Poly.Fat 2.1 g	Salt 1.4 g

☙☜

20) *Cottage cheese with granola* 👤 2   ⏰ 5 Min.

Ingredients:

400 g. Cottage cheese

2 tbsp. Water

Honey (to taste)

Crispy cereal granola (to taste)

Instructions:

1) Combine the cottage cheese with water and honey. Blend them all together. **2)** Add your favourite crispy cereal mix and blend everything together. Serve in two bowls.

Nutrition Facts:

Cal. 400	**Carbs**: 27.8 g	**Fat**: 5.8	Sat.Fat 3.5 g	Cholest. 20 mg
Protein 54.3 g	Diet. Fiber 3.8 g		Mon.Fat 1.7 g	Sodium 1525 mg
	Tot. Sugars 33.7 g		Poly.Fat 0.3 g	Salt 3.9 g

21) *Raisins couscous* 👤 2 ⏰ 7 Min.

Ingredients:

120 g. Couscous

50 g. Oatmeal flakes

40 g. Raisins

Agave nectar (to taste)

200 ml. Almond milk

Instructions:

1) Prepare the couscous according to the instructions. 2) Mix the couscous together with the other ingredients (oatmeal flakes and raisins) and let them soak for approx. 5 minutes. 3) Garnish everything with a bit of agave nectar.

Nutrition Facts:

Cal. 715	**Carbs**: 132.6 g	**Fat**: 7.1 g	Sat.Fat 1 g	Cholest. -
Protein 21.1 g	Diet. Fiber 13.2 g		Mon.Fat 2.7 g	Sodium 18 mg
	Tot. Sugars 27.4 g		Poly.Fat 2.3 g	Salt -

✿

22) *Granola with cranberries* 👤 2 ⏰ 25 Min.

Ingredients:

50 g. Vegan protein powder

2 tbsp. Olive oil

15 g. Sesam seeds

15 g. Cranberries

100 g. Rolled spelt flakes

Agave nectar (to taste)

400 g. nonfat Yogurt

Instructions:

1) Combine together oil, the spelt flakes and the agave nectar. Blend these ingredients together. 2) Spread the mixture on a baking sheet and bake at 320 °F (160 °C) for approx. 20 minutes. 3) Let everything cool and then mix the cereals with the yoghurt and the vegan protein powder. 4) Garnish with sesam seeds and cranberries.

Nutrition Facts:

Cal. 961	**Carbs**: 115.6 g	**Fat**: 22.2 g	Sat.Fat 14.5 g	Cholest. 8 mg
Protein 67 g	Diet. Fiber 16.3 g		Mon.Fat 0.7 g	Sodium 321 mg
	Tot. Sugars 45.3 g		Poly.Fat 2.8 g	Salt 0.8 g

23) *Blueberry porridge with banana* 👤 2   ⏰ 10 Min.

Ingredients:

500 ml. Water

2 Bananas

100 g. Rolled oats

Agave nectar (to taste)

90 g. Blueberries

Instructions:

1) Put the flakes and the water in a pot, let them boil and then let simmer for approx. 5 minutes. **2)** As the porridge starts to thicken, pour in the blueberries and agave nectar as a sweetener. **3)** Remove the pot from the heat. At the same time peel the bananas and cut them into small pieces. **4)** Mix the bananas with the porridge and serve them.

Nutrition Facts:

Cal. 658	**Carbs**: 115.7 g	**Fat**: 8.5 g	Sat.Fat 1.5 g	Cholest. -
Protein 15.1 g	Diet. Fiber 20.4 g		Mon.Fat 2.9 g	Sodium 26 mg
	Tot. Sugars 61.6 g		Poly.Fat 2.7 g	Salt -

ಊಎ

24) *Muffins with pumpkin* 👤 4   ⏰ 35 Min.

Ingredients:

80 g. Pumpkin

50 g. Whole-wheat flour

15 g. Rolled oats

1/3 Baking powder and oil

1/3 Egg

Agave nectar (to taste)

30 ml. Rice milk

Instructions:

1) Firstly, preheat the oven to 375 °F (190 °C). Secondly wash and prepare the pumpkin. Cut it into pieces and cook them in boiling water for 10 minutes until it becomes soft. **2)** Mix together the other dry ingredients. **3)** Purée the pumpkin with and blend it together with olive oil, milk and egg until it's very smooth. Fill the pan with the mixture and bake for approx. 25 minutes.

Nutrition Facts:

Cal. 489	**Carbs**: 83 g	**Fat**: 11 g	Sat.Fat 1.6 g	Cholest. 92 mg
Protein 12 g	Diet. Fiber 8 g		Mon.Fat 3.6 g	Sodium 240 mg
	Tot. Sugars 30 g		Poly.Fat 4 g	Salt 0.6 g

25) *Mustard sandwich* 👤 2   ⏰ 12 Min.

Ingredients:

4 slices Multigrain bread

100 g. slices Turkey breast

Tomato (to taste)

2 slices low-fat Cheese

Instructions:

1) Wash and slice the tomatoes. **2)** Lay over the bread slice cheese, tomatoes and turkey breast. **3)** Top the ingredients with the second slice of bread and heat the sandwich a little bit until it becomes slithly crispy.

Nutrition Facts:

Cal. 780	**Carbs**: 95.2 **Fat**: 17.2	Sat.Fat 8.1 g	Cholest. 88 mg
Protein 52.4	Diet. Fiber 9.8 g	Mon.Fat 4.7 g	Sodium 2851 mg
	Tot. Sugars 4.7 g	Poly.Fat 1.8 g	Salt 7.2 g

ಸಿಂ

26) *Couscous with peaches* 👤 2   ⏰ 10 Min.

Ingredients:

100 g. Couscous

3 Peaches

Agave nectar (to taste)

200 ml. Rice milk

Instructions:

1) Let the milk boil a bit and then combine it with the couscous. **2)** Let it swell and add a bit of agave nectar as you prefer. **3)** Wash and cut the peaches in small pieces (leave a few of them to garnish), add a little bit of sweetener and mash them. **4)** Pour the couscous into a bowl and mix it with the peaches, garnish it with the remaining pieces.

Nutrition Facts:

Cal. 670	**Carbs**: 112.3 **Fat**: 14 g	Sat.Fat 10 g	Cholest. -
Protein 18 g	Diet. Fiber 13 g	Mon.Fat 2 g	Sodium 47 mg
	Tot. Sugars 33 g	Poly.Fat 1 g	Salt -

27) *Quinoa chocolate snack*   👤 2   ⏰ 20 Min.

Ingredients:

200 g. Quinoa

500 ml. Cereal milk

2 tbsp. Agave nectar

4 tbsp. Dark cocoa powder

2 ripe Bananas

Instructions:

1) Rinse the quinoa with a strainer and then combine it with the cereal milk. Cook everything with low heat for approx. 15-20 minutes. **2)** Peel the bananas and mash them. Mix them with the agave nectar and the cocoa powder. **3)** As the quinoa is ready, remove it from the heat and mix it with the bananas.

Nutrition Facts:

Cal. 1170	**Carbs**: 189 g	**Fat**: 24.2 g	Sat.Fat 5.6 g	Cholest. -
Protein 34 g	Diet. Fiber 27.5 g		Mon.Fat 8.2 g	Sodium 112 mg
	Tot. Sugars 26 g		Poly.Fat 4.6 g	Salt -

๛ଓ

28) *Apple sauce with cinnamon*   👤 2   ⏰ 25 Min.

Ingredients:

500 g. Apples

130 ml. Water

2 tbsp. Lemongrass juice

Cinnamon (to taste)

Instructions:

1) Peel the apples and cut them into small pieces. **2)** Combine together apples, lemongrass juice, water and a bit of cinnamon as you prefer. Simmer over medium heat all the ingredients for approx. 15 minutes. **3)** Lastly, use a stamper to soften the fruits as you prefer.

Nutrition Facts:

Cal. 327	**Carbs**: 72 g	**Fat**: 0.4 g	Sat.Fat -	Cholest. -
Protein 2 g	Diet. Fiber 10 g		Mon.Fat -	Sodium 5 mg
	Tot. Sugars 66 g		Poly.Fat 0.2 g	Salt -

29) *Whole-wheat bread* 👤 4   ⏰ 45 Min.

Ingredients:

20 g. Yeast

230 ml. Lukewarm Water

340 g. Whole wheat flour

0.8 tsp. Salt

2 tbsp. Ground Flaxseed

2 tbsp. Pumpkin seeds

2 tbsp. Sunflower seeds

Instructions:

1) Firstly, preheat the oven to 400 °F (200 °C) and then mix the yeast with the water. Secondly, add the flour and most of the seeds to the mixture and knead everything with your hands into a homogenous dough. **2)** Use some flour to sprinkle a surface and give the form of a thick roll to the mixture. **3)** Cut some pieces (8-10) out of the dough. With your hands give them a ball form and place them on a baking sheet. **4)** Brush the loaves with some water and sprinkle them with te remaining seeds. **5)** Bake them for approx. 30 minutes.

Nutrition Facts:

Cal. 1254   **Carbs**: 198 g   **Fat**: 19 g   Sat.Fat 2.9 g   Cholest. -
Protein 49 g   Diet. Fiber 38 g   Mon.Fat 4.2 g   Sodium 1754 mg
                Tot. Sugars 4 g   Poly.Fat 9.7 g   Salt   4.5 g

༄༅

30) *Oatmeal blackberry waffle* 👤 2   ⏰ 20 Min.

Ingredients:

1 tbsp. Olive oil and Agave nectar

50 g. Whole-wheat flour and blackberries

30 g. Rolled oats and applesauce (unsweetened)

100 ml. Cereal milk

1/3 tsp. Baking powder

Instructions:

1) Mix together the dry ingredients. Now add the applesauce, cereal milk (or other you prefer), agave nectar and olive oil. Blend everything together. **2)** Add the blackberries and keep on mixing well. **3)** Brush the waffle iron with oliven oil and bake the waffles.

Nutrition Facts:

Cal. 450   **Carbs**: 63 g   **Fat**: 14 g   Sat.Fat 1.5 g   Cholest. -
Protein 10 g   Diet. Fiber 11 g   Mon.Fat 5.6 g   Sodium 203 mg
              Tot. Sugars 15 g   Poly.Fat 3.8 g   Salt   0.5 g

31) *Chickpea bread roll*   👤 2   ⏰ 20 Min.

Ingredients:

150 g. canned Chickpeas (unsweetened)

2 Tomatos and peppers

40 g. Spinach and Hummus

4 slices Whole grain bread

1 tbsp. Olive oil

Rosmary (to taste)

Instructions:

1) Firstly, you have to drain the chickpeas and mash them. Secondly, peel the tomatoes and chop them as well as the peppers. **2)** Combine together the chickpeas, olive oil, a bit os salt, peppers and hummus and mix them. **3)** Spread a slice of bread with tomatoes and spinach and then top the vegetables with the chickpeas mix and rosmary. Cover them with the second slice of bread.

Nutrition Facts:

Cal. 700	**Carbs**: 98	**Fat**: 16 g Sat.Fat 2.2 g	Cholest. -
Protein 28 g	Diet. Fiber 28 g	Mon.Fat 2.9 g	Sodium 1400 mg
	Tot. Sugars 16.6 g	Poly.Fat 7.3 g	Salt -

ಲ೧ಬ

32) *Sommer rice pudding*   👤 2   ⏰ 40 Min.

Ingredients:

100 g. Short-grain rice

400 ml. Milk (nonfat, unsweetened)

70 g. Strawberries

1 tbsp. Agave nectar

1 tbsp. Lemon juice

Instructions:

1) Bring to boil the rice and your favourite milk. **2)** Reduce the heat, cover the pot and let simmer for about 25 minutes. Stir if needed. **3)** Cut the strawberries in small pieces and, in another pot, mix them together with the agave nectar and lemon juice. **4)** Let the ingredients simmer over medium heat for another 5 minutes. **5)** Mix the berries with rice and taste.

Nutrition Facts:

Cal. 600	**Carbs**: 105 g	**Fat**: 7.2 g Sat.Fat 4.3 g	Cholest. 16 mg
Protein 21 g	Diet. Fiber 4.5 g	Mon.Fat 1.8 g	Sodium 194 mg
	Tot. Sugars 29.3 g	Poly.Fat 0.6 g	Salt 0.5 g

33) *Flaxseeds rye bread* 👤 4 ⏰ 150 Min.

Ingredients:

140 ml. warm Water

15 g. Yeast

1/3 tbsp. Salt

10 g. Flaxseeds

5 g. Sesam seeds and Poppy seeds

170 g. Rye flour

Instructions:

1) Firstly, crumble the yeast into a glass full of warm water and stir it with a spoon. Let the mixture rest for approx. 20 minutes and cover it with a towel. **2)** Combine together the three types of seeds with the rye flour. Now, combine the dry ingredients with the yeast mixture and knead them for approx. 10 minutes. **3)** After that, knead the dough shortly with your hands. Cover the dough with a towel and let it rest for 30 minutes in a warm place. **4)** Preheat the oven to 395 °F (200 °C). **5)** After that, knead the dough swiftly ince more and make a loaf. **6)** Bake it in an appropriate bowl with a bit of water next to it for 60 min. on the middle rack.

Nutrition Facts:

Cal. 670	**Carbs**: 127 g	**Fat**: 5.3 g	Sat.Fat 0.6 g	Cholest. -
Protein 19 g	Diet. Fiber 15.5 g		Mon.Fat 1 g	Sodium 270 mg
	Tot. Sugars 12 g		Poly.Fat 3 g	Salt 0.7 g

☙☯

34) *Yogurt and apricots pancakes* 👤 2 ⏰ 10 Min.

Ingredients:

100 g. Yoghurt (nonfat, unsweetened)

1 tbsp. Agave nectar

130 g. Wheat flour

1 tsp. Olive oil, baking powder

160 ml. Oat milk (unsweetened)

2 Canned apricots (unsweetened)

Instructions:

1) Mix together the wheat flour, agave nectar, baking powder and almond milk. **2)** Heat the olive oil in a pan and pour a small part of the batter in order to do the pancakes. Bake them for a couple of minutes until they're gold-brown. **3)** Strain the apricots and cut them in slices (or as you like) and serve them with the yoghurt and the pancakes.

Nutrition Facts:

Cal. 750	**Carbs**: 121 g	**Fat**: 22 g	Sat.Fat 11 g	Cholest. -
Protein 16 g	Diet. Fiber 5 g		Mon.Fat 4 g	Sodium 932 mg
	Tot. Sugars 19 g		Poly.Fat 3 g	Salt 2.4 g

35) *Pumpkin pancakes* 👤 2 ⏰ 40 Min.

Ingredients:

130 g. Pumpkin

3 tbsp. Agave nectar

1 tsp. Baking powder, lemon juice and oil

150 ml. Almond milk

80 ml. Water, ½ Egg

50 g. Raspberries

Instructions:

1) Firstly, remove the seeds from the pumpkin, cut it into small pieces and simmer it in hot water for approx. 10-12 minutes. **2)** Secondly, combine the flour, agave nectar and the baking powder. Mix them together. **3)** As the pumpkin softens, mix it with the egg and oil. **4)** Now, add the pumpkin mixture little by little to the flour and blend everything very well. Using a pan with heated oil, bake the batter into small pancakes. **5)** Separately, add the berries, agave and lemon juice in a pot and mix them together with an immersion blender. **6)** Serve the pancakes with the berries sauce.

Nutrition Facts:

Cal. 970	**Carbs**: 170 g	**Fat**: 16 g	Sat.Fat 2.4 g	Cholest. 139 mg
Protein 24 g	Diet. Fiber 20 g		Mon.Fat 6 g	Sodium 660 mg
	Tot. Sugars 60 g		Poly.Fat 6 g	Salt 1.5 g

ಐଓ

36) *Papaya salad* 👤 2 ⏰ 10 Min.

Ingredients:

2 tbsp. Sunflower seeds, chia seeds and pumpkin seeds

300 g. Papaya

2 Apples

2 Peaches

½ Lemon

Instructions:

1) Firstly, roast a little bit the pumpkin seeds and sunflower seeds and let them cool down a bit. **2)** Peel the apples and grate them in a bowl. The same thing with peaches and papaya. Cut them into small pieces and add them to the apples. **3)** Squeeze the lemon and add the juice to the bowl with the other ingredients. **4)** Mix all the fruits and add the sunflower, pumpkin and chia seeds.

Nutrition Facts:

Cal. 490	**Carbs**: 83 g	**Fat**: 5.7 g	Sat.Fat 1 g	Cholest. -
Protein 8.5 g	Diet. Fiber 16.5 g		Mon.Fat 1 g	Sodium 12 mg
	Tot. Sugars 81.3 g		Poly.Fat 3.3 g	Salt -

37) *Antioxidants salad* 👤 2   ⏰ 10 Min.

Ingredients:

3-4 tbsp. Yoghurt (nonfat, unsweetened)

25 g. Almonds

2 Bananas

3 peaches

200 g. Blueberries e raspberries

Instructions:

1) Pour in a bowl the yoghurt with the berries. **2)** Peel the bananas and cut them into pieces, as weel as the peaches. **3)** Add everything to the yoghurt and lastly, cut the almonds into small pieces and add them in the bowl with the other ingredients. **4)** Blend everything together and serve the salad.

Nutrition Facts:

Cal. 600	**Carbs**: 90 g	**Fat**: 12 g	Sat.Fat 1 g	Cholest. -
Protein 10 g	Diet. Fiber 26 g		Mon.Fat 6 g	Sodium 9 mg
	Tot. Sugars 83 g		Poly.Fat 4 g	Salt -

༄༅

38) *Orange oatmeal* 👤 2   ⏰ 12 Min.

Ingredients:

4 Oranges

100 g. Rolled oats

200 ml. Oat milk (unsweetened)

2 tbsp. Agave nectar and cocoa powder

2 tbsp. Cacao nibs (unsweetened) and walnuts

Instructions:

1) Squeeze and peel one orange, peel also a second one and be careful to remove the pith. After that, split the orange into small wedges. **2)** Combine the juice and gratings with the rolled oats, oat milks, the agave nectar and cocoa powder. Blend everything together and simmer over medium heat for approx. 3 minutes. Occasionally stirring. **3)** Add the oatmeal into the bowl and garnish everything with cacao nibs and walnuts.

Nutrition Facts:

Cal. 500	**Carbs**: 70 g	**Fat**: 11 g	Sat.Fat 4.3 g	Cholest. -
Protein 15 g	Diet. Fiber 18 g		Mon.Fat 3.5 g	Sodium 53 mg
	Tot. Sugars 40 g		Poly.Fat 2 g	Salt -

39) *Cinnamon pancakes* 👤 2 ⏰ 15 Min.

Ingredients:

150 g. Spelt flour

1 tsp. Baking powder, olive oil and cinnamon

½ tsp. Ground ginger

5 Walnuts

170 ml. Oat milk (unsweetened)

3 tbsp. Agave nectar

Instructions:

1) Blend together the flour, baking powder, salt, cinnamon, ground ginger, oat milk, and 2 tbsp. of agave nectar. **2)** Heat a pan with a bit of oil. **3)** Bake one pancake at the time for approx. 3 minutes until they become golden-brown. **4)** Garnish the pancakes with the remaining agave nectar and walnuts.

Nutrition Facts:

Cal. 700	**Carbs**: 115 g	**Fat**: 17 g	Sat.Fat 2 g	Cholest. -
Protein 16 g	Diet. Fiber 5 g		Mon.Fat 8 g	Sodium 600 mg
	Tot. Sugars 28 g		Poly.Fat 4 g	Salt 1.5 g

ಬೋಕ್ಸ್

40) *Vanilla soufflé* 👤 2 ⏰ 70 Min.

Ingredients:

2 tsp. Vanilla powder

500 g. Vanilla yoghurt (nonfat, unsweetened)

40 g. Vanilla pudding mix

250 ml. Almond milk

Cacao nibs and agave nectar (to taste)

Instructions:

1) Firstly, you have to preheat the oven to 320 °F (160 °C). Secondly, pour the vanilla powder, yoghurt, almond milk, agave nectar and pudding mix in a bowl and combine everything with a hand mixer. **2)** Transfer the mixture into a soufflé dish. **3)** Garnish it with cacao nibs (press them down slightly) and bake the dough for approx. 60 minutes.

Nutrition Facts:

Cal. 960	**Carbs**: 95 g	**Fat**: 19 g	Sat.Fat 7 g	Cholest. 570 mg
Protein 92 g	Diet. Fiber 2 g		Mon.Fat 6.8 g	Sodium 644 mg
	Tot. Sugars 60 g		Poly.Fat 2.8 g	Salt 1.6 g

41) *Rice pudding* 👤 2   ⏰ 50 Min.

Ingredients:

600 ml. Milk (nonfat)

100 g. Short-grain white rice

50 ml. Maple syrup

Instructions:

1) Pout the milk and the syrup into a pot and let them boil over medium heat. Add the rice and mix everything very well. **2)** Cover the pot with a lid, leaving between the two a small space. **3)** Let the rice simmer for approx. 45 minutes and stir occasionally.

Nutrition Facts:

Cal. 820	**Carbs**: 152 g	**Fat**: 10 g Sat.Fat 6.5 g	Cholest. 24 mg
Protein 27 g	Diet. Fiber 2 g	Mon.Fat 2.3 g	Sodium 292 mg
	Tot. Sugars 76 g	Poly.Fat 0.4 g	Salt -

෮෬

42) *Blueberry bagel* 👤 4   ⏰ 120 Min.

Ingredients:

150 ml. Lukewarm water

140 g. Blueberries

4 g. Dried yeast

230 g. Spelt Flour

100 g. Yoghurt (unsweetened)

¾ tbs. Salt

½ tbsp. Agave nectar

Instructions:

1) Mix well together water and yeast, let them there for approx. 5 minutes. In another bowl, mix together salt and flour. **2)** Now combine together flour, yeast and half of the blueberries. With your hands knead the mixture until it becomes a smooth dough. Cover with a towel and let it rest in a warm place for 1 hour. **3)** Combine the yoghurt with the blueberries and blend everything with an immersion blender. Bring some water to boil and preheat the oven to 395 °F (200 °C). **4)** Create 6-8 pieces and with your hands form a bagel. Bake each of them in the boiling water for 2 min. and remove it when it floats to the top. **5)** Put it on the baking sheet and bake them on th emiddle rack for approx. 20 minutes. **6)** Let them cool down and serve them with yoghurt.

Nutrition Facts:

Cal. 1000	**Carbs**: 173.8 g	**Fat**: 13.7 Sat.Fat 6.6 g	Cholest. 37 mg
Protein 30 g	Diet. Fiber 15.2 g	Mon.Fat 3.5 g	Sodium 638 mg
	Tot. Sugars 20.6 g	Poly.Fat 2.2 g	Salt 1.6 g

43) *Banana bread* 👤 4 ⏰ 65 Min.

Ingredients:

1 tbsp. Chia seeds, vanilla extract

2 ½ tbsp. Water

100 g. Rolled oats

1 tsp. Baking powder and salt

20 g. Butter

2 tsp. Agave nectar

2 ripe Bananas

Instructions:

1) Firstly, preheat the oven to 325 °F (170 °C) and let the chia seeds soak in water for approx. 5 minutes. **2)** Blend into a fine flour 80 g. of oat flakes with a mixer. Add the remaining flakes with salt and the baking powder. **3)** Take another bowl and combine together 1 ½ sliced bananas, butter, vanilla extract and the chia seeds. Mix it very well until it turns a smooth batter. **4)** Now, combine together the two mixtures. Line the batter over the bread tin and spread it smoothly and then add the remaining banana slices. **5)** Bake the banana bread on the middle rack for approx. 55 minutes.

Nutrition Facts:

Cal. 909	**Carbs**: 147 g	**Fat**: 22.3 g	Sat.Fat 2.8 g	Cholest. -
Protein 24 g	Diet. Fiber 20 g		Mon.Fat 8.6 g	Sodium 1016 mg
	Tot. Sugars 82 g		Poly.Fat 4.9 g	Salt 2.6 g

ಶಃಛ

44) *Sourdough Bread* 👤 4 ⏰ 180 Min.

Ingredients:

170 g. Rye flour

170 ml. lukewarm Water

60 g. Whole wheat flour

2 g. Salt

4 g. Dried yeast

Instructions:

1) SOURDOUGH MOTHER: 1 tbsp of rye flour and 1 tbsp of water, mix them together in a jar and keep them at room temp. for 1 day. For the next 3 days, add 1 tbsp of water and rye flour to the jar. Mix the ingredients together and after a few hour put the jar in the fridge. Now you have the starter and can feed it twice a week with the same procedure. **2) BREAD**: mix 1 tbsp. of starter + 200 g. rye flour and 200 ml. of lukewarm water. Cover the mixture with a towel and let it rise at room temp. for 24 h. Then, combine the mixture with the remaining rye flour, whole wheat flour and salt. **3)** Dissolve the yeast in 4 tbsp. of water and then add the remaining water and previously prepared sourdough. **4)** Prepare a floured surface and knead the ingredients until they have a smooth consistency. Cover with a towel and place it in a warm place for 90 min. Knead again to a loaf form and let sit for 30 min. **5)** Bake the bread to 400 °F (200 °C) for 45 Min. It's ready when you tap on it and it seems hollow.

Nutrition Facts:

Cal. 840	**Carbs**: 162 g	**Fat**: 2.8 g	Sat.Fat 0.5 g	Cholest. -
Protein 32 g	Diet. Fiber 12 g		Mon.Fat 0.4 g	Sodium 821 mg
	Tot. Sugars 15 g		Poly.Fat 1.2 g	Salt 2 g

45) Tomato bread   👤 4   ⏰ 70 Min.

Ingredients:

120 g. Whole wheat flour

100 g. plain Yoghurt

2/3 tbsp. Baking powder

9 g. Dried tomatoes (withour oil), sesam and pumpkin seeds

25 g. Egg and ricotta

20 ml. rice Milk (unsweetened)

Instructions:

1) Firstly, preheat the oven to 360 °F (180 °C) and secondly, use a bowl to mix together flour and salt. **2)** Now, chop the tomatoes and and divide into pieces the ricotta with your hands. **3)** Add these ingredients, together with milk, egg and yoghurt to the flour mixture and knead it until it becomes smooth. **4)** Place the dough in a bread pan and sprinkle it with sesam and pumpkin seeds. **5)** Bake the dough on the middle rack for approx. 60 minutes.

Nutrition Facts:

Cal. 647	**Carbs**: 84 g	**Fat**: 15.7 g	Sat.Fat 6.7 g	Cholest. 114 g
Protein 38 g	Diet. Fiber 5.2 g		Mon.Fat 4.7 g	Sodium 1663 mg
	Tot. Sugars 4.6 g		Poly.Fat 2.8 g	Salt 4.2 g

൝ൟ

46) Buckwheat bread   👤 4   ⏰ 110 Min.

Ingredients:

20 g. Yeast

200 ml. lukewarm Water

130 g. rice and buckwheat Flour

1 tbsp. Linseeds (or other your prefer)

½ tsp. Salt

1 tbsp. Olive oil

Instructions:

1) Firstly, dssolve the yeast in the lukewarm water and let sit for approx. 10-15 min. to activate. Secondly, mix together in a bowl the rice flour, linseeds and buckwheat flour. **2)** Combine together the flour and yeast mixture and mix them for 5 min. Cover the dough and let rise for approx. 30 min. **3)** With your damp hands create equal-sized balls and score a cross on top of them with a knife. Cover them and let them rise for 15 more min. **4)** Heat the oven to 360 °F (180 °C). **5)** Brush them with a bit of olive oil and bake them for approx. 40 min. until they're gold-braun. *!! Place in the oven a safe bowl of water.*

Nutrition Facts:

Cal. 1160	**Carbs**: 218 g	**Fat**: 17.5 g	Sat.Fat 2.1 g	Cholest. -
Protein 23.6 g	Diet. Fiber 12.7 g		Mon.Fat 7.6 g	Sodium 995 mg
	Tot. Sugars 1.5 g		Poly.Fat 4.8 g	Salt 2.5 g

47) *Cornbread*   👤 4   ⏰ 40 Min.

Ingredients:

50 g. Cornmeal and canned corn

60 g. Whole wheat flour

30 g. Agave nectar

1/3 tbsp. Baking powder and olive oil

90 g. Ricotta

50 g. Eggs

Instructions:

1) Firstly, preheat the oven to 400 °F (200 °C). Secondly, combine together the baking powder, cornmeal, flour and a bit of salt. Drain the corn. **2)** Set aside a tbsp. of agave nectar, while blend in a mixer the ricotta, corn, eggs, olive oil and the remaining honey and purée until it becomes smooth. **3)** Blend well together the ricotta with the flour mixture. **4)** Line a baking dish with appropriate paper and add the batter. Bake it for approx. 25-28 min. until it's golden-braun. **5)** Heat the remaining honey for 10 sec. and spread it over the cornbread.

Nutrition Facts:

Cal. 600	**Carbs**: 93 g	**Fat**: 12.3 g	Sat.Fat 2.6 g	Cholest. 186 mg
Protein 20 g	Diet. Fiber 11 g		Mon.Fat 5.8 g	Sodium 846 mg
	Tot. Sugars 28 g		Poly.Fat 2.6 g	Salt -

☙❧

48) *Gluten-free buns*   👤 4   ⏰ 115 Min.

Ingredients:

80 g. Potatoes and topioca flour

110 ml. Almond milk (unsweetened)

1 tbsp. Dry yeast

2 tbsp. Agave nectar, sesame and chia seeds

Salt (to taste)

Instructions:

1) Firstly, you have to peel and cut the potatoes. Add them in a pot, cover them with water and bring to boil. Let them simmer for about 15 min. Secondly, drain them and mash them with a fork. **2)** Heat the milk until it's lukewarm and dissolve the agave and yeast together. Cover and let sit for 10 min. **3)** Combine the flour, seeds and a bit of salt. Add the yeast mixture and potatoes and blend together for approx. 5 min. **4)** Create small balls with the dough, place them on a baking sheet and cross them with a cross. Let them rise for approx. one hour. **5)** Heat the oven to 360 °F (180 °C), place small jar with water in the oven and bake the bread for approx. 25 min.

Nutrition Facts:

Cal. 830	**Carbs**: 164	**Fat**: 10.8 g	Sat.Fat 1.7 g	Cholest. -
Protein 18 g	Diet. Fiber 26 g		Mon.Fat 2.6 g	Sodium 36 mg
	Tot. Sugars 18 g		Poly.Fat 2.8 g	Salt -

49) Raisin bread

👤 4   ⏰ 220 Min.

Ingredients:

6 g. Yeast

3 tbsp. Raisins

50 ml. Almond milk (unsweetened)

3 g. vegetable Butter

30 g. Applesauce

145 g. Whole wheat flour

Instructions:

1) Firstly, crumble the yeast into the lukewarm milk and make it dissolve using a fork. Secondly, cover it and let the yeast activate in a warm place for at least 10 min. (you see that bubbles start to form). **2)** Mix together flour, a bit of salt, the yeast mixture and applesauce. Knead with your hands for approx. 10 minutes until it's smooth. Cover and let it rise for 2 hour, when the volume is doubled. **3)** Add the raisins to the dough and divide it in 4- 5 equal-sized pieces. Cover and let them rise for approx. 30 min. **4)** Preheat the oven to 325 °F (170 °C) and bake the bread for approx. 40 min. **5)** Melt the butter and once the bread is baakes, spread it on top and let it cool down.

Nutrition Facts:

Cal. 600	**Carbs**: 118 g	**Fat**: 4.8 g	Sat.Fat 2.4 g	Cholest. 9 mg
Protein 17 g	Diet. Fiber 5.6 g		Mon.Fat 1.1 g	Sodium 89 mg
	Tot. Sugars 14.3 g		Poly.Fat 0.8 g	Salt -

૪౦ౚ

50) Caramel overnight oats

👤 2   ⏰ 80 Min.

Ingredients:

1 ripe Banana

80 g. rolled Oats

350 ml. Oat milk (unsweetened)

1 tbsp. Cinnamon and Vanilla powder

2 tbsp. Chia seeds

50 g. brown Sugar

Instructions:

1) Peel and slice half of the banana (and set aside), while mash the other half with a fork. **2)** Add the oatmeal flakes to the chia seeds, chia seeds and vanilla powder. Blend everything tigether. **3)** Cover the top and put the bowl in the fridge for aprrox. 45 min. (better overnight). **4) CARAMEL SAUCE**: blend together the milk, sugar and a bit of salt and let them boil for 60 sec. Low the heat and boil the mixture for approx. 40 minutes. Stir occasionally in order to have a thick sauce. **5)** Garnish the oats with the banana slices.

Nutrition Facts:

Cal. 900	**Carbs**: 144 g	**Fat**: 23 g	Sat.Fat 8.6 g	Cholest. -
Protein 18 g	Diet. Fiber 21.7 g		Mon.Fat 4.8 g	Sodium 55 mg
	Tot. Sugars 80 g		Poly.Fat 7.2 g	Salt -

51) *Red smoothie*   👤 2   ⏰ 5 Min.

Ingredients:

500 ml. Freshly squeezed orange juice

150 g. Strawberries (frozen)

1 ripe Banana (peeled, frozen)

140 g. Blackberry yoghurt

100 g. Pomegranate seeds

Instructions:

1) Slice the banana and combine it with all the other fruits. Keep a few pomegranate seeds aside to garnish the smoothie.
2) Blend very well with a mixer until you have a creamy puréè.
3) If you don't like seeds, strain the smoothie with a sieve into glasses. Finally, use the pomegranate seeds to garnish everything.

Nutrition Facts:

Cal. 500	**Carbs**: 96 g	**Fat**: 3 g	Sat.Fat 0.6 g	Cholest. -
Protein 11 g	Diet. Fiber 11 g		Mon.Fat 0.6 g	Sodium 32 mg
	Tot. Sugars 91 g		Poly.Fat 1.4 g	Salt -

ಶಂೞ

52) *Coconut smoothie*   👤 2   ⏰ 5 Min.

Ingredients:

150 g. Blueberries

100 g. rolled Oats

150 ml. Coconut milk (unsweetened)

2 tsp. Coconut flakes and cacao nibs

Instructions:

1) Take a mixer and finely purée the oatmeal flakes, blueberries and coconut milk. If you like add a few ice cubes.
2) Pour the smoothie in a glass and garnish with cacao and coconut flakes.

Nutrition Facts:

Cal. 620	**Carbs**: 98 g	**Fat**: 12.6 g	Sat.Fat 5.7 g	Cholest. -
Protein 16 g	Diet. Fiber 19.5 g		Mon.Fat 2.4 g	Sodium 13 mg
	Tot. Sugars 39.3 g		Poly.Fat 2.6 g	Salt -

53) *Pudding with spinach* 　 👤 2 　 ⏰ 60 Min.

Ingredients:

7 Dates (pitted)

500 ml. Rice milk (unsweetened)

100 g. Spinach

6 tbsp. Sesam seeds

1 Mango

1 ripe Banana

Instructions:

1) Blend well together the dates, rice milk and spinach in order to purée everything. Combine the smoothie with the sesam seeds, stir a few times and let rest for approx. 20 min. **2)** Cover and let in the fridge for at least 45 min. or better overnight. **3)** Peel the kiwi and mango and cut them into pieces, the same with the banana. **4)** Garnish the pudding with the prepared fruit.

Nutrition Facts:

Cal. 1100	**Carbs**: 172.5 g	**Fat**: 28.6 g	Sat.Fat 3.2 g	Cholest. -
Protein 22 g	Diet. Fiber 46 g		Mon.Fat 3.6 g	Sodium 105 mg
	Tot. Sugars 142 g		Poly.Fat 17 g	Salt -

☼☼

54) *Strawberry smoothie* 　 👤 2 　 ⏰ 5 Min.

Ingredients:

250 g. Strawberries

1 ripe Banana

200 g. Strawberry yoghurt (unsweetened)

Instructions:

1) Wash the strawberries, remove the stalk and put them in a blender. **2)** Peel and cut the banana in small pieces and add them to the blender with the other ingredients. **3)** Blend them until you have a smooth consistency.

Nutrition Facts:

Cal. 300	**Carbs**: 49 g	**Fat**: 4 g	Sat.Fat 2 g	Cholest. 7 mg
Protein 10 g	Diet. Fiber 7 g		Mon.Fat 1 g	Sodium 85 mg
	Tot. Sugars 45 g		Poly.Fat 1 g	Salt -

55) *Green smoothie* 2 👤   ⏰ 5 Min.

Ingredients:

150 g. Spinach

2 ripe Bananas

2 Celery stems

200 ml. Oat milk (unsweetened)

Mint (to taste)

Instructions:

1) Firstly, wash the spinach and dry it. Add the spinach into a blender. Squeeze the orange juice and add it into a blender. **2)** Peel the bananas, cut them into pieces and add them into the blender. **3)** Liquidize the green smoothie with the oat milk. Blend everything for approx. two minutes, fill a glass e add mint to taste.

Nutrition Facts:

Cal. 550	**Carbs**: 98 g **Fat**: 4.8 g Sat.Fat 0.5 g	Cholest. -
Protein 12 g	Diet. Fiber 18.3 g Mon.Fat 1 g	Sodium 81 mg
	Tot. Sugars 89.9 g Poly.Fat 1.5 g	Salt -

☙☼☙

56) *Blue smoothie* 👤 2   ⏰ 5 Min.

Ingredients:

250 g. Blueberries

100 g. Blackberry

1 ripe Banana

150 ml. Oat milk (unsweetened)

Instructions:

1) Wash and dry both kind of berries. **2)** Peel and sliced the banana into pieces and take a blender to mix everything together.

Nutrition Facts:

Cal. 350	**Carbs**: 55 g **Fat**: 3.5 g Sat.Fat 1.2 g	Cholest. 2 mg
Protein 14 g	Diet. Fiber 13 g Mon.Fat 0.7 g	Sodium 200 mg
	Tot. Sugars 54 g Poly.Fat 1.1 g	Salt -

57) *Coconut shake* 👤 2 ⏰ 5 Min.

Ingredients:

600 g. Coconut yoghurt

250 g. Blackberries

200 ml. Coconut milk (unsweetened)

Mint (to taste)

Instructions:

1) With a kitchen blender mix all the ingredients for approx. 2-3 minutes, until the mixture has a smooth consistency. **2)** Garnish with a few mint leaves (to taste).

Nutrition Facts:

Cal. 720	**Carbs**: 45 g	**Fat**: 12.8 g	Sat.Fat 9.3 g	Cholest. 14 mg
Protein 90 g	Diet. Fiber 13.9 g		Mon.Fat 1.8 g	Sodium 340 mg
	Tot. Sugars 44.5 g		Poly.Fat 1.1 g	Salt 0.8 g

❧☙

58) *Walnut shake* 👤 2 ⏰ 5 Min.

Ingredients:

300 g. plain Yoghurt (unsweetened)

600 ml. Walnut milk (unsweetened)

1 ripe Banana

3 tsp. Agave nectar

50 g. Walnuts (chopped)

Instructions:

1) Set aside a few walnuts to garnish the shake. **2)** Blend finely all the ingredients very well together. **3)** Pour the shake into a glass and garnish with the remaining walnuts.

Nutrition Facts:

Cal. 870	**Carbs**: 60 g	**Fat**: 44 g	Sat.Fat 4.3 g	Cholest. 3 mg
Protein 52 g	Diet. Fiber 7 g		Mon.Fat 8.1 g	Sodium 135 mg
	Tot. Sugars 52 g		Poly.Fat 27 g	Salt -

59) *Yellow smoothie*   👤 2   ⏰ 8 Min.

Ingredients:

2 Oranges

1 ripe Banana

200 ml. Oat milk (unsweetened)

Cinnamon (to taste)

Instructions:

1) Peel the banana, oranges and coarsely chop them. Take a kitchen blender and finely blend all the ingredients. **2)** Fill the glasses and garnish with cinnamon (to taste).

Nutrition Facts:

Cal. 430	**Carbs:** 75 g **Fat:** 4.9 g	Sat.Fat 0.8 g	Cholest. -
Protein 9 g	Diet. Fiber 12.4 g	Mon.Fat 2.4 g	Sodium 10 mg
	Tot. Sugars 54.6 g	Poly.Fat 1.3 g	Salt -

༄༅

60) *Cinnamon mix cream*   👤 2   ⏰ 5 Min.

Ingredients:

650 g. plain Yoghurt (unsweetened)

1 tsp. Cinnamon

Agave nectar (to taste)

40 g. Walnuts (chopped)

180 g. Applesauce (unsweetened)

Instructions:

1) CREAM: blend together the yoghurt with a a tbsp. of water, cinnamon and agave nectar (to taste). **2)** Pour a bit of the cream in a glass and with a spoon layer the applesauce and then some more cream. **3)** Use the chopped walnuts to garnish the cream.

Nutrition Facts:

Cal. 860	**Carbs:** 46.8 g **Fat:** 23 g	Sat.Fat 2.7 g	Cholest. 6 mg
Protein 103 g	Diet. Fiber 7.8 g	Mon.Fat 12.8 g	Sodium 283 mg
	Tot. Sugars 43.6 g	Poly.Fat 4.3 g	Salt -

61) *Mango smoothie* 👤 2   ⏰ 5 Min.

Ingredients:

- 2 fresh Mango
- 2 Oranges
- 80 g. fresh Spinach
- 100 ml. Rice milk
- 1 tsp. Chia seeds

Instructions:

1) Peel the mango and the oranges, cut them into pieces and use a blender to mix everything. **2)** Do the same thing with the spinach, rice milk and chia seeds. Blend everything together and pour both of the mixture together in a glass.

Nutrition Facts:

Cal. 400	**Carbs**: 70 g	**Fat**: 4 g	Sat.Fat 0.8 g	Cholest. -
Protein 9.6 g	Diet. Fiber 13 g		Mon.Fat 1.3 g	Sodium 50 mg
	Tot. Sugars 49 g		Poly.Fat 1.2 g	Salt -

൸ൄ

62) *Dates smoothie* 👤 2   ⏰ 15 Min.

Ingredients:

- 100 g. pitted Dates
- 1 small Banana
- 350 ml. Oat milk (unsweetened)

Instructions:

1) Use a pot and fill it with water, let it boil and let the dates soak for 10 minutes. Drain them and take a mixer. **2)** Peel the banana and with a mixer blend everything together until it has a creamy consistency.

Nutrition Facts:

Cal. 460	**Carbs**: 84 g	**Fat**: 9 g	Sat.Fat 0.7 g	Cholest. -
Protein 6.3 g	Diet. Fiber 11 g		Mon.Fat 5.7 g	Sodium 12 mg
	Tot. Sugars 82 g		Poly.Fat 2 g	Salt -

63) *Peach smoothie* 👤 2   ⏰ 5 Min.

Ingredients:

3 Peaches

1 Banana

1 tsp. Chia seeds

80 ml. Orange juice

140 ml. Oat milk (unsweetened)

Instructions:

1) Pit the peaches, peel the banana and cut in small pieces both fruits. **2)** Use a kitchen blender and add the remaining ingredients. Blend everything together and taste!

Nutrition Facts:

Cal. 345	**Carbs**: 60 g **Fat**: 5.3 g	Sat.Fat 0.6 g	Cholest. -
Protein 7 g	Diet. Fiber 10.6 g	Mon.Fat 1.1 g	Sodium 8 mg
	Tot. Sugars 40 g	Poly.Fat 2.3 g	Salt -

ಬ‍ಚ

64) *Peanut butter shake* 👤 2   ⏰ 5 Min.

Ingredients:

4 ripe Banana

400 ml. Almond milk (unsweetened)

2 tbsp. Peanut butter

Cinnamon (to taste)

Instructions:

1) Peel the bananas and cut them in small pieces. **2)** Combine them with the other ingredients and mix everything in a blender until it's creamy.

Nutrition Facts:

Cal. 970	**Carbs**: 152 g **Fat**: 26 g	Sat.Fat 4.7 g	Cholest. -
Protein 20 g	Diet. Fiber 17 g	Mon.Fat 11.6 g	Sodium 11 mg
	Tot. Sugars 117 g	Poly.Fat 8.7 g	Salt -

65) Summer smoothie 👤 2 ⏰ 5 Min.

Ingredients:

2 Mnago

3 ripe Bananas

3 Peaches

2 Apricot

1 Lemon

Mint (to taste)

Instructions:

1) Peel and pit the fruits and cut them into pieces. Squeeze the lemon. **2)** Use a blender to mix finely and garnish the smoothie with a few leaves of mint. Enjoy.

Nutrition Facts:

Cal. 550	**Carbs**: 111 g	**Fat**: 2.8 g	Sat.Fat 0.5 g	Cholest. -
Protein 7 g	Diet. Fiber 17.8 g		Mon.Fat 1 g	Sodium 30 mg
	Tot. Sugars 103 g		Poly.Fat 0.7 g	Salt -

ಲ೦ಜ

66) Kale smoothie 👤 2 ⏰ 5 Min.

Ingredients:

2 Tangerines

3 Carrots

70 g. fresh Kale

1 Lemon

Mint (to taste)

Instructions:

1) Peel and chop into pieces the fruits, wash and dry the kale and cut into pieces its leaves. **2)** Squeeze the lemon and ad its juice. Now, use a blender and combine together every ingredient and mix them finely. **3)** Pour the smoothie into a glass, garnish with a bit of mint (to taste) and taste.

Nutrition Facts:

Cal. 260	**Carbs**: 40 g	**Fat**: 2 g	Sat.Fat 0.5 g	Cholest. -
Protein 7.8 g	Diet. Fiber 17 g		Mon.Fat 0.2 g	Sodium 94 mg
	Tot. Sugars 39 g		Poly.Fat 1 g	Salt -

67) *Fried bananas* 👤 2   ⏰ 15 Min.

Ingredients:

- 3 ripe Bananas
- Agave nectar (to taste)
- 1 tsp. Cinnamon
- 1 tbsp. Coconut oil
- 1 tsp. Vanilla powder

Instructions:

1) Peel the bananas and cut them into slices. Take a bo[wl] mix together the agave nectar, cinnamon and vanilla p[owder].
2) Take a pan and heat the coconut oil, brush the banana slices with the agave mixture and fry both sides for approx. 2-3 minutes.

Nutrition Facts:

Cal. 350 **Carbs**: 61 g   **Fat**: 7.8 g   Sat.Fat 6.5 g   Cholest. -
Protein 3.6 g   Diet. Fiber 6.5 g   Mon.Fat 0.1 g   Sodium 4 mg
Tot. Sugars 53 g   Poly.Fat 0.3 g   Salt -

☯☪

68) *Sweet potatoes fries* 👤 2   ⏰ 40 Min.

Ingredients:

- 3 Sweet potatoes
- Rosmary and paprika powder (to taste)
- 2 tbsp. Olive oil
- 2 tbsp. Herbs mix
- 150 g. plain Yoghurt

Instructions:

1) Firstly, you have to peel the potatoes and slice them. Secondly, preheat the oven to 375 °F (190 °C) and in the meantime mix the rosmary, olive oil, paprika and other herbs in order to have a seasoning. 2) Brush the potatoes with this sauce and bake them for approx. 30 minutes. 3) Meanwhile, use the herbs mix to season the yoghurt and, once the potatoes are ready, garnish them with this dressing.

Nutrition Facts:

Cal. 550   **Carbs**: 103 g   **Fat**: 5.2 g   Sat.Fat 3.4 g   Cholest. 9 mg
Protein 17 g   Diet. Fiber 9 g   Mon.Fat 1.2 g   Sodium 1866 mg
Tot. Sugars 30 g   Poly.Fat 0.6 g   Salt 4.5 g

69) *Spiced veggie rolls* 👤 2   ⏰ 15 Min.

Ingredients:

8 pieces of Rice paper

2 Tomatoes

½ Avocado and lemon

250 g. Lettuce and chicken breast (smoked)

2 tsp. Olive oil

Garlic and herbs (to taste)

Instructions:

1) Firstly, you have to soak the rice paper in water and then place it on a paper towel. Secondly, peel the tomatoes and cut them into pieces, the same with the lettuce. **2)** Pit the avocado and mash it with a fork. Chop the garlic and mix it with the olive oil and avocado. Add some herbs (to taste) and lemon juice to spice the sauce. **3)** Spread the sauce on the rice paper and fill with the smoked chicken strips. **4)** Roll the paper and enjoy!

Nutrition Facts:

Cal. 910	**Carbs**: 76 g	**Fat**: 29 g	Sat.Fat 5.6 g	Cholest. -
Protein 73 g	Diet. Fiber 20 g		Mon.Fat 14.2 g	Sodium 400 mg
	Tot. Sugars 32 g		Poly.Fat 3.6 g	Salt 1 g

☙❧

70) *Veggie sticks with mustard* 👤 2   ⏰ 15 Min.

Ingredients:

2 Carrots and tomatoes

1 red pepper

Mustard and chives (to taste)

250 g. Turkey breast (sliced)

Instructions:

1) Firsly, prepare the vegetable, peel and slice the tomatoes, carrots and pepper. Secondly, spread the turkey slices with the mustard. **2)** Cut the chives and lay it as well as the vegetables on the turkey slices and roll them up. **3)** Secure them with a toothpick and serve.

Nutrition Facts:

Cal. 530	**Carbs**: 27 g	**Fat**: 20 g	Sat.Fat 10 g	Cholest. 135 mg
Protein 54 g	Diet. Fiber 12 g		Mon.Fat 5.9 g	Sodium 2680 mg
	Tot. Sugars 25 g		Poly.Fat 2.5 g	Salt 4 g

71) Tumeric latte with honey 👤 2 ⏰ 15 Min.

Ingredients:

400 ml. Oat milk

3 tsp. Honey

2 ½ tsp. Tumeric

1 tsp. Ginger

Instructions:

1) First of all, mix the oat milk (or your favourite one) with tumeric, ginger and honey in a small pan and warm over medium heat. **2)** Now, place the mixture in a heat-resistant glass and let t infuse for approx. 15 minutes and serve.

Nutrition Facts:

Cal. 280	**Carbs**: 40 g	**Fat**: 7.4 g	Sat.Fat 4.6 g	Cholest. 15 mg
Protein 14 g	Diet. Fiber 0.6 g		Mon.Fat 1.8 g	Sodium 193 mg
	Tot. Sugars 40 g		Poly.Fat 0.3 g	Salt -

ഗ്ര

72) Ginger muffins 👤 4 ⏰ 30 Min.

Ingredients:

70 g. Whole wheat flour

1 tsp. Ginger and cinnamon

½ tbsp. Olive oil

½ ripe Banana

30 g. Egg and yoghurt

2/3 tsp. Baking powder

Instructions:

1) First of all, preheat the ove to 325 °F (165 °C). Now, take a bowl and combine together cinnamon, flour, baking powder and ginger. **2)** In a second bowl mix together the olive oil, egg, ½ banana (mash it), honey and yoghurt. **3)** Now, add the dry ingredients into the mixture and blend everything together. **4)** Pour the batter into the muffins' molds and garnish them with the remaining banana slices. **5)** Bake the muffins for approx. 30 minutes and then let them cool down.

Nutrition Facts:

Cal. 540	**Carbs**: 85 g	**Fat**: 14 g	Sat.Fat 8.4 g	Cholest. 133 mg
Protein 14 g	Diet. Fiber 8.9 g		Mon.Fat 2.4 g	Sodium 460 mg
	Tot. Sugars 40 g		Poly.Fat 1.5 g	Salt 1 g

Lunch

73) Stuffed peppers   👤 4   ⏰ 45 Min.

Ingredients:

4 medium bell Peppers

2 tbsp. Olive oil

1 Onion

2 Tomatoes and zucchini

70 g. Brown rice

½ tsp. Garlic powder

Thyme (to taste)

Instructions:

1) First of all, cook the rice and when 5 minutes before the end of its cooking time, remove it from the heat. Preheat the oven to 375 °F (190 °C). Prepare the peppers (cut the top and remove the membrane and seeds). **2)** Wash and cut the tomatoes and zucchini, peel the onion and cut into small pieces. **3)** Take a bowl and mix very well together the vegetables with the rice, garlic powder, thyme and a bit of olive oil to blend everything. **4)** Fill the peppers with the mixture and let them cook for approx. 35 minutes. **5)** As approx. 20 min. has passed, remember to low the heat to 302 °F (150 °C) and finish the cooking.

Nutrition Facts:

Cal. 1500	**Carbs**: 180 g	**Fat**: 35.8 g	Sat.Fat 4.4 g	Cholest. 180 mg
Protein 150 g	Diet. Fiber 35 g		Mon.Fat 15 g	Sodium 372 mg
	Tot. Sugars 36 g		Poly.Fat 9.8 g	Salt 3 g

ஐ⊗

74) Sautéed artichokes   👤 4   ⏰ 20 Min.

Ingredients:

4 Artichokes

3 tbsp. Olive oil

2 Garlic gloves (minced)

Parsley (to taste)

Herbs mix (to taste)

Instructions:

1) First of all you, have to cut the artichokes in two halves and then in small slices. **Tip**: while you're cleaning and cutting them take a bucket and fill it with water and vinegar, soak the artichokes for aprrox. 4-7 minutes! In this way they won't oxidize. **2)** Rinse the artichokes and heat a pan with a bit of olive oil, parsley, minced garlic gloves and herbs mix. **3)** Cook them at medium heat for approx. 10-15 minutes and serve.

Nutrition Facts:

Cal. 260	**Carbs**: 32 g	**Fat**: 15 g	Sat.Fat 4 g	Cholest. -
Protein 10 g	Diet. Fiber 18 g		Mon.Fat 8 g	Sodium 600 mg
	Tot. Sugars 4 g		Poly.Fat 3 g	Salt -

75) Hummus wraps with avocado   👤 4   ⏰ 12 Min.

Ingredients:

80 g. canned Beans (low sodium, no-salt-added)

1 tbsp. Lemon juice and paprika

3 tbsp. Water

1 Avocado, cucumber, pepper

2 Tomatoes

4 Whole-grain wraps

Instructions:

1) HUMMUS: first of all, for the beans hummus you need to drain and rinse the beans (you can choose the type you prefer), pour them in a blender, add some lemon juice, olive oil and paprika and mix together until you have a creamy consistency. **2) WRAPS**: wash and slice the cucumber, tomatoes, pepper and avocado. Spread the hummus on the wraps leaving a small border around the edges. Lay down the vegetables on the wrap and roll it. Feel free to add any kind of vegetable you prefer.

Nutrition Facts:

Cal. 1380	**Carbs**: 197 g	**Fat**: 48.4 g	Sat.Fat 8.7 g	Cholest. -
Protein 53 g	Diet. Fiber 104 g		Mon.Fat 23.7 g	Sodium 352 mg
	Tot. Sugars 17 g		Poly.Fat 8 g	Salt 3 g

ఴఁ

76) Vegetables quiche   👤 4   ⏰ 60 Min.

Ingredients:

50 g. Leek (chopped)

50 g. Ricotta

300 g. Artichokes

1 package of Puff pastry

Instructions:

1) Prepare the vegetables: cut the artichokes in small pieces. Take a pan and heat the oil, sear the artichokes with a bit of garlic and salt and add the leek. **2)** Lay out the puff pastry and spread the vegetables and riotta cheese on top. **3)** Cook the quiche for approx. 40 minutes to 356 °F (180 °C). After approx. 20 minutes low the heat to 302 °F (150 °C).

Nutrition Facts:

Cal. 930	**Carbs**: 117 g	**Fat**: 25 g	Sat.Fat 4 g	Cholest. 24.5 g
Protein 80 g	Diet. Fiber 20 g		Mon.Fat 12 g	Sodium 1258 mg
	Tot. Sugars 23 g		Poly.Fat 3 g	Salt 2.3 g

77) *Pasta with tuna and broccoli* 👤 4 ⏰ 20 Min.

Ingredients:

320 g. Whole-grain pasta

180 g. Broccoli florets

1 can. (150 g.) Tuna (low sodium)

Olive oil and Parmesan cheese (to taste)

Instructions:

1) Prepare a pot with boiling water and 1 tbsp. of salt. Cook the whole-grain pasta according to the instructions you find on the package. **2)** Cut the broccoli and sear them with a bit of olive oil and seasoning herbs (to taste). **3)** A couple of minutes before the pasta would be cooked, rinse the pasta and put it again in the pot and add a bit of olive oil, the broccoli, tuna and cook approx. for other 2 minutes. Stir now and then. Braise the ingredients and your pasta is ready!

Nutrition Facts:

Cal. 1170	**Carbs**: 120 g	**Fat**: 28 g	Sat.Fat 13 g	Cholest. 120 mg
Protein 108 g	Diet. Fiber 4 g		Mon.Fat 7.3 g	Sodium 2480 mg
	Tot. Sugars 16 g		Poly.Fat 7.7 g	Salt 5 g

---

78) *Bean soup with chicken* 👤 4 ⏰ 20 Min.

Ingredients:

500 g. Chicken breast (boneless, skinless)

200 g. Baby spinach

2 bell Peppers

2 cups. Corn niblets (frozen)

1 can. White beans

Tortillas, paprika powder, rosemary, garlic, broth, salt, olive oil (to taste)

Instructions:

1) Slice the chicken, sprinkle a bit of rosmary, olive oil, salt and garlic on top and sear it for approx. 4-7 minutes. **2)** Take a pot and combine together the peppers (clean them, remove the seeds and slice them), corn niblets and 3 glasses of broth : cover and bring everything to boil. **3)** Rinse the beans and add them to the soup. The same with the baby spinach after you have cut them into pieces. Stir occasionally (add some broth if needed). **4)** As the soup is almost ready, add the chicken slices to add more flavour to the soup. Add some additional toppings if you like.

Nutrition Facts:

Cal. 1256	**Carbs**: 164 g	**Fat**: 16 g	Sat.Fat 5.7 g	Cholest. 340 mg
Protein 167 g	Diet. Fiber 45 g		Mon.Fat 4.6 g	Sodium 1239 mg
	Tot. Sugars 12 g		Poly.Fat 5.3	Salt 6 g

79) *Chickpea salad* 👤 4   ⏰ 5 Min.

Ingredients:

1 can. Chickpeas (low sodium, no-salt-added)

4 Tomatoes (medium)

2 Peppers and cucumbers

2 stalk celery

2 tbsp. Olive oil and lemon juice

Instructions:

1) Just a few minutes and you can taste this tasteful recipe. Drain and rinse the chickpeas. Wash, peel (if you prefer) and slice the tomatoes; the same thing do with the cucumbers, celery and peppers. **2)** Take a bowl and mix together all the ingredients. Add a bit of olive oil, lemon juice and salt to seasong the salad and serve.

Nutrition Facts:

Cal. 645	**Carbs**: 76 g	**Fat**: 12g	Sat.Fat 2 g	Cholest. -
Protein 27 g	Diet. Fiber 25 g		Mon.Fat 7 g	Sodium 160 mg
	Tot. Sugars 12 g		Poly.Fat 3g	Salt -

୭୧

80) *Black beans salad* 👤 4   ⏰ 5 Min.

Ingredients:

2 cans. Black beans and whole-kernel corn (no-salt-added, low-sodium)

2 cans. Tuna (low-sodium)

2 Tomatoes and bell peppers (medium)

Olive oil, garlic, lemon juice, herbs (to taste)

Instructions:

1) Drain and rinse the black beans and corn. Take a bowl (large size) and put everything together. **2)** Wash, peel and cut the tomatoes and peppers into pieces. Drain the tuna too and pour everything into the bowl. **3)** Season everything with a bit of lemon juice, garlic, herbs like rosemary and olive oil. **4)** Mix everything and serve.

Nutrition Facts:

Cal. 568	**Carbs**: 98 g	**Fat**: 7.9 g	Sat.Fat 3 g	Cholest. -
Protein 24 g	Diet. Fiber 25 g		Mon.Fat 2.4 g	Sodium 44 mg
	Tot. Sugars 21.7 g		Poly.Fat 2.5 g	Salt 2 g

81) *Chicken with herbs and pumpkin* 👤 4 ⏰ 20 Min.

Ingredients:

50 ml. Water

½ tsp. Garlic and onion powder, dried thyme

3 g. Salt

4 Chicken breast halves (boneless, skinless)

100 g. Tomatoes

1 Pumpkin (small)

1 Shallot

Instructions:

1) First of all, mix the herbs in a bowl with a bit of salt and with your fingers press this mixture to the chicken. **2)** Heat a bit of oil into a skillet, add a bit of salt to add flavor and cook the chicken on both sides for 5 min. Remove the chicken from the skillet and keep warm. **3)** Using the same skillet, add a bit of oil, 50 ml. of water and add the small pumpkin (in pieces), tomatoes and shallot (cut into pieces). Stir frequently and cook for approx. 10 min. until the water evaporate and the veggies are ready. **4)** Serve the chicken with the vegetables.

Nutrition Facts:

Cal. 988	**Carbs**: 80 g	**Fat**: 24.5 g	Sat.Fat 3 g	Cholest. 256 mg
Protein 108	Diet. Fiber 8 g		Mon.Fat 8 g	Sodium 1384 mg
	Tot. Sugars 12 g		Poly.Fat 3.6 g	Salt 3 g

☙❧

82) *Tacos mix* 👤 4 ⏰ 15 Min.

Ingredients:

5 Toamtoes (medium)

140 g. Ricotta

Paprika, garlic powder, lemon juice, olive oil (to taste)

70 g. Olive (pitted) and baby spinach

200 g. Roasted chicken filet (boneless)

4-6 Corn tortillas

Instructions:

1) Heat up the roasted chicken and prepare the tortillas following the package directions. **2)** Prepare the vegetables. Wash and peel the tomatoes and slice them. Take a pan and with a bit of olive oil, garlic powder and paprika sear the spinach for a few minutes. **3)** Take a bowl and mix together the vegetables, tomatoes, roasted chicken, olives and garnish with a bit of lemon juice. **4)** Take the tortillas and fill them with the ingredients. Garnish the tortillas cutting into pieces the ricotta. **5)** Wrap up the tortillas and serve.

Nutrition Facts:

Cal. 1275	**Carbs**: 147 g	**Fat**: 20 g	Sat.Fat 5 g	Cholest. 305 mg
Protein 123 g	Diet. Fiber 30 g		Mon.Fat 9.8 g	Sodium 880 mg
	Tot. Sugars 26 g		Poly.Fat 5 g	Salt 5.4 g

83) Spinach quiche with sweet potato 👤 4 ⏰ 50 Min.

Ingredients:

2 sweet Potatoes, shallot

5-7 slices. Turkey bacon (nitrate-free)

200 g. Spinach

Olive oil, a bit of salt (to taste)

2 large eggs + 4 egg whites

100 g. Ricotta

35 ml. Oat milk

Instructions:

1) Heat the oven to 400 °F (200 °C). Grate the potatoes and cover with baking paper a plate. Spread the potatoes pressing with the fingers on the bottom of it. **2)** Now, cook the potato crust for approx. 20 min. and then remove from the heat and reduce the temperature to 350 °F (170 °C). **3)** Take a pan and heat a bit of oil over medium-high heat for about 5-7 min.; then add the slices of bacon, shallots (cut into pieces) and spinach. Cook for 2-4 min. and stir frequently. Remove from the heat and spread the mixture on top of the sweet potatoes. **4)** Prepare the eggs and milk, use a fork to whisk the mixture in the plate. Garnish everything with the ricotta cheese on top. **5)** Cook until the eggs are set (approx. 40 min.). Let it cool down and serve.

Nutrition Facts:

Cal. 547	**Carbs**: 44 g	**Fat**: 18 g	Sat.Fat 5.6 g	Cholest. 348 mg
Protein 53 g	Diet. Fiber 12.5 g		Mon.Fat 8 g	Sodium 1832 mg
	Tot. Sugars 12.7 g		Poly.Fat 4.4 g	Salt 2 g

୫୦ଓଷ

84) Mexican salad 👤 4 ⏰ 10 Min.

Ingredients:

200 g. Tuna (canned, low-sodium, no-salt-added)

7 Tomatoes (diced)

1 Shallot, green jalapeño pepper, lemon, cucumber and clove garlic

Cilantro, lettuce, black pepper (to taste)

Instructions:

1) First of all, prepare the pico de gallo: chop the jalapeño pepper (use half of it if you don't want it very spicy), the shallot, black pepper, cilantro, squeeze the lemon, wash and dice the tomatoes and mince the garlic. Combine these ingredients in a bowl. **2)** Add the tuna and cucumber to the pico de gallo and mix together. Use the lettuce a dish to serve the tuna with pico de gallo and taste.

Nutrition Facts:

Cal. 748	**Carbs**: 60 g	**Fat**: 12.4 g	Sat.Fat 3.6 g	Cholest. 156 mg
Protein 108	Diet. Fiber 24 g		Mon.Fat 3.2 g	Sodium 432 mg
	Tot. Sugars 28 g		Poly.Fat 5.6 g	Salt -

85) *Stuffed tomatoes with salmon* 👤 4   ⏰ 30 Min.

Ingredients:

4 large Tomatoes

150 g. smoked Salmon (low-sodium, no-salt-added)

2 Shallot

160 g. Zucchini

50 g. bread crumbs

Olive oil, salt, pepper, rosmary, thyme, basil (to taste)

Instructions:

1) Take a bowl, add the bread crumbs, the tomatoes' pulp, shallots (cut them into pieces), olive oil, salt, pepper, thyme, basil, smoked salmon and zucchini (clean them and cut them into pieces). **2)** Wash and prepare the tomatoes. Fill them with the mixture and cook them for approx. 25 min. to 392 °F (200 °C).

Nutrition Facts:

Cal. 924	**Carbs**: 63.5 g	**Fat**: 28.5	Sat.Fat 7.6 g	Cholest. 172 mg
Protein 108 g	Diet. Fiber 24.5 g		Mon.Fat 8.3 g	Sodium 756 mg
	Tot. Sugars 36 g		Poly.Fat 8 g	Salt 4.6 g

༄༅

86) *Cauliflower rice with salmon* 👤 4   ⏰ 20 Min.

Ingredients:

250 g. Salmon fillet

250 g. Brown rice

Balsamic vinegar, herbs, olive oil, orange juice (to taste)

1 tsp. Sesame seeds

1 Shallot

1 head Cauliflower (chopped)

Instructions:

1) First of all, prepare the rice according to the instructions on the package. Secondly, prepare and chop the shallot. **2)** Chop the cauliflower and sear it for a few minutes together with the shallot. Season everything with some herbs and a bit of olive oil (to taste). **3)** Use some herbs and olive oil to season the salmon's fillets. Moreover, it's important to brush it with a bit of oil on the whole salmon. Squeeze an orange and sprinkle the juice on top of the salmon too. Cook the fillets for approx. 2-4 min. on both sides. **4)** As the rice is ready, serve it with the cauliflower and the fillets. If you like, sprinkle a bit of balsamic vinegar and sesam seeds on top of the vegetables too.

Nutrition Facts:

Cal. 1176	**Carbs**: 35.7 g	**Fat**: 33.7 g	Sat.Fat 8.3 g	Cholest. 305 mg
Protein 144	Diet. Fiber 11.5 g		Mon.Fat 18.4 g	Sodium 1710 mg
	Tot. Sugars 12 g		Poly.Fat 7 g	Salt -

87) *Chicken rice with broccoli* 👤 4   ⏰ 30 Min.

Ingredients:

200 g. Brown rice

350 g. Broccoli

4 Chicken breast fillets

100 ml. Water

2 tsp. Sesame seeds

Paprika, rosmary, olive oil, tumeric (to taste)

Instructions:

1) First of all, cook the brown rice according to the instructions. In the meantime, prepare the broccoli chopping them and boiling them for approx. 4-8 min. 2) Secondly, cut the chicken fillets into small pieces and fry them in a pan with some herbs, a bit of water, olive oil and rosmary. 3) If necessary, add some water and sprinkle tumeric and paprika to the fillets (to taste). Let simmer until the water is absorbed. 4) Sprinkle the fillets with the sesame seeds before serving on a plate.

Nutrition Facts:

Cal. 1857	**Carbs**: 209 g	**Fat**: 19 g	Sat.Fat 4.3 g	Cholest. 348 mg
Protein 180	Diet. Fiber 21.6 g		Mon.Fat 6.9 g	Sodium 3379 mg
	Tot. Sugars 54.6 g		Poly.Fat 7.4 g	Salt 8.6 g

---

88) *Chicken veggie mix*   👤 4   ⏰ 20 Min.

Ingredients:

200 g. Chicken fillet

700 g. Potatoes

120 ml. Vegetable broth

1 Red and yellow bell pepper

2 Shallots

200 g. Beans

Olive oil, paprika, herbs (to taste)

Instructions:

1) Firstly, wash and boil the beans for approx. 5 min. Secondly, slice the fillets in small pieces and season them with herbs, a bit of paprika, rismary or others you prefer. Sautée with a bit of oil in a pan. 2) Remove the chicken and prepare the potatoes. Peel and cut them into pieces and sauté the potatoes in the pan. 3) Now, wash and cut the shallots and bell peppers into pieces and add them in the pan. Braise all the ingredients and stir them now and then. 4) Add the fillets once again for approx. others 5 min. and serve.

Nutrition Facts:

Cal. 1189	**Carbs**: 161 g	**Fat**: 18.4 g	Sat.Fat 5.8 g	Cholest. 116 mg
Protein 73 g	Diet. Fiber 26.8 g		Mon.Fat 6.3 g	Sodium 462 mg
	Tot. Sugars 35 g		Poly.Fat 6.3 g	Salt 1.3 g

89) *Stuffed chicken with spinach* 👤 4   ⏰ 50 Min.

Ingredients:

4 Chicken breast fillets

4-6 tbsp. Ricotta cheese

400 g. Spinach (fresh)

1 Egg

50 g. Bread crumbs

Paprika, olive oil, herbs (to taste)

Instructions:

1) Firstly, wash and boil the spinach in saltwater for approx. 2-3 min. Dry them and cut them into pieces. Secondly, wash the chicken breast and cut them in the middle creating a hole. **2)** Use the spinach, paprika and ricotta to create a filling and and stuff the fillets. **3)** Prepare a bowl and crack the egg, toss the fillets in the egg and than wrap them up with the bread crumbs. **4)** Prepare a baking sheet and place the fillets. **5)** Cook them at 350 °F (175 °C) for approx. 25 min.

Nutrition Facts:

Cal. 1113   **Carbs**: 35 g   **Fat**: 21.2 g   Sat.Fat   7.3 g   Cholest. 639 mg
Protein 175 g   Diet. Fiber 9.2 g   Mon.Fat   6.2 g   Sodium   1205 mg
                 Tot. Sugars 6.8 g   Poly.Fat 3.9 g   Salt   2 g

༄༅

90) *Sweet potatoes with avocado* 👤 4   ⏰ 15 Min.

Ingredients:

4 Large sweet potatoes

2 Eggs

1 tsp. Tumeric

1 Avocado

180 g. Yoghurt (non-fat)

Salt, paprika (to taste)

Instructions:

1) Clean and open the potatoes halfway and heat them using the microwave on the highest setting for approx. 4-7 min. **2)** Once the potatoes has softened, remove them carefully and peel them with a spoon. **3)** Mash the inner part and combine together with the egg. **4)** Fry this mixture in a pan without oil until you see that the egg is cooked. **5)** Fill the potato again with this mixture. **6)** Cut the avocado into pieces and garnish the potatoes with it on top of them. Mix together the paprika and yoghurt and serve with this sauce.

Nutrition Facts:

Cal. 2148   **Carbs**: 289 g   **Fat**: 57 g   Sat.Fat   14.6 g   Cholest. 1106 mg
Protein 58 g   Diet. Fiber 45.3 g   Mon.Fat   27.4 g   Sodium   543 mg
                 Tot. Sugars 71.3 g   Poly.Fat 7.9 g   Salt   1.4 g

91) *Chicken curry and rice* 👤 4   ⏰ 30 Min.

Ingredients:

200 g. Basmati rice

2 Chicken breast fillets

2 medium Peppers

400 ml. Canned oat milk (or other, low-fat)

Herbs, curry powder, olive oil (to taste)

Water (just enough)

Instructions:

1) First of all, prepare the rice according to the instructions you read on the package. Secondly, slice in small pieces the chicken breast fillets and fry them in a pan with a bit of water. **2)** Cut the peppers in small pieces. Add them to the chicken and fry everything for approx. 15 min. Season everything with some herbs (to taste). **3)** As you see the chicken turns light brown, use the milk to deglaze the pan. **4)** Add the curry powder and others spices (to taste). Blend everything and serve.

Nutrition Facts:

Cal. 1167	**Carbs**: 128 g	**Fat**: 30 g	Sat.Fat 21.5 g	Cholest. 172 mg
Protein 90 g	Diet. Fiber 12 g		Mon.Fat 5.4 g	Sodium 378 mg
	Tot. Sugars 22 g		Poly.Fat 2.7 g	Salt 0.7 g

༄༅

92) *Spiced roasted chicken with potatoes* 👤 4   ⏰ 45 Min.

Ingredients:

4 Chicken breast fillets

1 Shallot

400 g. Potatoes and zucchini

½ Lemon

Rosmary, olive oil, herbs (to taste)

Instructions:

1) First of all, prepare the chicken breasts and fry them on both sides on high heat. Secondly, wash and slice the shallot and add it to the pan with 2 tsp. of olive oil. **2)** Season the chicken breasts with rosemary and other herbs. **3)** Wash the potatoes in small pieces and spread them on a baking sheet. Add some seasoning to add flavour and add the chicken breast on the sheet covering with a bit of oil, salt and rosmary. Cook them in the oven at 360 °F (180 °C) for approx. 30 min. (until the potatoes are crispy). **4)** Cook the zucchini with a bit of oil and shallott's pieces for a few minutes. **5)** Squeeze and drizzle with some lemon juize, serve.

Nutrition Facts:

Cal. 1500	**Carbs**: 113 g	**Fat**: 40 g	Sat.Fat 7 g	Cholest. 348 mg
Protein 160	Diet. Fiber 18.9 g		Mon.Fat 21.9 g	Sodium 426 mg
	Tot. Sugars 26.4 g		Poly.Fat 6.7 g	Salt 1 g

93) *Chickpea curry and rice* 👤 4 ⏰ 30 Min.

Ingredients:

250 g. Basmati rice

2 Garlic gloves

1 Shallot

3 tsp. Olive oil and curry powder

500 g. Chickpea and tomatoes (canned, low-sodium)

300 ml. Rice milk (low-fat)

Instructions:

1) First of all, prepare and cook the rice according to the package instructions. Than keep the rice warm. 2) Peel and chop the shallot and sauté the shallot with a bit of oil. Mix the milk and diced tomatoes and let them simmer for a few min. 3) Wash the chickpeas and drain very well. Combine the chickpeas with the curry powder, herbs and cook approx. 15 minutes. 4) Serve the rice and season with herbs and chili powder.

Nutrition Facts:

Cal. 2160	**Carbs**: 324 g **Fat**: 56 g	Sat.Fat 36 g	Cholest. -
Protein 70 g	Diet. Fiber 39 g	Mon.Fat 5.6 g	Sodium 2580 mg
	Tot. Sugars 34 g	Poly.Fat 10 g	Salt 4 g

෨෬

94) *Chickpea salad with dressing* 👤 4 ⏰ 15 Min.

Ingredients:

50 g. Ricotta cheese (low-fat)

300 g. Chickpeas (canned, low-sodium, low-salt)

150 g. Tuna

150 g. Broccoli, pepper

½ Shallot

Lemon juice, herbs mix, turmeric (to taste)

100 g. Yoghurt (non-fat)

Instructions:

1) First of all, cut the broccoli into small pieces. Use a pot, add some water and cook the broccoli for approx. 5 min. 2) Secondly, finaly chop the shallot and combine it with the yoghurt, the lemon juice, herbs and turmeric. Mix together in a bowl. 3) Now, crumble the ricotta and add the cheese to the bowl. 4) Drain the broccoli and chickpeas and than add these ingredients to the bowl. 5) Lastly, prepare and cut the peppers into small pieces. Serve the salad with the yoghurt dressing.

Nutrition Facts:

Cal. 568	**Carbs**: 60 g **Fat**: 8.2 g	Sat.Fat 2.6 g	Cholest. 20 mg
Protein 42 g	Diet. Fiber 32 g	Mon.Fat 1 g	Sodium 455 mg
	Tot. Sugars 19 g	Poly.Fat 2.3 g	Salt 1 g

95) *Spinach and potato pie* 👤 4 ⏰ 45 Min.

Ingredients:

700 g. Potatoes and spinach

2 tbsp. Olive oil

250 ml. Rice milk (unsweetened) and vegetable broth

240 g. Ricotta cheese

50 g. Parmesan

20 g. Whole wheat flour

2 Shallots

Instructions:

1) Firstly, take a casserole dish and lay down the potatoes once they are sliced. Slice the shallots in small pieces. **2)** Use a bit of olive oil, vegetable broth and flour in a pan. **3)** Add the spinach and shallot and cook until it starts to shrivel. Add a bit of flavor with rosmary and/or the herbs mix or spices that you prefer. **4)** Cut the ricotta into small pieces and, together with the parmesan, prinkle these cheeses on top of it. **5)** Cook in the preheated oven at 360 °F (180 °C) for approx. 30 minutes and serve.

Nutrition Facts:

Cal. 1750	**Carbs**: 140 g	**Fat**: 78 g	Sat.Fat 50 g	Cholest. 215 mg
Protein 100 g	Diet. Fiber 26 g		Mon.Fat 16.9 g	Sodium 2375 mg
	Tot. Sugars 26 g		Poly.Fat 3.8 g	Salt 4 g

☙❦

96) *Cucumber mixed salad* 👤 4 ⏰ 20 Min.

Ingredients:

700 g. Potatoes

600 g. Cucumber

120 g. plain Yoghurt

Parsley, dill, lemon juice (to taste)

Instructions:

1) First of all, take a pot, peel and cook the potatoes for approx. 20 minutes. In the meantime, wash and finely slice the cucumber and parsley. **2)** Secondly, put the cucumber- and parsley's slices into a bowl and mix well with a bit of dill, lemon juice and yohurt. **3)** As the potatoes are ready, cut them and mix them with the cucumber mix. Serve.

Nutrition Facts:

Cal. 680	**Carbs**: 125 g	**Fat**: 2.5 g	Sat.Fat 0.6 g	Cholest. -
Protein 22 g	Diet. Fiber 16.3 g		Mon.Fat 0.2 g	Sodium 71 mg
	Tot. Sugars 20 g		Poly.Fat 1.4 g	Salt -

97) *Chicken tortillas* 👤 4   ⏰ 20 Min.

Ingredients:

300 g. Chicken breast

1 Shallot

100 g. Ricotta

2 Bell pepper

4 whole-grain Tortillas

Olive oil, herbs, lemon juice (to taste)

Instructions:

1) Firstly, wash and dry the chicken breasts and slice them into pieces. Place the breasts in a pan and fry on both sides. Season with some herbs and lemon juice (to taste). 2) Secondly, slice the shallot and chop the ricotta cheese and set aside for the moment. 3) Cut the peppers in small pieces and sear them for a couple of minutes. 4) If you like add you fav. Low-sodium and low-fat sauce on the tortillas, otherwise combine together all the igredients, add a bit of olive oil and spread them on the tortillas. 5) Carefully roll them together and cut them in two halves. If you like sear them in a pan and serve.

Nutrition Facts:

Cal. 1875	**Carbs**: 158 g	**Fat**: 79.7 g	Sat.Fat 19.5 g	Cholest. 230 mg
Protein 120 g	Diet. Fiber 7 g		Mon.Fat 47.7 g	Sodium 3078 mg
	Tot. Sugars 12.4 g		Poly.Fat 12.8 g	Salt 3 g

☼☾

98) *Ground beef chili* 👤 4   ⏰ 30 Min.

Ingredients:

4 Tomatoes and carrots

2 Shallots and garlic gloves

2 Chili peppers

2 tsp. Olive oil

400 g. Ground beef

400 ml. Water

180 g. Kidney beans (canned, low-sodium, no-salt added)

30 g. Fresh ginger and coriander

Instructions:

1) First of all, prepare the vegetables. Rinse and drain the beans, slice the carrots and cut into pieces the tomatoes. Take the coriander and chop it. Secondly, finely chop the garlic gloves, shallots and chili peppers. 2) Take a pan and heat the olive oil, braise the garlic, shallots, chili peppers and carrots for a few minutes. In the same pan, add the ground beef and braise on high heat for approx. 5 more min. 3) Deglaze with the other ingredients (tomatoes, water and beans) and let everything boil on medium heat for approx. 15 minutes. 4) Lastly, season with ginger, herbs mix and coriander (to taste). Serve.

Nutrition Facts:

Cal. 1320	**Carbs**: 84 g	**Fat**: 74 g	Sat.Fat 38 g	Cholest. 240 mg
Protein 105 g	Diet. Fiber 39 g		Mon.Fat 26.7 g	Sodium 864 mg
	Tot. Sugars 62 g		Poly.Fat 4.3 g	Salt 2 g

99) Vegetable chili

👤 4   ⏰ 35 Min.

Ingredients:

70 g. Shallots + 1 Avocado

½ Bell peppers

1 tbsp. Olive oil + 3 tbsp. Tomato paste, lemon juice

380 ml. Vegetable broth

150 g. Quinoa

Paprika powder, cilantro (to taste)

400 g. Diced tomatoes, kidney beans, corn (canned, low-sodium, no-salt added))

Instructions:

1) First of all, cut the shallots into small pieces and sauté in a large pan with a bit of olive oil. Rinse briefly the quinoa with warm water using a strainer, so you get rid of its bitterness. **2)** Brown the quinoa in the pan for approx. 3-4 min. **3)** Wash and rinse the beans and diced tomatoes. Deglaze with the vegetable broth, diced tomatoes, beans, tomato paste and corn. Let everything simmer for approx. 30 min. **4)** Add the paprika powder, cilantro and combine very well. **5)** Lastly, pit the avocado and cut it into small cubes and sprinkle them, with the lemon juice, on top of the chili.

Nutrition Facts:

Cal. 1769	**Carbs**: 230 g **Fat**: 57 g	Sat.Fat 10 g	Cholest. -
Protein 83 g	Diet. Fiber 79 g	Mon.Fat 30 g	Sodium 4034 mg
	Tot. Sugars 33 g	Poly.Fat 12.4 g	Salt 5 g

༺✿༻

100) Caprese wraps

👤 4   ⏰ 8 Min.

Ingredients:

4 Whole wheat tortillas

200 g. Ricotta (or other low-fat cheese you like)

60 g. Cranberries

150 g. Turkey breast (organic, sliced)

60 g. fresh Spinach

4 small tomatoes

Instructions:

1) Take the tortillas and spread them with the ricotta and sprinkle with cranberries. **2)** Now, create a layer on the tortillas with spinach and turkey breasts. **3)** Roll the tortillas from bottom to the top, cut in half and serve.

Nutrition Facts:

Cal. 1300	**Carbs**: 200 g **Fat**: 23.4 g	Sat.Fat 13 g	Cholest. 69 mg
Protein 82 g	Diet. Fiber 22 g	Mon.Fat 2 g	Sodium 3290 mg
	Tot. Sugars 42.3 g	Poly.Fat 2.5 g	Salt 4 g

101) *Stuffed potatoes with vegetables* 👤 4   ⏰ 2,5 h.

Ingredients:

60 ml. Olive oil

600 g. Potatoes

100 g. Tomatoes + 10 g. shallot

4 Bell peppers

30 g. Ricotta cheese

70 g. Corn (canned, no-salt added)

260 g. Black beans (canned, unsweetened, no-salt added)

40 ml. Vinegar (red wine)

Instructions:

1) Firstly, consider the vegetable filling: take the tomatoes, shallots and peppers, wash and cut them into small pieces. Take a bowl and add the beans (rinse them), corn, olive oil and vinegar. **2)** Now, season with some herbs mix or Worcester sauce (to taste). Let everything cool in the fridge for approx. 1 ½ hours. **3)** Now, let's prepare the potatoes: wash them and create a hole inside them with a fork. Place them in the oven at 395 °F (200 °C) for approx. 50-60 minutes. **4)** As the potatoes are cooked, remove them from the heat, cut them open and fill them with the vegetable mix. **5)** Garnish them with the ricotta and serve.

Nutrition Facts:

Cal. 1000	**Carbs**: 157 g	**Fat**: 23 g	Sat.Fat 8.9 g	Cholest. 30 mg
Protein 35.3 g	Diet. Fiber 33.4 g		Mon.Fat 10 g	Sodium 1278 mg
	Tot. Sugars 20 g		Poly.Fat 2.3 g	Salt 3 g

ೞಚ

102) *Greens chicken quinoa* 👤 4   ⏰ 15 Min.

Ingredients:

200 g. Quinoa

3 tsp. Olive oil, lemon juice

4 Chicken breasts

3 Tomaotes and bell peppers

2 Cucumber

400 g. Broccoli (frozen)

Herbs mix (to taste)

Instructions:

1) First of all, prepare the quinoa according to the instructions of the package and thaw the broccoli. Secondly, take a pan and fry the chicken breasts on both sides until they become crispy. Add a bit of flavour with some herbs mix (to taste). Once cooked, set them aside for now. **2)** Prepare the peppers and tomatoes: remove the seeds and slice them. **3)** Use the same pan of the chicken and add the vegetables. Stew them for approx. 5-7 min. **4)** Combine all the ingredients with the quinoa, season with a bit of herbs mix and lemon juice (to taste) and serve.

Nutrition Facts:

Cal. 1500	**Carbs**: 132 g	**Fat**: 33 g	Sat.Fat 5 g	Cholest. 328 mg
Protein 180 g	Diet. Fiber 35 g		Mon.Fat 14 g	Sodium 450 mg
	Tot. Sugars 26 g		Poly.Fat 8.3 g	Salt 1 g

103) Crispy nuggets with greens   👤 4   ⏰ 30 Min.

Ingredients:

200 g. Corn flakes (unsweetened)

2 Eggs

800 g. Chicken breast fillets

150 g. Iceberg salad

2 Bell peppers

2 tsp. Vinegar, lemon juice, sesam and oumpkin seeds.

Instructions:

1) Firstly, put the corn flakes in a bag and crush them. Then take the eggs and scrumble them in a bowl with a fork. 2) Now, slice the chicken breasts into nugget-sized pieces and add some seasoning you prefer on both sides (such as the herbs mix). 3) Wrap up the nuggets into the eggs first and second into the corn flakes. Place the nuggets onto a baking sheet and cook them at 395 °F (200 °C) for approx. 15-18 minutes. 4) Now, prepare the vegetables. Wash the tomatoes and bell peppers and cut them into pieces. Season with a bit of olive oil. 5) Serve the nuggets on top of the vegetables and sprinkle a bit of vinegar, sesam and pumpkin seeds and a bit of lemon juice (to taste).

Nutrition Facts:

Cal. 1986	**Carbs**: 155 g	**Fat**: 28 g	Sat.Fat 7.4 g	Cholest. 1132 mg
Protein 260 g	Diet. Fiber 11 g		Mon.Fat 9.1 g	Sodium 2654 mg
	Tot. Sugars 38 g		Poly.Fat 5.9 g	Salt 5.7 g

☙☸

104) Paella with peas   👤 4   ⏰ 50 Min.

Ingredients:

4 Chicken breast fillets

2 Shallots, lemons, bell peppers, green onions

250 g. Paella rice

800 ml. Vegetable broth

180 g. Frozen peas

Paprika powder, herbs mix, olive oil (to taste)

Instructions:

1) Firstly, marinate the chicken breasts after cutting them into small pieces. Combine together 1 tsp. of oil and paprika powder and marinate with this mixture. After that, cover and let the chicken sit in the fridge for approx. 20 min. 2) In the meantime, peel the shallots and cut them, as well as the garlic and bell peppers. 3) Use 1 tsp. of oil in a pan and fry both sides of the chicken bites. Lightly braise the onions and peppers for approx. 3-5 min. Add the rice, season with a bit of herbs mix and paprika and braise for 10 more minutes. 4) Add the vegetables broth and bring to boil. 5) Now, add the peas and chicken and cook for approx. 25-28 min. at 375 °F (190 °C). 6) Wash the green onions (cut them in rings) and lemons (cut them into pieces). Serve.

Nutrition Facts:

Cal. 2650	**Carbs**: 212 g	**Fat**: 92 g	Sat.Fat 21.3 g	Cholest. 580 mg
Protein 214 g	Diet. Fiber 31 g		Mon.Fat 44.2 g	Sodium 1754 mg
	Tot. Sugars 35 g		Poly.Fat 18.6 g	Salt 3 g

105) *Greens-stuffed mushrooms* 👤 4 ⏰ 30 Min.

Ingredients:

2 Tomatoes and garlic cloves

2 tbsp. Olive oil

4 tsp. Tomato paste

8 big Mushrooms

2 Zucchini and shallots

1 bell Pepper

Herbs mix, paprika powder (to taste)

Instructions:

1) First of all, prepare the zucchini. Cut them, as well as the garlic cloves and shallots. **2)** Score the tomatoes and gently pour the boiling water over the top and carefully peel them. Cut them into pieces, as well as the pepper. **3)** Heat a tbsp. of olive oil and sauté all these ingredients. Now, stir the herbs mix with the tomato paste, salt and pepper. **4)** Wash the mushrooms and clean them removing stems and gills. **5)** Stuffed them with the vegetables and bake in the oven at 395 °F (200°C) for approx. 8-10 minutes. Serve.

Nutrition Facts:

Cal. 438	**Carbs**: 16 g	**Fat**: 28 g Sat.Fat 4 g	Cholest. -
Protein 28 g	Diet. Fiber 15 g	Mon.Fat 18 g	Sodium 269 mg
	Tot. Sugars 14 g	Poly.Fat 3.2 g	Salt -

☙☬

106) *Chicken with snap peas* 👤 4 ⏰ 30 Min.

Ingredients:

4 Sweet potatoes

2 Shallots

4 Chicken breast fillets

3 tsp. Olive oil

250 g. Snap peas

Paprika powder, turmeric, herbs mix (to taste)

Instructions:

1) First of all, peel the potatoes and cut into pieces. Bring some water to boil and cook the potatoes for approx. 8-12 minutes. Then drain them. **2)** Now, finely chop the shallots and season the chicken breasts both sides until it turns golden-brown. Add a bit of oil if necessary. Keep warm. **3)** Using the same pan, add the peas with a dash of water and sauté for approx. 10 minutes. Garnish them with some herbs mix. **4)** Now, mash the potatoes and add a bit of turmeric and paprika powder (to taste). **5)** Cut the chicken into small strips and serve them with peas and potatoes.

Nutrition Facts:

Cal. 1500	**Carbs**: 168 g	**Fat**: 23 g Sat.Fat 5 g	Cholest. 248 mg
Protein 120 g	Diet. Fiber 28 g	Mon.Fat 11 g	Sodium 312 mg
	Tot. Sugars 40 g	Poly.Fat 4 g	Salt -

107) *Veggie ratatouille* 👤 4   ⏰ 1 h.

Ingredients:

3 Onions, garlic gloves

1 tsp. Olive oil

2 tbsp. Vinegar (balsamic)

6 Tomatoes

3 Zucchini, eggplants

1 Pepper

450 g. Diced tomatoes (canned, low sodium, so salt added)

Lemon, fresh basil (to taste)

Instructions:

1) First of all, peel and finely chop the garlic gloves and the onions too. Take a pan and using a tsp. of oil sauté both of them. **2)** Secondly, add the diced tomatoes with 1 tbsp. of vinegar. Garnish with a few leaves of basil and cook everything for approx. 3-4 min. **3)** Now, wash the pepper, cut it into small pieces and add them to the tomato sauce. Spread all the sauce over the casserole dish. **4)** Now, prepare the other vegetables. Take the eggplants, zucchini and tomatoes, wash them and cut them into thin rings. With the rings, create a layer over the tomatoes sauce. **5)** Cook everything at 360 °F (180 °C) for approx. 40 minutes. **6)** Garnish everything with others basil leaves and luemon juice. Serve.

Nutrition Facts:

Cal. 611	**Carbs**: 71.1 g	**Fat**: 12.3 g	Sat.Fat 2.3 g	Cholest. -
Protein 29.4 g	Diet. Fiber 32.6 g		Mon.Fat 5.4 g	Sodium 866 mg
	Tot. Sugars 67.3 g		Poly.Fat 3.4 g	Salt 1.8 g

☘☘

108) *Spinach pizza* 👤 4   ⏰ 50 Min.

Ingredients:

400. Whole-wheat flour

200 ml. Water

7 g. Dried Yeast

5 tbsp. Olive oil

200 g. Cherry tomatoes

Oregano, basil, pepper (to taste) + 1 onion, 3 garlic gloves

300 g. Leaf spinach

150 g. Tomato purée + 100 g. ricotta

Instructions:

1) CRUST: Combine together the flour, water, yeast, a bit of salt and 1 tbsp. of olive oil. Knead everything together, cover and let sit in a warm place for approx. 30-40 minutes. **2)** In the meantime, prepare the tomatoes. Cut them in half and set aside for now. Garnish the tomato purée with oregano, a bit of salt and pepper and set aside these ingredients too. **3)** Now, finely chop the onion and garlic and sauté in a pan with 2-3 tbsp. of olive oil and add the leafy spinach. **4)** As 40 min. has passed and the dough has rested, roll it very thinly and lay it down on a baking sheet. Spread the tomatoes sauce on top. **5)** Distribute the spinach, ricotta cheese and cherry tomatoes and cook at 395 °F (200 °C) for approx. 20 minutes. Serve.

Nutrition Facts:

Cal. 1845	**Carbs**: 314.2 g	**Fat**: 33 g	Sat.Fat 4.8 g	Cholest. -
Protein 57.2 g	Diet. Fiber 24 g		Mon.Fat 20 g	Sodium 242 mg
	Tot. Sugars 23 g		Poly.Fat 5.5 g	Salt 0.5 g

109) *Mango mix sandwich* 👤 4 ⏰ 15 Min.

Ingredients:

2 Chicken breast fillet

8 slices Whole-wheat bread

3 tsp. Olive oil

1 Mango

50 g. Ricotta

150 g. Tomatoes

Arugola, lemon juice, herbs mix, rosmary (to taste)

Instructions:

1) Firstly, cut the chicken breasts into strips and sauté them in a pan with a bit of olive oil and season them with a bit of herbs mix or rosmary. **2)** In the meantime, prepare the mango. Cut it into pieces and place them in a bowl. Heat a little bit the whole-wheat bread. **3)** Top the bread slices with the mango pieces, tomatoes, chicken breasts slices and arugola. Add a little bit of lemon juice to garnish everything. **4)** Cover with another slice of bread and serve.

Nutrition Facts:

Cal. 1402	**Carbs**: 150 g	**Fat**: 36 g	Sat.Fat 13 g	Cholest. 207 mg
Protein 97 g	Diet. Fiber 31 g		Mon.Fat 14.3 g	Sodium 1897 mg
	Tot. Sugars 32 g		Poly.Fat 4.7 g	Salt 2.6 g

ಐ಩

110) *Cauliflower greens rice* 👤 4 ⏰ 20 Min.

Ingredients:

2 Shallots

4 Garlic gloves

5 tsp. Olive oil

700 g. Frozen peas and carrots (mixed together)

2 kg. Cauliflower

6 tbsp. Balsamic vinegar

Herbs mix, rosmary (to taste)

Instructions:

1) First of all, use a mixer and finely grate the cauliflower. Secondly, prepare the shallots and garlic gloves. Finely chop them and sauté with a bit of olive oil in a pan. **2)** Now, add the slightly-thawed mix of peas and carrots and cook for approx. 5-8 minutes. **3)** Stir the cauliflowers and cook them for others 5-6 minutes. **4)** Lastly, garnish them with the balsamic vinegar and herbs mix (to taste).

Nutrition Facts:

Cal. 1428	**Carbs**: 140 g	**Fat**: 36 g	Sat.Fat 5.4 g	Cholest. -
Protein 87 g	Diet. Fiber 91 g		Mon.Fat 20 g	Sodium 5340 mg
	Tot. Sugars 91.5 g		Poly.Fat 7 g	Salt 13 g

111) *Cucumber wraps* 👤 4 ⏰ 15 Min.

Ingredients:

8 Whole-wheat tortillas

2 Cucumbers

100 g. Lettuce

250 g. Ricotta

320 g. Kidney beans (low-sodium, no-salt added)

Olive oil, lemon juice (to taste)

Instructions:

1) Firstly, heat a little bit the tortillas at 120 °F (50 °F) for approx. 10-12 minutes. **2)** Secondly, cut the cucumber into slices, rinse and drain the beans and cut the lettuce into small pieces. **3)** Spread the ricotta cheese over the warm tortillas, add the lettuce, beans and cucumbers. Garnish with a bit of olive oil and lemon juice. **4)** Roll the wraps up, tuck in the sides and serve.

Nutrition Facts:

Cal. 2345	**Carbs**: 375 g	**Fat**: 33 g	Sat.Fat 18 g	Cholest. 120 mg
Protein 136 g	Diet. Fiber 33 g		Mon.Fat 1.5 g	Sodium 5200 mg
	Tot. Sugars 17 g		Poly.Fat 4.6 g	Salt 10 g

₨☏

112) *Rice with beets* 👤 4 ⏰ 40 Min.

Ingredients:

2 Garlic gloves and shallots

2 tsp. Olive oil and Agave nectar

350 g. Risotto rice

1 L. Vegetable broth

3 Beets

50 g. Parmesan

Rosmary, herbs mix (to taste)

Instructions:

1) Firtly, peel and finely chop the shallots and garlic gloves. Braise them in a pan with a bit of olive oil. **2)** Secondly, prepare the beets. Peel the and cut them into pieces. Add a tbsp. of agave nectar and blend well. **3)** Now, add the rice to the beets and sautée for approx. 5 minutes. **4)** Now, take a pot and put the vegetable broth to boil. Use the broth to deglaze the rice, adding the broth hradually. Continue stitting until the broth is evaporated and the rice is ready (approx. After 20 min). **5)** Garnish with herbs mix, parmesan and a bit of olive oil. Serve.

Nutrition Facts:

Cal. 1723	**Carbs**: 313 g	**Fat**: 24.5 g	Sat.Fat 10.5 g	Cholest. 33 mg
Protein 45 g	Diet. Fiber 16 g		Mon.Fat 10 g	Sodium 3410 mg
	Tot. Sugars 50 g		Poly.Fat 2.2 g	Salt 6.8 g

113) *Curry loin rice* 👤 4   ⏰ 30 Min.

Ingredients:

250 g. Rice

500 g. Pork loin

500 g. Potatoes

3 Carrots and shallots

5 tsp. Olive oil

1,5 L. Water

25 g. Curry powder

Instructions:

1) First of all, prepare the rice according the package instructions. In the meantime, peel the potatoes and shallots. Cut them as well as the carrots and pork loin into thick cubes. **2)** Heat the olive oil in a pot and fry the loin for approx. 5 min. Garnish it with a bit of herbs mix. Add the potatoes and cook for another 3-5 min. **3)** Add the carrots and shallots and sauté for a few minutes. **4)** Regarding the water, pour 3 tbsp. in a bowl and the rest in the pot and let everything simmer for approx. 10-15 min. **5)** Mix the 3 tbsp. of water with the curry powder and blend very well. Serve this sauce with the rice.

Nutrition Facts:

Cal. 2230	**Carbs**: 320 g	**Fat**: 28 g	Sat.Fat 13.7 g	Cholest. 309 mg
Protein 147 g	Diet. Fiber 30 g		Mon.Fat 9.2 g	Sodium 873 mg
	Tot. Sugars 54.6 g		Poly.Fat 3 g	Salt 2 g

☙☜

114) *Chicken fricassee with peas* 👤 4   ⏰ 30 Min.

Ingredients:

250 g. Long grain rice

2 Shallots and carrots

750 ml. Vegetable broth

500. Chicken breasts fillets

300 g. Peas (canned, no salt-added, unsweetened)

200 ml. Milk (low-fat)

Herbs mix, olive oil (to taste)

3 tsp. Potato starch

Instructions:

1) Firtly, prepare the rice according to the package instructions. Secondly, peel and chop the onions. **2)** Now, take a large pot, chop ½ of a carrot and add it to the pot with the vegetable broth. Bring everything to boil. **3)** Add the chicken breasts and simmer over low heat for approx. 15 min (after 7 min. turn the chicken once). Garnish with herbs mix (to taste). **4)** Cut the other carrots into small pieces and drain the peas. Remove the chicken and blend the other ingredients with an immersion blender. Add the milk and mix well. **5)** Add the peas and carrots to the purée and bring everything to boil. **6)** Cut the breasts into small slices and add the to the pot again and let them simmer for others 3-5 min. **7)** Combine the starch with a bit of cold water and blend into the pot. Serve with the rice.

Nutrition Facts:

Cal. 1932	**Carbs**: 260 g	**Fat**: 15 g	Sat.Fat 5 g	Cholest. 268 mg
Protein 165 g	Diet. Fiber 34.2 g		Mon.Fat 3.6 g	Sodium 3200 mg
	Tot. Sugars 48 g		Poly.Fat 3.7 g	Salt 6 g

115) *Fish & chips with greens*   👤 4   ⏰ 55 Min.

Ingredients:

5 Potatoes and carrots

1 Broccoli head

3 tbsp. Olive oil

3 Fish fillets (to taste)

1 Egg

5 g. Potato starch

100 g. Bread crumbs

Instructions:

1) Firstly, heat the oven to 390 °F (200 °C). Secondly, cut the potatoes into pieces and garnish with a bit of olive oil and herbs mix. **2)** Spread the potatoes on the baking sheet (previously covered with baking paper) and bake on the middle rack for approx 30 min. Turn them now and then. **3)** Now, cut the fish fillets into pieces very carefully. Beat the egg with a fork. Dip each piece of the fillets first in the starch, secondly in the egg and lastly in the bread crumbs. **4)** Place them onto another baking sheet (covered with paper). **5)** Separate the broccoli in small pieces and slice the other greens (carrots). Mix them with the remaining olive oil, garnish with a bit of herbs mix and add to the sheet with the fillets. Put the chips to the lowest rack after 30 min. and the fish one on the middle. **6)** Bake both of them for 15 minutes.

Nutrition Facts:

Cal. 1576   **Carbs**: 170 g   **Fat**: 40 g   Sat.Fat 7 g   Cholest. 430 mg
Protein 120 g   Diet. Fiber 31 g   Mon.Fat 22.8 g   Sodium 996 mg
                Tot. Sugars 40 g   Poly.Fat 6.4 g Salt   2 g

☎☎

116) *Multigrain turkey sandwich*   👤 4   ⏰ 10 Min.

Ingredients:

8 slices. Multigrain bread

4 tbsp. Horseradish

100 g. Feta

100 g. Lettuce and tomatoes

200 g. Turkey breast (sliced)

Instructions:

1) First of all, warmp up the bread for a few minutes. Wash and skiced the tomatoes. **2)** Once the bread is warmed up and crispy, spread the horseradish on each side. **3)** Add the lettuce, tomatoes, turkey breast and feta and cover with a second bread slice. Enjoy!

Nutrition Facts:

Cal. 1620   **Carbs**: 190 g   **Fat**: 40 g   Sat.Fat 20.2 g   Cholest. 175 mg
Protein 110 g   Diet. Fiber 19.3 g   Mon.Fat 11 g   Sodium 5700 mg
                Tot. Sugars 9 g   Poly.Fat 3.6 g   Salt   14 g

117) *Beef rice*

👤 4　　⏰ 25 Min.

Ingredients:

400 g. Short grain rice

1 Carrot

2 Bell peppers

300 g. Beef

2 tbsp. Olive oil and sesame seeds

40 g. Corn and peas (canned, low-sodium, unsweetened)

Parsley, herbs mix (to taste)

Instructions:

1) First of all, prepare the rice according to the instructions of the package. In the meantime, wash the vegetables and cut them into pieces (peppers and carrot). Wash and rinse the peas and corn. **2)** Secondly, heat half of the oil in a pan and sauté both vegetables for no more than 3-4 min. Just before the 3 minutes have passed, add the peas and corn and set aside. **3)** Garnish the beef (to taste) and fry it with the remaining olive oil for 5 min. more or less. **4)** At the same time, roast the sesame seeds until they turn golden-brown. **5)** Combine and stir all the ingredients together and garnish with a bit of parsly.

Nutrition Facts:

Cal. 2098	**Carbs**: 330 g	**Fat**: 38 g	Sat.Fat 8.7 g	Cholest. 136 mg
Protein 93 g	Diet. Fiber 20 g		Mon.Fat 14.9 g	Sodium 280 mg
	Tot. Sugars 18 g		Poly.Fat 11.8 g	Salt -

☯☪

118) *Cod salad*

👤 4　　⏰ 25 Min.

Ingredients:

4 Oranges (organic)

2 tbsp. Agave nectar and lemon juice

1 tbsp. Balsamic vinegar

800 g. Cod fillet

2 Shallots

Herbs mix, fresh chives (to taste)

150 g. Cherry tomatoes

Instructions:

1) First of all, preheat the oven to 450 °F (230 °C) and cut 2 oranges in halves. Slice one of the halves. Squeeze the juice of one half and cut the remaining two halves into pieces. **2)** Blend together the orange juice with the agave nectar, lemon juice and vinegar in order to create a sauce for the dressing. **3)** Take a baking sheet, cover it with baking paper and lay the cod fillet on top. Add a bit of flavour with salt and pepper, sprinkle a bit of orange dressing and roast in the oven for approx. 15 min. **4)** Peel and cut the remaining oranges, cherry tomatoes, shallots and chives and stir together all the ingredients. **5)** Serve this mixed salad with the fillets.

Nutrition Facts:

Cal. 1300	**Carbs**: 140 g	**Fat**: 8 g	Sat.Fat 1.3 g	Cholest. 270 mg
Protein 156 g	Diet. Fiber 28 g		Mon.Fat 1.2 g	Sodium 1450 mg
	Tot. Sugars 138 g		Poly.Fat 3.6 g	Salt 3.4 g

119) *Melon-chicken salad* 👤 4 ⏰ 40 Min.

Ingredients:

40 ml. Vinegar

1 Lemon

800 g. Chicken breast fillet

4 tsp. Olive oil

1 Melon

130 g. Asparagus

400 g. Spinach

60 g. Basmati rice

Instructions:

1) Firstly, preheat the oven at 250 °F (120 °C). **2)** Secondly, take a pan, heat a bit of oil and and fry both sides of the chicken. Add a bit of flavour with herbs mix (to taste). Add the vinegar and lemon juice and sauté briefly. **3)** Thirdly, cook the chicken in the preheated oven for approx. 20 minutes. **4)** Now, prepare the basmati rice according to the package instructions and at the same time prepare the melon. Cut its pulp into bite-sized pieces. **5)** Prepare and lightly cook the asparagus and the spinach with a bit of olive oil and the remaining lemon juice. **6)** Distribute the greens onto a plate, add the melon and the rice. Serve.

Nutrition Facts:

Cal. 1870	**Carbs**: 123 g	**Fat**: 45 g	Sat.Fat 8 g	Cholest. 460 mg	
Protein 212 g	Diet. Fiber 13 g		Mon.Fat 23 g	Sodium 3110 mg	
	Tot. Sugars 107 g		Poly.Fat 8 g	Salt 4 g	

☙☼

120) *Roasted greens risotto* 👤 4 ⏰ 45 Min.

Ingredients:

2 Bell peppers and zucchini

300 g. Cherry tomatoes

2 Shallots

2 tbsp. Olive oil

450 ml. Vegetable broth

Herbs mix, basil, chives (to taste)

250 g. Arborio rice

Instructions:

1) First of all, preheat the oven to 360 °F (180 °C). **2)** Secondly, prepare the vegetables removing the seeds from the pepper and cut them into pieces. Same ting with the zucchini, slice them and the cherry tomatoes. **3)** Use a casserole to place the greens, season them as you prefer and add a bit of olive oil. Stir well together and cook them on the middle rack for approx. 25 minutes. **4)** Peel and cut in to pieces the shallots and sauté them with a bit of oil for approx. 8-10 min. **5)** Add the rice to the pot and use the vegetable broth to deglaze the risotto. **6)** Lastly, add the roasted vegetables to the pot and simmer for the last 5 minutes. Serve.

Nutrition Facts:

Cal. 1500	**Carbs**: 240 g	**Fat**: 40 g	Sat.Fat 6 g	Cholest. -	
Protein 38 g	Diet. Fiber 29 g		Mon.Fat 24.5 g	Sodium 1460 mg	
	Tot. Sugars 54 g		Poly.Fat 6 g	Salt 3 g	

121) *Lentil Sloppy Joe*   👤 4   ⏰ 30 Min.

Ingredients:

200 g. Lentils

200 ml. Vegetable broth and water

4 Whole-grain bread rolls

2 Shallots

1 Bell pepper

2 tbsp. Olive oil

400 g. Tomato purée

Paprika powder, chili powder, cumin, salt and pepper (to taste)

Instructions:

1) First of all, prepare and pour the lentils, borth and water in a pot and bring to boil. Stir occasionally, reduce the heat and simmer for approx. 20 minutes. **2)** Secondly, prepare the shallots cutting them into rings and the peppers into small cubes. **3)** Take a pan and heat the oil, add the shallots and peppers and sauté everything together for approx. 5 minutes. **4)** Now, add the chili and paprika powder, tomato purée and other herbs mix you like to add flavour. Mix well. **5)** Add the lentils and let the pan simmer for others 5 minutes. Stir when necessary. **6)** Prepare the bread. Cut the bread rolls in two halves and garnish with the lentils, greens and shallots pieces. Close with the other halves and serve.

Nutrition Facts:

Cal. 1560	**Carbs**: 239 g	**Fat**: 23 g	Sat.Fat 3.5 g	Cholest. -
Protein 77 g	Diet. Fiber 47 g		Mon.Fat 11 g	Sodium 2093 mg
	Tot. Sugars 36 g		Poly.Fat 5.3 g	Salt 4 g

༺༻

122) *Chicken fruit skewers*   👤 4   ⏰ 50 Min.

Ingredients:

500 g. Chicken breasts fillets

3 Garlic gloves

4 tbsp. Balsamic vinegar

1 tbsp. Olive oil

200 g. Red grapes

250 g. Cherry tomatoes

10 or more. Wood or metal skewers

Lemon juice (to taste)

Instructions:

1) First of all, peel and chop the garlic gloves into pieces and slice the chicken breasts. **2)** Secondly, combine the chicken breasts with the gloves, vinegar, olive oil in one bowl. Cover, put in the fridge and let marinate for approx. 30 minutes. **3)** Prepare the grill with medium heat. **4)** Now, prepare the grapes, remove them from the bunch. Cut the tomatoes in two halves and alternate in the skewers the tomatoes with the chicken breasts. **5)** Grill these two ingredients and complete the skewers with the grape. **6)** Garnish everything with the vinegar and lemon juice (to taste) and serve.

Nutrition Facts:

Cal. 750	**Carbs**: 24 g	**Fat**: 20 g	Sat.Fat 3 g	Cholest. 261 mg
Protein 105 g	Diet. Fiber 4 g		Mon.Fat 4.8 g	Sodium 1150 mg
	Tot. Sugars 21 g		Poly.Fat 8.5 g	Salt 3 g

123) *Turmeric chicken risotto* 👤 4   ⏰ 40 Min.

Ingredients:

3 Chicken breasts

2 Shallots and celery ribs

1 tbsp. Olive oil and turmeric

1 tsp. Dried oregano

250 g. Whole-grain rice

600 ml. Water

Herbs mix, paprika powder, rosmary (to taste)

Instructions:

1) First of all, slice the celery ribs, finely chop the shallots and cut into cubes the chicken breasts. Take a pan, heat the olive oil and fry both sides of the chicken breasts for approx. 5-8 minutes until it's golden-brown. **2)** Now, add the ingredients in this sequence: the celery and shallots and fry for 5 more minutes. Add the turmeric, rosmary and oregano and fry for 1 minute. **3)** Now, prepare the rice according to the package instructions. **4)** Pour the water to the pan, bring to boil and let simmer over low heat for approx. 15 minutes. Stir and mix well. (**!!**You can add 20 g. potato starch to let the sauce thicken) **5)** Season the chicken as you prefer and serve with the rice.

Nutrition Facts:

Cal. 1730	**Carbs**: 230 g	**Fat**: 23.3 g	Sat.Fat 4.2 g	Cholest. 260 mg
Protein 130 g	Diet. Fiber 14.2 g		Mon.Fat 12.3 g	Sodium 650 mg
	Tot. Sugars 21 g		Poly.Fat 4 g	Salt 1.6 g

☙☷

124) *Stuffed pumpkins* 👤 4   ⏰ 50 Min.

Ingredients:

2 kg. Pumpkins

2 tbsp. Olive oi

2 Shallots + 1 apple

130 g. Spinach and peppers

350 g. Quinoa

200 g. plain Yoghurt (low-fat)

2 tbsp. Lemon juice

70 g. Walnuts

Instructions:

1) First of all, prepare the oven and preheat it to 400 °F (200 °C). **2)** Secondly, prepare the pumpkins. Cut them in half, remove the seeds and brush them with a bit of olive oil. Season them as you prefer and place them on a baking sheet cut-side down to roast for approx. 20 minutes. **3)** After 20 minutes, flip them up and cook them for other 20 minutes. **4)** Prepare the quinoa according to the instructions and prepare and cut the shallots into small pieces. **5)** Now, finely cut the spinach. Quarter the apple, remove the seeds and cut it into small pieces. **6)** Combine the quinoa with with the apple pieces, walnuts, shallots and spinach. Garnish with the plain yoghurt. Mix weel and stuff the pumpkins, serve.

Nutrition Facts:

Cal. 2800	**Carbs**: 515 g	**Fat**: 53 g	Sat.Fat 7 g	Cholest. 12 mg
Protein 80 g	Diet. Fiber 72 g		Mon.Fat 24.3 g	Sodium 410 mg
	Tot. Sugars 105 g		Poly.Fat 14 g	Salt 1 g

125) *Asian spicy chicken* 👤 4   ⏰ 40 Min.

Ingredients:

250 g. Whole grain rice

6 tbsp. Balsamic vinegar

2 Garlic gloves and peppers

2 tbsp. Ginger

150 g. Peas, broccoli (both frozen)

600 g. Chicken breasts (boneless, skinless)

Herbs mix, olive oil (to taste)

!! Use tofu for the vegetarian version

Instructions:

1) First of all, prepare the whole-grain rice according to the instructions. **2)** Secondly, peel and dice the garlic gloves and ginger. **3)** Heat a pan with a bit of olive oil, add the chicken breasts (previously cut in small pieces), add the garlic gloves and ginger and season as you prefer with herbs mix or others. Cook approx. For 8 minutes and transfer to a plate. **4)** Now, prepare the peppers dicing them. **5)** In the same pan, add a bit of oil, peas and broccoli and mix well together and cook for approx. 5 minutes. **6)** Add the chicken to this sauce and cook for approx. other 5 minutes. Serve with the rice.

Nutrition Facts:

Cal. 2160	**Carbs**: 242 g	**Fat**: 37 g	Sat.Fat 6 g	Cholest. 350 mg
Protein 190 g	Diet. Fiber 26 g		Mon.Fat 12 g	Sodium 5260 mg
	Tot. Sugars 56 g		Poly.Fat 12.9 g	Salt 9 g

ꊛꊛ

126) *Rice salad with beets* 👤 4   ⏰ 30 Min.

Ingredients:

4 Sweet potatoes

4 Beets (precooked)

450 g. Basmati rice

5 tbsp. Olive oil

8 tbsp. Balsamic vinegar

Herbs mix (to taste)

Instructions:

1) Firstly, preheat the oven to 395 °F (200 °C) and line a baking sheet with the appropriate paper. Prepare the potatoes, peel and cut them into small pieces. **2)** Secondly, prepare the beets. Cut them into small cubes and spread them and the potatoes on the baking sheet. Season them with a bit of oil and herbs mix. **3)** Cook them on the middle rack for approx. 18 min. **4)** Now, prepare the rice according to the instructions. **5)** Combine the rice with the vegetables and serve.

Nutrition Facts:

Cal. 3000	**Carbs**: 510 g	**Fat**: 65 g	Sat.Fat 11 g	Cholest. 37 mg
Protein 66 g	Diet. Fiber 40 g		Mon.Fat 41 g	Sodium 840 mg
	Tot. Sugars 96 g		Poly.Fat 8.2 g	Salt 2 g

127) *Boston baked beans (quick version)* 👤 4   ⏰ 50 Min.

Ingredients:

900 g. Navy beans (canned, low-sodium)

1 Onion

120 g. Whole grain rice syrup

60 g. Tomato pasta

2 tbsp. Vinegar

½ tsp. Ground cloves

Paprika powder, rosmary, herbs mix, pepper (to taste)

Instructions:

1) First of all, preheat the oven to 350 °F (170 °C). **2)** Secondly, prepare the beans. Drain and rinse the beans, dice the onion and add both ingredients to a bowl. **3)** Take another bowl and blend together the rice syrup, tomato paste, vinegar, herbs mix and paprika. **4)** Add these ingredients to the beans and mix together very well. **5)** Pour this mixture into a baking dish and bake everything for approx. 40-45 minutes. Serve.

Nutrition Facts:

Cal. 1000	**Carbs**: 180 g	**Fat**: 5.6 g	Sat.Fat 1.1. g	Cholest. 18 mg
Protein 58 g	Diet. Fiber 22.2 g		Mon.Fat 1 g	Sodium 2000 mg
	Tot. Sugars 99.1 g		Poly.Fat 2.3 g	Salt 5.1 g

༺༻

128) *Colorful Thanksgiving* 👤 4   ⏰ 30 Min.

Ingredients:

½ Head cauliflower

1 Pepper, zucchini, celery stick, shallot

150 g. Red cabbage

10 g. Parsley

1 Pomegranate

Rosmary, cumin, paparika and turmeric powder (to taste)

1 Lime (squeezed)

Instructions:

1) First of all, take a big bowl and prepare the vegetables. Finely grate the cauliflower, carrot and zucchini. Then, slice the shallot and celery. Add everything to this bowl and stir. **2)** Secondly, remove the seeds from the pepper, cut it into small cubes and add the pepper to the bowl too. **3)** Pluck the parsley leaves and chop its stick. Cut into pieces even the cabbage and add everything yo the bowl, pomegranate seeds included. **4)** Mix very well and garnish with cumin, paprima, rosmary and turmeric powder. **5)** On top sprinkle the lemon juice and stir well.

Nutrition Facts:

Cal. 360	**Carbs**: 50 g	**Fat**: 3.4 g	Sat.Fat 0.5 g	Cholest. -
Protein 16.2 g	Diet. Fiber 27.2 g		Mon.Fat 0.4 g	Sodium 250 mg
	Tot. Sugars 44.5 g		Poly.Fat 1.8 g	Salt 0.3 g

129) *Black beans burger* 👤 4   ⏰ 60 Min.

Ingredients:

90 g. Quinoa and lettuce

1 tbsp. Olive oil

½ Red onion

100 g. Champignons and cooked beets

450 g. Black beans (canned, low-sodium)

1 Tomato + 4 slices Feta

Rosmary, herbs mix (to taste)

4 Hamburgers buns

Instructions:

1) First of all, prepare the quinoa following the instructions and set aside. **2)** Secondly, take a skillet and heat a bit of olive oil. Now, dice the onion, wash and cut the champignons into small pieces and add to the pan. **3)** Mix well and sauté everything for approx. 10 minutes. Add a bit of flavour with herbs mix (to taste). **4)** Prepare the beets dicing them and add them to the pan. Add a bit of flavor (to taste) and cook for others 5 minutes. **5)** Drain and rinse the beans and add them to the other ingredients. Remove from the geat the pan and mix the ingredients with the cooked quinoa. **6)** Smash the mixture and create a few burgers. Leave them 1 hour in the fridge. **7)** Preheat the oven 375 °F (190°C) and cook the burgers for 30 min. until both sides are golden-brown. **8)** Slice the tomatoes, lettuce, feta and cover with the other half of the bun. Srve.

Nutrition Facts:

Cal. 2400	**Carbs**: 360 g	**Fat**: 60 g	Sat.Fat 19 g	Cholest. 70 mg
Protein 80 g	Diet. Fiber 43 g		Mon.Fat 18 g	Sodium 2630 mg
	Tot. Sugars 20 g		Poly.Fat 5.3 g	Salt 5.6 g

☼☽

130) *Kidney beans gumbo* 👤 4   ⏰ 60 Min.

Ingredients:

40 g. Whole grain flour

2 Bell peppers, celery ribs

1 Shallot

500 ml. Vegetable broth

450 g. Champignons and diced tomatoes, kidney beans (canned, low-sodium)

4 tbsp. Rice oil

340 g. Basmati rice

Instructions:

1) Firstly, take a large pot and heat the rice oil, add the flour and stir into a paste. Cook it for approx. 10 minutes, avoid burning and stir frequently. **2)** Secondly, dice the peppers, celery ribs and add the paste. Cook for approx. 10 minutes until the greens has softened. **3)** Dice the champignons and the shallot and add everything to the pot, beans and diced tomatoes included. Add a bit of flavor with some herbs mix (to taste), cover the pot and let simmer for approx. 10 minutes. **4)** In the meantime, prepare the rice according to the instructions. Once ready, serve the soup and garnish it with basmati rice.

Nutrition Facts:

Cal. 2680	**Carbs**: 385 g	**Fat**: 60 g	Sat.Fat 6.3 g	Cholest. -
Protein 105 g	Diet. Fiber 78 g		Mon.Fat 26.2 g	Sodium 2300 mg
	Tot. Sugars 42 g		Poly.Fat 17 g	Salt 3 g

131) *Orange salad* 👤 4   ⏰ 15 Min.

Ingredients:

4 tbsp. Sesame seeds, pumpkin seeds

4 Apricots and apples

500 g. Papaya

2 Mangos

1 Lemon

Instructions:

1) Firstly, roast the seeds in a pan and then set aside. **2)** Secondly, take a bowl and grate the apples. **3)** Prepare the apricots and peel and cut into pieces the mangos and papaya. Add them to the grated apples. **4)** Mix the fruits together and squeeze the lemon. Garnish with the roasted seeds (add others if you like) and serve.

Nutrition Facts:

Cal. 950	**Carbs**: 168 g	**Fat**: 11.2 g	Sat.Fat 1.5 g	Cholest. -
Protein 16.5 g	Diet. Fiber 32 g		Mon.Fat 2.3 g	Sodium 27
	Tot. Sugars 166 g		Poly.Fat 6.2 g	Salt -

☼☼

132) *Shrimps risotto* 👤 4   ⏰ 40 Min.

Ingredients:

3 Garlic gloves

1 tbsp. Olive oil

250 g. Risotto rice

800 ml. Vegetable broth

300 g. Shrimps (fresh and cleaned) and asparagus

Parmesan, rosmary powder (to taste)

Instructions:

1) First of all, prepare the rice according to the instructions, add gradually the vegetable broth and stir regularly. **2)** Secondly, in the meantime peel the garlic gloves and sauté them in a pot with a bit of oil. **3)** Now, prepare the asparagus cutting the woody edges and cut them into pieces. Wash the shrimps. **4)** Cook them lightly with the garlic gloves and then add them to the risotto a couple of minutes before it's ready. **5)** Mix well, garnish with a bit of parmesan and rosmary to add flavour and serve.

Nutrition Facts:

Cal. 1240	**Carbs**: 194 g	**Fat**: 30 g	Sat.Fat 5 g	Cholest. -
Protein 39 g	Diet. Fiber 19.2 g		Mon.Fat 16 g	Sodium 2300 mg
	Tot. Sugars 17 g		Poly.Fat 3.7 g	Salt 4.9 g

133) *Spinach pasta* 👤 4 ⏰ 20 Min.

Ingredients:

3 Zucchini

400 g. Spinach (fresh)

400 g. Whole-grain spaghetti

300 g. Peas (frozen)

1 Shallots

1 Lemon

Parmesan, rosmary, paprika powder (too taste)

Instructions:

1) First of all, take a pot and prepare the whole-grain spaghetti following the instructions. (Usually approx. 12 minutes) **2)** Secondly, wash and prepare the vegetables. Cut the zucchini, take a pot and combine together the spinach, zucchini and thaw peas and cook the lightly for a few minutes. Garnish them with a bit of oil and rosmary. **3)** A couple of minutes before the pasta is ready, drain the spaghetti and put them into the pot again. **4)** Add the vegetables and mix everything together. Cook for another 2 minutes. Garnish with parmesan (to taste) and serve.

Nutrition Facts:

Cal. 2240	**Carbs**: 300 g	**Fat**: 52 g	Sat.Fat 8.3 g	Cholest. 295 mg
Protein 98 g	Diet. Fiber 71 g		Mon.Fat 24 g	Sodium 335 mg
	Tot. Sugars 23 g		Poly.Fat 11 g	Salt 0.6 g

෮෬

134) *Rye pasta with spinach* 👤 4 ⏰ 15 Min.

Ingredients:

300 g. Rye pasta (to taste)

500 g. Spinach (fresh)

3 Garlic gloves

120 g. Ricotta

200 g. Cherry tomatoes

Walnuts, parmesan, rosmary, herbs mix (to taste)

Instructions:

1) Firstly, prepare the pasta according to the instructions (usually it takes approx. 8-12 minutes). **2)** Secondly, wash the spinach and cut them into small pieces, peel the garlic and slice the gloves too. Wash and cut the cherry tomatoes. **3)** Take a pan and add the garlic, spinach and tomatoes. Let everything cook for several minutes and season them with herbs mix, rosmary and a bit of oil. **4)** As the pasta is almost ready, drain and pour it again in the pot adding the vegetables. Stir everything together for another 2-3 minutes. **5)** Garnish with a parmesan and walnuts pieces and serve.

Nutrition Facts:

Cal. 2300	**Carbs**: 250 g	**Fat**: 83 g	Sat.Fat 25 g	Cholest. 624 mg
Protein 125 g	Diet. Fiber 53 g		Mon.Fat 33 g	Sodium 1689 mg
	Tot. Sugars 6.4 g		Poly.Fat 15 g	Salt 4.2 g

135) *Greens casserole* 👤 4 ⏰ 70 Min.

Ingredients:

- 500 g. Zucchini
- 300 g. Tomatoes
- 400 g. Potatoes
- 1 Shallot
- 160 g. Feta
- 200 g. Cottage cheese
- Rosmary, olive oil, paprika powder (to taste)

Instructions:

1) Firstly, preheat the oven to 395 °F (200 °C) and prepare the vegetables. Cut the zucchini, peel and slice the potatoes and the tomatoes. 2) Secondly, peel the garlic and cut into small pieces both cheeses. Mix them together. Season with a bit of rosmary and oil. 3) Brush the casserole with a bit of oil and create a layer firstly with the zucchini and then with potatoes and cheese mixture. 4) Create multiple layers and spread the tomatoes on top. 5) Sprinkle a bit of olive oil and other seasoning and cook in the oven on th emiddle rack for approx. 60 minutes.

Nutrition Facts:

Cal. 1560	**Carbs**: 91 g	Fat: 87 g	Sat.Fat 50 g	Cholest. 207 mg
Protein 90 g	Diet. Fiber 13.2 g		Mon.Fat 26.5 g	Sodium 2160 mg
	Tot. Sugars 26.4 g		Poly.Fat 4.3 g	Salt 5.4 g

---

136) *Greens muffins* 👤 4 ⏰ 40 Min.

Ingredients:

- 2 Eggs
- 180 g. Spinach (fresh)
- 60 g. Ricotta
- Herbs mix, olive oil, paprika powder, pepper (to taste)

Instructions:

1) First of all, preheat the oven to 320 °F (160 °C). 2) Secondly, take a pan and heat the spinach over medium heat. 3) Now, combine the other ingredientes. Mix well together the eggs, the ricotta and season them with olive oil, herbs mix and a bit of salt and pepper. 4) Add the spinach and mix well. Fill the muffin molds and bake for approx. 30 minutes.

Nutrition Facts:

Cal. 315	**Carbs**: 3 g	Fat: 22 g	Sat.Fat 11.2 g	Cholest. 402 mg
Protein 24 g	Diet. Fiber 3 g		Mon.Fat 6.3 g	Sodium 760 mg
	Tot. Sugars 2.2 g		Poly.Fat 2.1 g	Salt 1.4 g

137) *Roasted salmon with roasted greens* 👤 4 ⏰ 40 Min.

Ingredients:

5 Zucchini

3 Shallots and 4 garlic gloves

500 g. Tomaotes

600 g. Salmon fillets

2 Lemons (squeezed)

Olive oil, herbs mix, paprika powder, basil, thyme (to taste)

Instructions:

1) First of all, take a bowl and cut the zucchini and shallots. Prepare the tomatoes: peel and cut them into pieces. Add all three ingredients to a bowl. 2) Secondly, season them with herbs and distribute the vegetables on the baking sheet. 3) Place the salmon fillets on top and sprinkle them with the garlic cloves and lemon juice. 4) Bake everything at 360 °F (180 °C) for approx. 25-30 minutes. Check the veggis color, when they turn slightly brown, they're ready. 5) Lastly, remove them from the oven and sprinkle them with some herbs, basil and thyme. Serve.

Nutrition Facts:

Cal. 1825 **Carbs**: 56 g **Fat**: 103 g Sat.Fat 20 g Cholest. 348 mg
Protein 148 g Diet. Fiber 24 g Mon.Fat 42 g Sodium 450 mg
Tot. Sugars 49 g Poly.Fat 25.3 g Salt 1 g

൭൬

138) *Fried fish with spinach* 👤 4 ⏰ 20 Min.

Ingredients:

2 Shallots

4 tbsp. Olive oil

Curry powder, turmeric powder, lemon juice, herbs mix (to taste)

800 g. Kingfish fillets

600 g. Spinach (fresh)

500 ml. Coconut milk (low-fat)

Instructions:

1) First of all, prepare a pan. Chop the shallots and garlic gloves, add them to the pan and fry with the olive oil for a few minutes. 2) Secondly, move everything to one side of the pan and use the space to brown the fillets. 3) Garnish them with the spices mix and deglaze with the milk. 4) Lastly, add the spinach and the curry powder and cook on a medium heat for 10-15 minutes. Serve.

Nutrition Facts:

Cal. 1748 **Carbs**: 68 g **Fat**: 75 g Sat.Fat 57.9 g Cholest. 560 mg
Protein 187 g Diet. Fiber 22 g Mon.Fat 8 g Sodium 735 mg
Tot. Sugars 41 g Poly.Fat 5.7 g Salt 2 g

139) *Scrambled eggs with ricotta* 👤 4 ⏰ 10 Min.

Ingredients:

5 Tomatoes (big one)

4 tbsp. Olive oil

5 Eggs

400 g. Ricotta

300 g. Spinach (fresh)

1 Lemon

Herbs mix, rosmary, turmeric, paparika powder (to taste)

Instructions:

1) Prepare the vegetables. Cut the tomatoes into small pieces. Wash and coarsely cut the spinach. Add both vegetables in a pan and lightly brown with a bit of oil. Season them with your favourite herbs mix. **2)** Scramble the eggs in a plate and add a bit of salt and the lemon juice to take away the eggs' flavour. **3)** Add the eggs to the pan and mix very well. **4)** As the eggs starts to thicken crumble the ricotta with your hand and sprinkle it over the other ingredients. **5)** Let everything cook for a minute and than serve.

Nutrition Facts:

Cal. 1680	**Carbs**: 24 g	**Fat**: 123 g	Sat.Fat	54 g	Cholest.	2850 mg
Protein 168 g	Diet. Fiber 6 g		Mon.Fat	25.6 g	Sodium	1200 mg
	Tot. Sugars 25 g		Poly.Fat	11.3 g	Salt	5 g

ಸಂಞ

140) *Tomato omelet* 👤 4 ⏰ 15 Min.

Ingredients:

6 Eggs

2 Shallots

3 Tomatoes

Olive oil, rosmary(to taste)

100 g. Cherry tomatoes and artichokes

60 ml. Sparkling water

120 g. Ricotta

1 Lemon

Instructions:

1) Prepare the artichockes. Cut them into small pieces and sauté them into a pan with a bit of oil and half of a shallot for approx. 10 minutes. **2)** In the meantime, peel and finely slice the remaining shallots and cut into pieces the tomatoes. **3)** Stir the eggs using a fork and add the sparkling water. Season with a bit of salt and pepper or others spices. Add the lemon juice to remove the eggs flavour. **4)** Put the shallots in a pan and sautè them for a few minutes. Add the tomatoes, artichokes and ricotta. **5)** Fry over medium heat and let set. Serve.

Nutrition Facts:

Cal. 1040	**Carbs**: 21 g	**Fat**: 87.4 g	Sat.Fat	28 g	Cholest.	1430 mg
Protein 65 g	Diet. Fiber 6.7 g		Mon.Fat	39.3 g	Sodium	1380 mg
	Tot. Sugars 21.4 g		Poly.Fat	9.2 g	Salt	2 g

141) *Couscous soup* 👤 4 ⏰ 30 Min.

Ingredients:

700 ml. Vegetable broth

2 tbsp. Olive oil

3 Tomatoes + 2 onions

100 g. Peas (canned, unsweetened)

100 g. Beans (canned, low-sodium, unsweetened)

70 g. Couscous

Paprika powder, parsley (to taste)

Instructions:

1) Drain and rinse the peas, wash the onions and tomatoes and cut them into cubes. **2)** Take a pot, add some olive oil and add the onions, tomatoes and peas. Season as you prefer and sauté for 2-4 minutes. **3)** Add the couscous, the drained and rinsed beans and pour gradually the vegetable broth. **4)** Let everything simmer for approx. 15-20 minutes. **5)** Season with paprika and parsley (to taste).

Nutrition Facts:

Cal. 670 **Carbs**: 67.8 g **Fat**: 30 g Sat.Fat 4.8 g Cholest. -
Protein 22 g Diet. Fiber 15 g Mon.Fat 20 g Sodium 2540 mg
Tot. Sugars 24 g Poly.Fat 4 g Salt 4.6 g

ಬಿಲ

142) *Classic olive salad* 👤 4 ⏰ 10 Min.

Ingredients:

4 Cucumbers

250 g. Green olives (pitted)

5 Tomatoes

500 g. Mix of lettuce and arugola

2 Lemons + 2 tsp. Chia seeds

650 g. Tuna (in water canned, no-salt added, low-sodium)

Olive oil, herbs mix (to taste)

200 g. Beans (in water canned)

Instructions:

1) Take a big bowl. Drain and rinse the tuna and beans. Add the to the bowl. **2)** Cut in pieces the olives (or keep it whole) and the tomatoes and add the to the bowl. **3)** Take the lettuce mixed with arugola and cut the lettuce in bite-sized pieces and mix everything with the other ingredients. **4)** Peel the cucumber and add them too. **5)** Season them with olive oil, vinegar and lemon juice and prinkle on top of them the chia seeds. Serve and enjoy.

Nutrition Facts:

Cal. 2200 **Carbs**: 60 g **Fat**: 112 g Sat.Fat 24.9 g Cholest. -
Protein 220 g Diet. Fiber 28 g Mon.Fat 60 g Sodium 1400 mg
Tot. Sugars 50 g Poly.Fat 16 g Salt 3.7 g

143) *Millet with greens* 👤 4   ⏰ 20 Min.

Ingredients:

250 g. Millet

5 Tomatoes

1 Shallot

300 g. Peas and beans mixture

3 Carrots

450 ml. Vegetable broth

Olive oil, turmeric powder and pepper (to taste)

Instructions:

1) First of all, prepare the millet according to the directions you find in the package. **2)** Secondly, prepare the vegetables. Peel and cut the tomatoes into small pieces and slice the shallots. Take a pan and lightly braise these two ingredients with a bit of olive oil. **3)** Add the peas and beans mixture and the carrots (cut them into pieces). **4)** Now, add the vegetable brothe and let everything simmer for approx. 12 minutes. **5)** Serve the vegetables with the millet and season everything with the turmeric powder and pepper.

Nutrition Facts:

Cal. 1420   **Carbs**: 220 g   **Fat**: 22.4 g   Sat.Fat 2.5 g   Cholest. -
Protein 55 g   Diet. Fiber 48 g   Mon.Fat 10.2 g   Sodium 1720 mg
              Tot. Sugars 53 g   Poly.Fat 6.4 g   Salt 2.3 g

☼☾

144) *Coconut curry with rice* 👤 4   ⏰ 30 Min.

Ingredients:

250 g. Basmati rice

2 Onions and garlic gloves

4 tsp. Curry powder

550 g. Diced tomatoes (canned)

300 ml. Coconut milk (low-fat)

530 g. Chickpeas (canned, low-sodium)

Basil, herbs mix, oregano (to taste)

Instructions:

1) Firstly, cook the rice according the instructions of the package and keep warm. **2)** Secondly, take a pan, heat a bit of olive oil and sauté the garlic gloves and onions after cutting them. **3)** Add the tomatoes and the milk and let everything simmer for approx. 10 minutes. **4)** Now, wash and drain the chickpeas, season them with the curry powder and your favourite herbs mix and cook them for approx. 10-15 minutes. **5)** As everything is ready, serve the vegetables with the rice. Add a bit of flavour if necessary.

Nutrition Facts:

Cal. 1870   **Carbs**: 324 g   **Fat**: 56 g   Sat.Fat 36 g   Cholest. -
Protein 69 g   Diet. Fiber 40 g   Mon.Fat 5.3 g   Sodium 2379 mg
              Tot. Sugars 34 g   Poly.Fat 9.8 g   Salt 3.5 g

145) *Roasted chickpeas with avocado* 👤 4 ⏰ 40 Min.

Ingredients:

250 g. Quinoa

800 g. Chickpeas

5 Tomatoes

2 Avocado

200 g. Lettuce

Olive oil, oregano, parsely, thyme, other herbs (to taste)

Instructions:

1) First of all, take a pot with water, bring to boil and prepare the quinoa. Let simmer approx. For 10 minutes. **2)** Secondly, drain the chickpeas and put them into a bowl. Season the chickpeas with a bit of olive oil, oregano and the herbs mix you prefer. Mix well together. **3)** Cover a baking sheet with baking paper and spread the chickpeas. Place in the oven at 430 °F (220 °C) and cook for approx. 25 minutes. (Low the heat the last 10 minutes). **4)** Wash and prepare the lettuce and season the quinoa. Peel and cut the avocados. **5)** Serve with the chickpeas.

Nutrition Facts:

Cal. 2358	**Carbs**: 250 g	**Fat**: 105 g	Sat.Fat 15 g	Cholest. -
Protein 103 g	Diet. Fiber 113 g		Mon.Fat 60 g	Sodium 70 mg
	Tot. Sugars 30 g		Poly.Fat 20 g	Salt -

ಬಚ

146) *Quick avocado toast with tomatoes* 👤 4 ⏰ 8 Min.

Ingredients:

8 slices. Whole grain bread

4 Avocado

12 Cherry tomatoes

Olive oil, lemon juice, basil, oregano (to taste)

Instructions:

1) Firstly, toast the bread slices until they're crispy. **2)** Secondly, peel and cut the avocados and mash them with a fork. **3)** Spread the avocadoes on the bread slices. **4)** Cut the tomatoes and season them with olive oil, basil and oregano. Mix well together and lay them over the avocados. **5)** Sprinkle the sandwiches with lemon juice.

Nutrition Facts:

Cal. 1680	**Carbs**: 118 g	**Fat**: 143 g	Sat.Fat 30.3 g	Cholest. 6 mg
Protein 30 g	Diet. Fiber 50 g		Mon.Fat 93.2 g	Sodium 850 mg
	Tot. Sugars 37.2 g		Poly.Fat 19 g	Salt 2 g

147) *Creamy mushrooms* 👤 4 ⏰ 15 Min.

Ingredients:

900 g. Champignons

5 Garlic gloves + 1 Shallot

2 tbsp. Paprika powder and tomato paste

280 ml. Vegetable broth

50 ml. White wine

30 g. Chives

Herbs mix, turmeric, paprika powder (to taste)

Instructions:

1) First of all, wash the champignons and cut them into pieces. Take a pan, heat a bit of oil and sauté the mushrooms. In the meantime, peel and finely slice the shallot and garlic gloves. Add them to the pan and cook for other 5 minutes. **2)** Slowly mix the tomato paste, paprika powder, white wine and vegetable broth and let everything cook. **3)** Now, cut and add the chives to the pan. **4)** Season with a bit of paprika powder, mix very well and serve.

Nutrition Facts:

Cal. 1020	**Carbs**: 30 g	**Fat**: 75 g	Sat.Fat 12 g	Cholest. -
Protein 47 g	Diet. Fiber 26 g		Mon.Fat 35.6 g	Sodium 1003 mg
	Tot. Sugars 25 g		Poly.Fat 27.4 g	Salt 2 g

☙☜

148) *Eggplant -potato mix* 👤 4 ⏰ 40 Min.

Ingredients:

900 g. Potatoes

2 Shallots

500 g. Chsmpignons

500 g. Eggplants

500 ml. Vegetable broth

Parsley, parmesan, rosmary, oregano, olive oil, curry powder (to taste)

Instructions:

1) First of all, wash, peel and cut the potatoes, the champignons and the eggplant. Peel and slice the shallots too. **2)** Secondly, use a pan, heat a bit of oil and add the shallots slices and rosmary. Add the potatoes and roast them for approx. 5 minutes. **3)** Add the mushrooms and eggplants. Mix weel ad deglaze with the vegetable broth. Let cook on medium heat for approx. 30 minutes and the broth should evaporate. **4)** Garnish with parmesan, parsley and curry powder and serve.

Nutrition Facts:

Cal. 1930	**Carbs**: 175 g	**Fat**: 115 g	Sat.Fat 116 g	Cholest. -
Protein 52 g	Diet. Fiber 35 g		Mon.Fat 24 g	Sodium 1340 mg
	Tot. Sugars 33 g		Poly.Fat 5.2 g	Salt 3.7 g

149) *Summer bruschetta* 👤 4   ⏰ 15 Min.

Ingredients:

300 g. Whole grain bread

4-6 Tomatoes

100 g. Olives (pitted)

2 Avocados

200 g. Tuna (in water canned)

Lemon juice, parsley, herbs mix, olive oil (to taste)

Instructions:

1) First of all, slice the bread, take a pan and warm it until it become crispy. 2) Secondly, prepare the tomatoes. Peel and cut them into pieces. Season them with a bit of olive oil and oregano and mix well. 3) Take a bowl, peel and smash the avocadoes with a fork. Add a bit of lemon juice and olive oil and mix well. Drain and rinse the olives. 4) As the bread is crispy, spread the avocado on the bread slices and garnish with tomatoes, drained tuna and olives. Season with your favorite herbs mix and parsley. Serve.

Nutrition Facts:

Cal. 1740	**Carbs**: 147 g	**Fat**: 105 g	Sat.Fat 20 g	Cholest. -
Protein 36 g	Diet. Fiber 43 g		Mon.Fat 68 g	Sodium 1187 mg
	Tot. Sugars 50 g		Poly.Fat 14 g	Salt 3.1 g

☙❧

150) *Leek with eggplants* 👤 4   ⏰ 40 Min.

Ingredients:

3 Garlic gloves

540 g. Tofu (organic)

3 tbsp. Olive oil

500 g. Leek

350 g. Eggplants

3 tbsp. White wine

½ Lemon (organic)

Rosmary, oregano (to taste)

Instructions:

1) First of all, slice the eggplants and grill them. Season them with a bit of olive oil, 1 ½ garlic gloves (cut them) and parsley. 2) In the meantime, press the tofu to remove the excess of water and cut it into thick cubes. 3) Take a pan and cook together the garlic gloves, tofu and grated lemon. Remove from the heat as the cubes of tofu turn golden. 4) Cut and slice the leek and lightly cook the rings for approx. 10 minutes. 5) When the leek is ready, mix it together with the eggplants and tofu and garnish with a bit of lemon juice, rosmary and oregano (to taste).

Nutrition Facts:

Cal. 1280	**Carbs**: 48 g	**Fat**: 69 g	Sat.Fat 11 g	Cholest. -
Protein 113 g	Diet. Fiber 26 g		Mon.Fat 32 g	Sodium 3276 mg
	Tot. Sugars 24 g		Poly.Fat 24 g	Salt 7.5 g

151) *Colorful crusted salmon*   👤 4   ⏰ 20 Min.

Ingredients:

1 Avocado and mango

350 g. Tomatoes

250 g. Ricotta

2 tbsp. Honey

2 tbsp. Olive oil

4 Salmon fillets

100 g. Arugola

Lemon juice, paprika powder, parsley (to taste)

Instructions:

1) First of all, peel the onion, the avocado and mango and cut them into pieces. **2)** Mix all together the fruits, ricotta and herbs mix. **3)** Now, blend together a bit of paprika powder, lemon juice, honey, olive oil and parsley (cut it very finely). Brush this mix onto the fillets and cook bothe sides for 3-5 minutes. **4)** In the meantime, prepare and wash the arugola. Divide onto plate and serve the fillets with the fruits and ricotta mix.

Nutrition Facts:

Cal. 2450	**Carbs**: 96.2 g	**Fat**: 165 g	Sat.Fat 67 g	Cholest. 550 mg
Protein 172 g	Diet. Fiber 21 g		Mon.Fat 57 g	Sodium 715 mg
	Tot. Sugars 84 g		Poly.Fat 25 g	Salt 1.5 g

---

152) *Honey walnut shrimps mix*   👤 4   ⏰ 40 Min.

Ingredients:

250 g. Basmati rice

5 tbsp. Honey and water

1 head Broccoli

60 g. Walnuts (chopped)

450 g. Shrimps (peeled)

2 tbsp. Plain yoghurt

2 tbsp. Olive oil

Lemon juice, parsley (to taste)

Instructions:

1) First of all, prepare the basmati rice according to the package instructions and use 2 tbsp. of honey and water to pour them into a pan and heat them. **2)** Add the walnuts pieces and let them caramelize for 5 minutes until the water has evaporated. **3)** Take a baking sheet and spread the walnuts and let them cool down. **4)** Prepare the vegetables. Wash and cut into florets the broccoli. Take a pot, pour a small amount of water, cover and stew the broccoli over medium heat for approx. 5 minutes. **5)** On one pot, create a sauce with yoghurt and the remaining honey and on another pot add the shrimps and sauté them with a bit of oil, lemon juice and parsley. **6)** Serve the rice with the shrimps, sauce and broccoli. Season to taste.

Nutrition Facts:

Cal. 3050	**Carbs**: 291 g	**Fat**: 150 g	Sat.Fat 41 g	Cholest. 1040 mg
Protein 130 g	Diet. Fiber 17.4 g		Mon.Fat 43 g	Sodium 1258 mg
	Tot. Sugars 85.6 g		Poly.Fat 53 g	Salt 3 g

153) *Quiche with kale and pumpkin* 👤 4 ⏰ 1 h.

Ingredients:

200 g. Pastry dough

50 g. Kale (fresh) and pumpkin

1 Onion, pear

30 g. Walnuts

200 g. Ricotta

2 Eggs

Rosmary, olive oil, herbs, turmeric powder (to taste)

Instructions:

1) First of all, preheat the oven to 360 °F (180 °C). **2)** Secondly, take a quiche pan and press the pastry down. **3)** Take another pan, peel and cut the onion into pieces. Prepare the kale, wash it and cut the leaves into pieces. **4)** Heat a bit of olive oil and sauté the onion fro a couple of minutes. Stir regularly and add the kale. Cook for others 3-5 minutes. Season everything with rosmary, herbs mix and turmeric powder. **5)** Prepare the pumpkin cutting it into small cubes. **6)** Now, prepare the pear removing the seeds and cut it into slices. Crumble up the ricotta and mix it well with the kale. **7)** Create some holes into the pastry dough and fill them with the kale mixture. Garnish with the pumpkin cubes, turmeric powder, walnuts and pear pieces. **8)** Cook for 30 min. and serve.

Nutrition Facts:

Cal. 1870	**Carbs**: 128.4 g	**Fat**: 138.6 g	Sat.Fat 67.5 g	Cholest. 735 mg
Protein 40 g	Diet. Fiber 9.3 g		Mon.Fat 38.4 g	Sodium 345 mg
	Tot. Sugars 46.5 g		Poly.Fat 23.5 g	Salt -

൦൬

154) *Taleggio bowl with cranberries* 👤 4 ⏰ 20 Min.

Ingredients:

250 g. Taleggio cheese

250 g. Couscous

10 Cherry tomatoes

200 g. Red cabbage

100 g. Cranberries (jarred)

200 g. Tuna (in water canned)

150 g. Corn (in water canned)

Olive oil, vinegar, lemon juice, herbs mix (to taste)

Instructions:

1) First of all, prepare the couscous according to the package instructions. **2)** Secondly, cut the ends of the cabbage and lightly slice it. Take a bowl and start adding the ingredients. **3)** Drain and rinse the corn and cranberries and add them to the bowl. Do the same fot the tuna and add it to the bowl. **4)** Wash and cut the cherry tomatoes and add them to the bowl. **5)** Season all the ingredients with lemon juice, olive oil, a bit of vinegar (to taste) and / or other spices. Mix very well. **6)** As the couscous is ready, split it into bowl and serve with all the vegetables and pieces of taleggio.

Nutrition Facts:

Cal. 2340	**Carbs**: 260 g	**Fat**: 88 g	Sat.Fat 35.4 g	Cholest. 142 mg
Protein 92 g	Diet. Fiber 32 g		Mon.Fat 21 g	Sodium 1637 mg
	Tot. Sugars 110 g		Poly.Fat 24.5 g	Salt 4.2 g

155) *Kale mixed salad* 👤 4   ⏰ 15 Min.

Ingredients:

80 g. Quinoa

200 g. Kale (fresh)

60 g. Ricotta

4 tbsp. Lemon juice and olive oil

80 g. Walnuts

2 tbsp. Raisin

2 Pears

Instructions:

1) Firstly, prepare the quinoa according to the instructions. In the meantime wash and prepare the kale. Cut the leaves into small piecesa, wash and dry them. **2)** Secondly, peel and slice the pears and add to a bowl. Crumble the walnuts and add the pieces too. Add the kale and ricotta. **3)** Season with a bit of olive oil and lemon juice. Sprinkle a bit of raisin on top and add the couscous. **4)** Mix everything together and serve.

Nutrition Facts:

Cal. 2010 **Carbs**: 201 g **Fat**: 110 g Sat.Fat 16.4 g Cholest. 40 mg
Protein 39.3 g Diet. Fiber 26 g   Mon.Fat 41 g   Sodium 330 mg
         Tot. Sugars 138.2 g   Poly.Fat 48.2 g Salt -

☼☼

156) *Mexican cheesy nachos* 👤 4   ⏰ 40 Min.

Ingredients:

100 g. Hard

1 Shallot

2 tbsp. Olive oil

250 g. Tomatoes (puréed)

8 Eggs

150 g. Kidney beans (in water, canned)

150 g. Corn (in water canned)

Paprika powder, rosmary (to taste)

Instructions:

1) First of all, cover with baking paper the baking sheet and lay down the cheese. Bake at 480 °F (250 °C) for approx. 10 minutes until the cheese turn golden-brown. Then remove the cheese from the oven and let cool down. **2)** Give the cheese the triangle shape. Now, prepare the shallot and slice it. Briefly sauté in a sauce pan with a bit of oil and rosmary. **3)** Add the beans, corn, paprika powder and and herbs mix. Heat for approx. 4-7 minutes. **4)** Add the tomatoes and cook for others 5 minutes. In a separate pan fry the eggs and season them with parsley and a bit of pepper and paprika powder. **5)** Serve the cheesy nachos with the beans sauce.

Nutrition Facts:

Cal. 1540   **Carbs**: 52 g **Fat**: 100 g Sat.Fat 30 g   Cholest. 2207 mg
Protein 113 g Diet. Fiber 14 g   Mon.Fat 46 g   Sodium 2167 mg
         Tot. Sugars 26 g   Poly.Fat 13 g Salt 4 g

157) *Summer skewers* 👤 4   ⏰ 10 Min.

Ingredients:

1 Garlic gloves

1 Lemon

140 g. Shrimps (peeled)

140 g. Pineapple

10 Cherry tomatoes

Parsley, thyme, olive oil (to taste)

At least 4-6 skewers

Instructions:

1) First of all, prepare and grilled the shrimps. Heat a bit of oil in a pan and add the shrimps. Season them with a bit of olive oil, lemon juice, thyme and parsley. Grilled them for 3-4 minutes. **2)** Secondly, peel and cut the ananas into small pieces. Do the same with the tomatoes, cut them in two halves. **3)** As the shrimps are ready, start to fill the skewers. Alternate the shrimps with the tomatoes and with the ananas. Sprinkle with a bit of lemon juice and serve.

Nutrition Facts:

Cal. 190	**Carbs**: 14.3 g **Fat**: 5.3 g	Sat.Fat 1.2 g	Cholest. 150 mg
Protein 20 g	Diet. Fiber 1.3 g	Mon.Fat 2.4 g	Sodium 180 mg
	Tot. Sugars 12.4 g	Poly.Fat 1 g	Salt -

☙☕

158) *Shrimps mixed salad* 👤 4   ⏰ 10 Min.

Ingredients:

2 Lemons

4 Tomatoes

2 Avocados

300 g. Shrimps

200 g. Corn (in water canned)

200 g. Tuna (in water canned)

100 g. Olives (pitted)

Olive oil, parsley (to taste)

Instructions:

1) First of all, take a pan and grill the shrimps for 3-4 minutes with a bit of olive oil and lemon juice. **2)** In the meantime, take a big bowl and mix together the other ingredients little by little. **3)** Peel the avocados and cut them into pieces, as well as the tomatoes. Drain and rinse the corn, olives and tuna and add everything to the bowl. **4)** Season everything with a bit of olive oil, lemon juice and your favorite herbs mix and serve.

Nutrition Facts:

Cal. 1189	**Carbs**: 91 g **Fat**: 68 g	Sat.Fat 14.3 g	Cholest. 470 mg
Protein 80 g	Diet. Fiber 43 g	Mon.Fat 37.2 g	Sodium 1569 mg
	Tot. Sugars 32.5 g	Poly.Fat 11.3 g	Salt 3.2 g

159) *Spinach quesadilla* 👤 4   ⏰ 30 Min.

Ingredients:

4 Eggs and eggs white

350 g. Ricotta

2 tsp. Paprika powder

20 g. Rice flour

Olive oil, salt, oregano (to taste)

100 g. Spinach (fresh)

300 g. Feta

Instructions:

1) First of all, preheat the oven to 400 °F (200 °C). Take a bowl and mix together the eggs, eggs white, rice flour, organo, some salt and the ricotta. Mix well together and let rest. **2)** Take the dough and give it the form of the tortillas and bake for approx. 10 minutes until it become crispy. **3)** Let them cool down and remove from the baking sheet. **4)** Take a pan and heat some oil. Add the number of tortillas the pan allows and spread them with the spinach, feta and season with oregano and paprika powder. **5)** Top with the second tortilla and cook both sides until the filling is warm and the cheese soften. Serve.

Nutrition Facts:

Cal. 2140	**Carbs**: 32 g	**Fat**: 210 g	Sat.Fat 119 g	Cholest. 1230 mg
Protein 168 g	Diet. Fiber 16.5 g		Mon.Fat 51 g	Sodium 3280 mg
	Tot. Sugars 16.3 g		Poly.Fat 9.3 g	Salt 6.7 g

☯☪

160) *Spinach mixed eggs* 👤 4   ⏰ 15 Min.

Ingredients:

6 Eggs

1 Lemon

3 tbsp. Olive oil

250 g. Spinach (fresh)

4 slices. Baked ham (organic, low-sodium, no salt added)

Parmesan, oregano, turmeric, herbs mix (to taste)

Instructions:

1) First of all, beat the eggs and add the lemon juice from the squeezed lemon to remove the taste of the eggs. Season with a bit of oregano and your favourite herbs mix. **2)** Secondly, slice the ham and spinach in small pieces and add them to th eggs. Mix well. **3)** Heat the pan with a bit of olive oil and add the eggs. Cook for a few minutes and serve.

Nutrition Facts:

Cal. 920	**Carbs**: 8.7 g	**Fat**: 69 g	Sat.Fat 17 g	Cholest. 1620 mg
Protein 64 g	Diet. Fiber 0.3 g		Mon.Fat 36.2 g	Sodium 1120 mg
	Tot. Sugars 7.8 g		Poly.Fat 9.2 g	Salt 2.4 g

161) *Lemon pasta* 👤 4   ⏰ 15

Ingredients:

300 g. Whole grain pasta

1 Lemon

300 g. Cherry tomatoees

180 g. Tuna

100 g. Olives (pitted)

Olive oil, herbs mix (to taste)

Instructions:

1) Firstly, prepare the whole grain pasta according to the instructions of the package. **2)** Secondly, prapare the vegetables. Wash and cut into pieces the cherry tomatoes, rinse and drain the olives. **3)** 2-3 minutes before the pasta is ready (see the cooking time on the package), drain the pasta and put it again on the pot. **4)** Add the tomatoes, tuna and olives. Squeeze the lemon and add a bit of olive oil and herbs mix (to taste). **5)** Cook for another 2-3 minutes. Serve.

Nutrition Facts:

Cal. 1568	**Carbs**: 206 g	**Fat**: 62 g	Sat.Fat 7.3 g	Cholest. 234 mg
Protein 52 g	Diet. Fiber 41 g		Mon.Fat 37.3 g	Sodium 74 mg
	Tot. Sugars 14 g		Poly.Fat 12.2 g	Salt -

꧁꧂

162) *Yellow rice salad* 👤 4   ⏰ 15 Min.

Ingredients:

300 g. Basmati rice

2 Mango

2 Cucumber

1 Lime

150 g. Olives (pitted)

Thyme, turmeric, herbs mix (to taste)

Instructions:

1) Firstly, prepare the basmati rice according to the package instructions and then let cool a few minutes. **2)** Secondly, peel and cut the cucumbers and mango and cut into small pieces. **3)** Mix togethe the rice and the other ingredients. Squeeze the lime and sprinkle the juice on them. Season with the turmeric, thyme and other herbs mix according to your taste.

Nutrition Facts:

Cal. 1340	**Carbs**: 240 g	**Fat**: 34 g	Sat.Fat 5.2 g	Cholest. -
Protein 27 g	Diet. Fiber 18 g		Mon.Fat 20 g	Sodium 75 mg
	Tot. Sugars 67 g		Poly.Fat 5 g	Salt -

163) *Rice noodles with tomatoes* 👤 4   ⏰ 15 Min.

Ingredients:

300 g. Rice noodles

200 g. Tomatoes

150 g. Ricotta

150 g. Olives (pitted)

90 g. Corn (in water canned)

Olive oil, paprika powder, rosmary (to taste)

Instructions:

1) First of all, prepare the rice noodles according to the package. **2)** In the meantime, wash and cut into pieces the tomatoes. Cut the ricotta into pieces and drain and rinse the corn. **3)** As the noodles are almost ready, drain and put it into the pot with the other ingredients. Mix well together the corn, ricotta, tomatoes and noodles

Nutrition Facts:

Cal. 1950	**Carbs**: 230 g	**Fat**: 55 g	Sat.Fat 8.2 g	Cholest. -
Protein 100 g	Diet. Fiber 25 g		Mon.Fat 16.5 g	Sodium 2680 mg
	Tot. Sugars 13 g		Poly.Fat 24.8 g	Salt 3.2 g

☯☪

164) *Whole grain rice with string beans* 👤 4   ⏰ 15 Min.

Ingredients:

280 g. String beans

340 g. Whole grain rice

200 g. Tomatoes

80 g. Little artichokes (marinated in oil, low-sodium)

2 Garlic cloves

Olive oil, parsley (to taste)

Instructions:

1) First of all, prepare the whole grain rice according to the package instructions and let cool. **2)** Prepare the tomatoes, wash them, remove the seeds and cut the pulp. Drain the artichockes and cut them in 2-3 pieces. **3)** Cut the ends of the string beans and lightly cook them in a pan with a bit of olive oil, garlic gloves (finely cut them) and parsley. **4)** Mix together the rice, tomatoes and the artichockes. Serve the string beans aside and season as you prefer.

Nutrition Facts:

Cal. 1560	**Carbs**: 238 g	**Fat**: 42 g	Sat.Fat 26.7 g	Cholest. -
Protein 52 g	Diet. Fiber 30 g		Mon.Fat 4.1 g	Sodium 1730 mg
	Tot. Sugars 24 g		Poly.Fat 7.3 g	Salt 2.5 g

165) *Thyme pasta with walnuts* 👤 4 ⏰ 15 Min.

Ingredients:

300 g. Whole grain spaghetti

3 Garlic cloves

3 tsp. Thyme (dried)

5 tbsp. Pistachios (chopped)

50 g. Walnuts (crumbled)

50 g. Ricotta

Oregano, olive oil (to taste)

Instructions:

1) First of all, prepare the spaghetti according to the instructions. 2) Secondly, prepare the pistachios and walnuts. As the pasta is almost ready, drain it and pour it in the pot again. 3) Mix the spaghetti with walnuts, thyme, garlic gloves, and crumbled ricotta. Season with a bit of olive oil and herbs mix. 4) Sprinkle on top the pistachios mix.

Nutrition Facts:

Cal. 1678	**Carbs**: 223 g **Fat**: 70 g	Sat.Fat 30 g	Cholest. 121 mg
Protein 62 g	Diet. Fiber 14 g	Mon.Fat 27.2 g	Sodium 176 mg
	Tot. Sugars 10 g	Poly.Fat 4.2 g	Salt -

☼☽

166) *Green mix noodles* 👤 4 ⏰ 15 Min.

Ingredients:

280 g. Rye pasta

100 g. Pistachios (chopped)

500 g. Zucchini

Mint (fesh leaves, to taste)

3 tsp. Chia sesamen and pumpkin seeds

2 Garlic gloves

Olive oil, parsley, rosmary (to taste)

Instructions:

1) Firstly, prepare the pasta according to the instructions. 2) Secondly, prepare the zucchini, cut them into thick slices and lightly cook them with a bit of olive oil and garlic gloves. 3) As the pasta is almost ready, drain and finish the cooking adding the seeds, rosmary, pistachios and the zucchini. 4) Season a bit if necessary and serve.

Nutrition Facts:

Cal. 2145	**Carbs**: 261 g **Fat**: 132.4 g	Sat.Fat 14.7 g	Cholest. -
Protein 44 g	Diet. Fiber 21.5 g	Mon.Fat 56.9 g	Sodium 547 mg
	Tot. Sugars 18.5 g	Poly.Fat 41.7 g	Salt 1.2 g

167) *Roasted Brussel sprouts mix* 👤 4   ⏰ 35 Min.

Ingredients:

700 g. Brussel sprouts

550 g. Sweet potatoes

60 g. Leek

4 tbsp. Walnuts

1 Shallot

Olive oil, rosmary, white wine, pine nuts (to taste)

Instructions:

1) First of all, you have to preheat the oven to 400 °F (200 °C). Secondly, you have to to prepare the potatoes. **2)** Peel and cut them into pieces and take a baking sheet. Lay daown the sprouts and the potatoes. **3)** Season with a bit of olive oil and rosemary and roast for approx. 25 minutes. **4)** In the meantime, prepare and cut the leeks and shallot. Lightly cook them with a bit of olive oil and white wine. **5)** When both the sprouts mix and the leeks are ready, mix them very well together. Garnish with the pine nuts and walnuts pieces and serve.

Nutrition Facts:

Cal. 1560	**Carbs**: 190 g	**Fat**: 50 g	Sat.Fat 6.8 g	Cholest. -
Protein 53 g	Diet. Fiber 62 g		Mon.Fat 61 g	Sodium 100 mg
	Tot. Sugars 56 g		Poly.Fat 56 g	Salt -

☼☺

168) *Griddled beef (Italian version)* 👤 4   ⏰ 20 Min.

Ingredients:

500 g. Beef (very thin slices)

3 tbsp. Herbs mix: rosmary, paprika powder, a bit of salt, oregano

2 tbsp. Olive oil

2 Lemons

3 Bell peppers

10 Cherry tomatoes

40 g. Arugola

3 Garlic cloves

Instructions:

1) First of all, preheat the griddle. 2) As you open the package with the thin slices of beef you have to brush them with a bit of olive oil in order to be able to turn them on both sides and remove them from the griddle without crumble them. **2)** Prepare a big bowl with 2 tbsp. of olive oil, the garlic cloves (cut them into small pieces) and herbs mix. As you cook them on both sides (approx. 1 minutes for each side), remove them from the griddle and put them on the bowl with the seasoning. Sprinkle the lemon juice on top of them and mix very well. **3)** Prepare the vegetables, cut the bell peppers in small pieces, wash and cut the tomatoes in 4 pieces and wash the arugola. Put them into a second bowl and season them with olive oil, lemon juice and apple vinegar. **4)** Serve with the beef.

Nutrition Facts:

Cal. 560	**Carbs**: 22 g	**Fat**: 52 g	Sat.Fat 11 g	Cholest. 78 mg
Protein 88 g	Diet. Fiber 11 g		Mon.Fat 34 g	Sodium 47 mg
	Tot. Sugars 3.2 g		Poly.Fat 4 g	Salt 3.2 g

169) *Griddled beef quinoa* 👤 4 ⏰ 20 Min.

Ingredients:

250 g. Beef (very thin slices)

300 g. Quinoa

5 Tomatoes

150 g. Artichoke

Garlic cloves, lemon juice, rosmary herbs mix (to taste)

Instructions:

1) First of all, prepare the quinoa according to the package instructions. **2)** Secondly, heat the griddle and brush them with a bit of olive oil. Griddle them on each side and as they're ready put them in a bowl with olive oil, lemon juice and herbs mix to season them. **3)** Prepare the vegetables. Wash and cut the tomatoes and cut in small pieces the artichokes. **4)** Lightly cook the artichokes with a bit of olive oil, rosmary, a couple of crumbled garlic cloves and lemon juice. **5)** As the quinoa is ready, combine the quinoa with the tomatoes and artichokes. Serve with the beef aside and season if necessary.

Nutrition Facts:

Cal. 2134	**Carbs**: 170 g	**Fat**: 78.9 g	Sat.Fat 12 g	Cholest. 327 mg
Protein 180 g	Diet. Fiber 32.6 g		Mon.Fat 43.5 g	Sodium 1589 mg
	Tot. Sugars 37.6 g		Poly.Fat 13.5 g	Salt 3.2 g

༄༅

170) *Greens tartlets* 👤 4 ⏰ 30 Min.

Ingredients:

100 g. Spinach

8 Egg whites

100 g. Ricotta

250 g. Tomatoes

Olive oil, parmesan, herbs mix (to taste)

Instructions:

1) First of all, preheat the oven to 350 °F (180 °C). **2)** Prepare the vegetables. Cut the spinach into small pieces. The same with the tomatoes, wash and slice them. **3)** Mix together the vegetables with the ricotta. **4)** Season everything with a bit of olive oil, parmesan and herbs mix. **5)** Create small tartlets and cook for approx. 30 minutes. Low the heat as 22 minutes have passed.

Nutrition Facts:

Cal. 652	**Carbs**: 8.2 g	**Fat**: 36-8 g	Sat.Fat 20 g	Cholest. 612 mg
Protein 66.2 g	Diet. Fiber 3.1 g		Mon.Fat 10.2 g	Sodium 1879 mg
	Tot. Sugars 7.2 g		Poly.Fat 3.3 g	Salt 4.3 g

171) *Sweetly spiced chips* 👤 4   ⏰ 40 Min.

Ingredients:

500 g. Sweet potatoes

50 g. Corn starch

500 g. Yoghurt (low fat)

4 tbsp. Balsamic vinegar

Rosmary, oregano, turmeric, paprika powder, herbs mix, chive (to taste)

Instructions:

1) First thing first, peel the potatoes and cut them into thick slices lenghtwise. **2)** Secondly, mix the herbs / spices listed and / or add your favourites. Put them in a bowl and mix. **3)** Add the potatoes and add the vinegar. Mix everything together. **4)** Place the potatoes on a baking sheet and bake at 375 °F (200 °C) for approx. 30 minutes. **5)** Meanwhile, season the yoghurt with the herbs mix and chive and pour it into a bowl. **6)** Serve with the fries.

Nutrition Facts:

Cal. 1167	**Carbs**: 210 g	**Fat**: 13.2 g	Sat.Fat 7.1 g	Cholest. 24 mg
Protein 35.5 g	Diet. Fiber 20 g		Mon.Fat 2.7 g	Sodium 3250 mg
	Tot. Sugars 60 g		Poly.Fat 1.4 g	Salt 9.2 g

☙☞

172) *Greens quick fritters* 👤 4   ⏰ 30 Min.

Ingredients:

500 g. Zucchini

4 Tomatoes and eggs

4 tbsp. Olive oil, parsley (chopped), lemon juice, quick cooking rolled oats

Oregano, herbs mix (to taste)

500 g. Plain yoghurt (low-fat)

2 Garlic cloves

Instructions:

1) Prepare the zucchini and tomatoes. Wash and cut the tomatoes into small pieces, while use a grater for the zucchini. **2)** Secondly, mix together with the oats, eggs, 1 tbsp of lemon juice, garlic cloves (chopped) and season with with a bit of salt and pepper. **3)** Take a pan, heat with a bit of oil and add some of the mixture to cook the fritters. Repeat the process until you have cooked all the mixture. **4)** Season the yogurt with some of the herbs mix (and/ or your favorite herbs) and serve with the fritters.

Nutrition Facts:

Cal. 1690	**Carbs**: 88.3 g	**Fat**: 87 g	Sat.Fat 18.2 g	Cholest. 1080 mg
Protein 121 g	Diet. Fiber 27 g		Mon.Fat 50 g	Sodium 800 mg
	Tot. Sugars 72.4 g		Poly.Fat 11 g	Salt 2 g

173) *Spinach and ricotta tart* 👤 4 ⏰ 30 Min.

Ingredients:

6 Potatoes

400 g. Spinach

4 Tomatoes

3 tbsp. Sesam oil

2 Eggs

250 g. Ricotta

Basil, paprika powder, herbs mix (to taste)

Instructions:

1) First of all, preheat the oven to 320 °F (160 °C). **2)** Secondly, peel and slice the potatoes, wash and slice the tomatoes and spinach. **3)** Sauté the potato slices using a bit of sesam oil and over medium heat for approx. 5 minutes. **4)** Mix together all the ingredients. Use the baking paper to prepare the pan and cover the botttom with the potatoes as they're ready. **5)** Fill the pan with the other ingredients and cook in the oven for approx. 20 minutes. Low the heat as 12 min. have passed.

Nutrition Facts:

Cal. 1370 **Carbs**: 93 g **Fat**: 90 g Sat.Fat 45 g   Cholest. 720 mg
Protein 78 g Diet. Fiber 14.2 g Mon.Fat 28 g Sodium 1349 mg
  Tot. Sugars 8.3 g Poly.Fat 8 g Salt 4.2 g

༺༻

174) *Italian classic rice* 👤 4 ⏰ 30 Min.

Ingredients:

2 Shallors

1 L. plain Water

300 g. Risottto rice

200 g. Tomato sauce (organic)

Basil, olive oil, parmesan (to taste)

!! You can use whole-grain alternatives too

Instructions:

1) First of all, prepare the risotto according to the package. Pour 1 L of plain cold water into a pot and bring it to boil. Put a bit of salt and pour the rice. Read the cooking time on the package. **2)** As the rice is almost ready, rinse and put it back again on the pot. **3)** Add the tomato sauce and 3-5 tbsp. of olive oil. Season it with parmesan likewise and blend it very well. **4)** Serve the risotto with 2 leaves of basil on top.

Nutrition Facts:

Cal. 1430 **Carbs**: 312 g **Fat**: 18 g Sat.Fat 3 g Cholest. -
Protein 35 g Diet. Fiber 18 g Mon.Fat 11 g Sodium 3200 mg
  Tot. Sugars 24 g Poly.Fat 3 g Salt 2 g

Dinner

175) *Cauliflower sweet soup* 👤 4 ⏰ 35 Min.

Ingredients:

250 g. Potatoes

250 g. Zucchini

300 g. Cauliflower

850 ml. Vegetable broth

2 tsp. Rosmary (dried powder and fresh leaves)

4 slices. Whole grain bread

Olive oil (to taste)

Instructions:

1) First of all, peel and cook the potatoes in boiling water for approx. 15 minutes. **2)** Secondly, prepare the vegetables. Cut the zucchini and cauliflower in small pieces. **3)** Remove the potatoes from the water, drain and place them in another pot together with the vegetable broth, zucchini and cauliflower. Cook everything on medium heat for approx. 20 minutes. **4)** Cut the bread slices into small squared pieces and brown them for a few minutes with olive oil and 1 tsp. dried rosmary powder. **5)** As the 20 minutes passed, blend the vegetables with a hand blender until it's a homogeneous mass. **6)** Serve with a drizzle of oil and garnish the soup with a few bread pieces.

Nutrition Facts:

Cal. 410	**Carbs**: 50 g	**Fat**: 2.8 g	Sat.Fat 2.1 g	Cholest. -
Protein 29 g	Diet. Fiber 24.1 g		Mon.Fat 0.2 g	Sodium 1980 mg
	Tot. Sugars 24.5 g		Poly.Fat 0.5 g	Salt 2 g

༒༒

176) *Mediterranean red soup* 👤 4 ⏰ 30 Min.

Ingredients:

1 kg. Tomatoes

2 Shallots

4 tbsp. Olive oil

800 ml. Vegetable broth

2 tbsp. Tomato paste

Fresh basil, whole grain bread (to taste)

Instructions:

1) First of all, wash and peel with tomatoes. (An easy method can be pouring boiling water on them). After that cut them into pieces. **2)** Finely chop the shallots and sauté with a bit of oil in a pan for approx. 20 minutes. **3)** In the meantime briefly sear the bread slices with a bit of oil to make them crispy. **4)** As 15 minutes has passed, add the broth and the tomato paste to the tomatoes and bring to boil. **5)** Garnish with the bread slices and fresh basil leaves.

Nutrition Facts:

Cal. 750	**Carbs**: 39 g	**Fat**: 56.8 g	Sat.Fat 8.2 g	Cholest. -
Protein 13.8 g	Diet. Fiber 16.2 g		Mon.Fat 39 g	Sodium 2140 mg
	Tot. Sugars 35.2 g		Poly.Fat 6 g	Salt 2.2 g

177) *Couscous greens soup*   👤 4   ⏰ 25 Min.

Ingredients:

1 Shallot

2 Zucchini

3 Tomatoes

1 tin. Beans (in water canned)

800 ml. Vegetable broth

70 g. Couscous

Dried rosmary, herbs mix, turmeric (to taste)

Instructions:

1) Firstly, wash the zucchini and tomatoes and cut them into cubes. **2)** Secondly, cut and prepare the zucchini and tomatoes. Finely slice the shallot and put them together in a pan. Add a bit of olive oil and sauté for 2-4 minutes. **3)** Drain and rinse the beans. Add the broth and the remaining ingredients (beans and couscous) and let simmer on medium heat for approx. 15 minutes. **4)** Season with your favourite herbs, dried rosmary and turmeric. Serve.

Nutrition Facts:

Cal. 650	**Carbs**: 68 g	**Fat**: 30 g	Sat.Fat 4.6 g	Cholest. -
Protein 22 g	Diet. Fiber 15 g		Mon.Fat 19.4 g	Sodium 2180 mg
	Tot. Sugars 24 g		Poly.Fat 4 g	Salt 4.6 g

ಸಿಜಿ

178) *Italian minestrone*   👤 4   ⏰ 1 h.

Ingredients:

500 g. Zucchini

1 Potato and onion

2 Garlic cloves and carrots

60 g. Celery, leek

3 Tomatoes

1 tin. Cannellini beans (both in water canned)

1 tin. Peas (in water canned, no sugar /salt added)

Oregano, olive oil (to taste)

Instructions:

1) First of all, prepare the vegetabels. Drain and rinse the peas and beans and put them in a large bowl. **2)** Peel and cut the potatoes, tomatoes, carrots and zucchini. Cut them into small pieces. Do the same with leek, celery and onion. **3)** Put everything in a big pot and add as much water as the vegetables are covered. Add a bit of salt and oregano and cook on low heat for aprrox. 60 minutes. **4)** As the minestrone is ready, season with a bit of olive oil and herbs mix and serve.

Nutrition Facts:

Cal. 140	**Carbs**: 32 g	**Fat**: 5.3 g	Sat.Fat 1 g	Cholest. -
Protein 11.4 g	Diet. Fiber 5 g		Mon.Fat 2 g	Sodium 1430 mg
	Tot. Sugars 6.8 g		Poly.Fat 2.3 g	Salt 1 g

179) *Yellow turmeric soup* 👤 4 ⏰ 30 Min.

Ingredients:

2 Celery stalks

2 Leeks

1 Shallot

450 g. Pumpkin

500 ml. Vegetable broth

Olive oil, turmeric, paprika powder, rosmary, oregano (to taste)

Instructions:

1) First of all, prepare the pumpkin and carrots and cut them into small pieces. Slice the shallot, leeks and celery stalks and put them into a pan to to cook for approx. 15 minutes. Add the broth and season them with a bit of olive oil and turmeric. 2) As the 15 minutes have passed, take a hand blender and mix very well until it's an omogeneous mass. 3) Season if necessary with a bit of rosmary and paprika powder and serve.

Nutrition Facts:

Cal. 104	**Carbs**: 28 g	**Fat**: 21 g	Sat.Fat 13.7 g	Cholest. -
Protein 6 g	Diet. Fiber 5 g		Mon.Fat 4.6 g	Sodium 15 mg
	Tot. Sugars 12 g		Poly.Fat 2.2 g	Salt -

☙☕

180) *Sweet ginger soup* 👤 4 ⏰ 30 Min.

Ingredients:

300 g. Carrots

2 tsp. Ginger

2 Garlic cloves

300 g. Beets

400 ml. Vegetable broth

1 Potato

Paprika powder, olive oil (to taste)

Instructions:

1) First of all, prepare the carrots, potato and the beets. Cut them into pieces and put everything into a large pot. **2)** Crush the garlic cloves and add them to the pot too. Cover with the broth and cook for approx. 10 minutes. **3)** As you see the vegetables are ready, use a hand blender and purée everything. **4)** Season with the ginger powder, rosmary and a drizzle of oil.

Nutrition Facts:

Cal. 140	**Carbs**: 35 g	**Fat**: 15 g	Sat.Fat 12.2 g	Cholest. -
Protein 10 g	Diet. Fiber 6 g		Mon.Fat 3.2 g	Sodium 19 mg
	Tot. Sugars 9 g		Poly.Fat 2.1 g	Salt -

181) *Leek – lentil soup* 👤 4   ⏰ 55 Min.

Ingredients:

- 200 g. Lentils (organic)
- 3 Leeks
- 2 Shallots
- 3 Potatoes
- 700 ml. Vegetable broth
- Whole grain bread (slices, to taste)

Instructions:

1) First of all, take a large pot and bring the vegetable broth to a boil. 2) Secondly, add the lentils and the shallots (finely sliced). Simmer for approx. 45 minutes. 3) Meanwhile, brown the bread slices until they become crispy and keep warm. 4) Wash, peel and cut the potatoes and leeks and, as 35 minutes have passed, put them into the pot. Cook everything for other 10 minutes. 5) Season if necessary and serve with crispy bread.

Nutrition Facts:

Cal. 800 **Carbs**: 136 g **Fat**: 5.7 g Sat.Fat 1.2 g Cholest. -
Protein 48 g Diet. Fiber 43 g Mon.Fat - Sodium 1760 mg
  Tot. Sugars 34 g Poly.Fat 2 g Salt 3.7 g

---

182) *Summer corn soup* 👤 4   ⏰ 30 Min.

Ingredients:

- 2 Shallots
- 2 tsp. Turmeric powder
- 200 g. Chickpeas
- 6 Potatoes
- 800 ml. Vegetable broth
- 500 g. Corn (in water canned)
- Olive oil, herbs mix (to taste)

Instructions:

1) First of all, peel and cut the shallots and potatoes. Take a pan and heat a bit of oil. Add the potatoes and shallots and cook for aprox. 5 minutes. 2) Drain and rinse the corn and chickpeas. Add them to the pot, together with the broth and simmer for approx. 5-8 minutes. (Read the directions on the tins if useful). 3) Add the turmeric and blend everything with an immersion blender to purée everything. 4) Let the soup simmer for approx. 10 minutes. Garnish with a drizzle of oil and serve.

Nutrition Facts:

Cal. 1209 **Carbs**: 145 g **Fat**: 36 g Sat.Fat 3.2 g Cholest. -
Protein 28 g Diet. Fiber 23 g Mon.Fat 19 g Sodium 2987 mg
  Tot. Sugars 22 g Poly.Fat 5.7 g Salt 4 g

183) *Fresh shrimps - cuttlefish soup* 👤 4   ⏰ 45 Min.

Ingredients:

4 Garlic cloves

200 g. Cuttlefish (fresh, already cleaned)

200 g. Shrimps (fresh, already cleaned)

800 ml. Vegetable broth

200 g. Diced tomatoes (in water canned)

Parsly, rosmary, olive oil, celery, herbs mix (to taste)

Instructions:

1) Frst of all, prepare the fish. Rinse the cuttlefish and shrimps. Take a pan and add the vegetable broth and a bit of olive oil. **2)** Drain the tomatoes and add them to the pot. Bring to boil. **3)** Press the garlic cloves and add them. Season everything with parsly, rosmary and celery (cut it into pieces). **4)** Add the cuttlefish and cook them for approx. 25 minutes. Not much more than that as they become hard. **5)** In the last 5-7 minutes add the shrimps and finish the cooking. **6)** Garnish with parsly, rosmary and herbs mix and serve.

Nutrition Facts:

Cal. 1004   **Carbs**: 49.6 g   **Fat**: 31.2 g   Sat.Fat   31.2 g   Cholest. 505 mg
Protein 129 g   Diet. Fiber   22.4 g   Mon.Fat   6.2 g   Sodium   1780 mg
                Tot. Sugars   43.2 g   Poly.Fat   8.2 g   Salt   5.4 g

ಲ೦ಣ

184) *Green broccoli pureed soup* 👤 4   ⏰ 15 Min.

Ingredients:

500 g. Broccoli

4 Garlic cloves

4 Zucchine

40 g. Walnuts (crushed)

300 ml. Vegetable broth

Parmesan, olive oil (to taste)

Instructions:

1) Firstly, dive the broccoli into florets. Peel and finely chop the garlic cloves and cut the zucchini. **2)** Take a pan, add the broccoli and zucchini. Cook them in boiling water for 5 minutes. **3)** Drain the water from the vegetables and add the broth, olive oil and garlic. **4)** Use an immersion blender to blend everything until the soup is uniform and simmer for 5 minutes. **5)** Garnish with the parmesan and walnuts and serve.

Nutrition Facts:

Cal. 1370   **Carbs**: 62 g   **Fat**: 72 g   Sat.Fat   72.4 g   Cholest. 195 mg
Protein 117 g   Diet. Fiber   28 g   Mon.Fat   47.5 g   Sodium   2460 mg
                Tot. Sugars   62 g   Poly.Fat   3.2 g   Salt   4.5 g

185) *Classic goulash* 👤 4   ⏰ 115 Min.

Ingredients:

- 1 Kg. Stewing beef
- 4 Onions + 2 Shallots
- 100 g. Tomato puree
- 1 L. Meat broth
- 1 Tomato + 4 Potatoes
- 2 tbsp. Sweet chili powder (be abundant) + 2 tbsp. Spicy chili powder (be abundant)
- Olive oil (to taste)

Instructions:

1) First of all, prepare the meat and cut it into small pieces. Secondly, peel and slice the onions and shallots. Take a pot, add the tomatoes and the peeled potatoes. Sautée everything for approx. 5 minutes with a bit of olive oil. Add the meat and the tomato puree and cook on high heat for 5 minutes. **2)** Add the broth gradually and season with both types of chili powder and olive oil. Let everything cook for at least 1 hour (100 minutes it's fine). **3)** Stir very frequently and serve.

Nutrition Facts:

Cal. 980	**Carbs:** 54.6 g	**Fat:** 40 g	Sat.Fat 11.5 g	Cholest. 285 mg
Protein 105 g	Diet. Fiber 4.3 g		Mon.Fat 17.6 g	Sodium 312 mg
	Tot. Sugars 3.2 g		Poly.Fat 3.7 g	Salt 3 g

---

186) *Veggie Goulash* 👤 4   ⏰ 40 Min.

Ingredients:

- 500 g. Smoked tofu
- 4 Bell peppers + 1 Shallots
- 600 g. Vegetable broth
- 3 Tomato and potatoes
- 2 tbsp. Sweet chili powder (be abundant) + 2 tbsp. Spicy chili powder (be abundant)
- Olive oil, parsley (to taste)

Instructions:

1) First of all, peel the potatoes and cut them into small pieces. Secondly, peel and finely slice the shallot. **2)** Now, cut in thin slices the peppers, the tomatoes and tofu into cubes. **3)** Take a pot, add the sliced shallot, peppers, half of the chili powders and potatoes and sautèe everything for approx. 5 minutes. **4)** Now, deglaze with the vegetable broth, add the remaining chili powder, cover and simmer for others 10 minutes. **5)** Now, add the tomatoes and tofu for others 5-8 minutes. **6)** Sprinkle the parsley on top and add a bit of olive oil. Serve

Nutrition Facts:

Cal. 1980	**Carbs:** 170 g	**Fat:** 78 g	Sat.Fat 10.6 g	Cholest. -
Protein 108 g	Diet. Fiber 47 g		Mon.Fat 37.5 g	Sodium 1897 mg
	Tot. Sugars 70 g		Poly.Fat 19.3 g	Salt 3 g

187) *Mexican pozole mix* 👤 4 ⏰ 40 Min.

Ingredients:

1 Onion, garlic clove, green jalapeño pepper, avocado

1 tsp. Cumin, oregano, cilantro

220 g. Tomatillos (fresh)

430 g. Chickpeas

800 g. Pinto beans (in water canned)

900 ml. Vegetable broth

2 Limes, radishes

Instructions:

1) First of all, take a pot and heat the olive oil on medium heat. Prepare the onion and cut it into small pieces. Sautée everything for a few minutes until it's fragrant. **2)** Now, dice the jalapeño and garlic clove and add them to the pot together with the cumin and oregano. Stir and cook for approx. 2-3 minutes. **3)** Prepare the tomatillos into small pieces and add them to the pot together with the chickpeas (drain and rinse them). Add the broth and pinto beans too. **4)** Bring the pot to boil and low the heat. Let simmer for approx. 20 minutes. **5)** Slice the radishes and avocado and set aside. **6)** Divide the stew into bowls and garnish with lime juice, sliced avocado, cilantro and radishes. Serve and enjoy.

Nutrition Facts:

Cal. 2207	**Carbs**: 323 g	**Fat**: 57.7 g	Sat.Fat 11.2 g	Cholest. -
Protein 92 g	Diet. Fiber 107 g		Mon.Fat 31.1 g	Sodium 3840 mg
	Tot. Sugars 44 g		Poly.Fat 11.3 g	Salt 8 g

☙❦

188) *Cashew salad mix* 👤 4 ⏰ 15 Min.

Ingredients:

140 g. Smoked tofu

Olive oil, vinegar (to taste)

100 g. Cashew

300 g. Lettuce

500 g. Tomatoes and chickpeas

200 g. Tuna (in water canned)

Roasmary powder, herbs mix (to taste)

Instructions:

1) First of all, cut the tofu into small cubes. Take a pan and heat 1 tbsp of olive oil and add the tofu. Sautée for approx. 5 minutes. **2)** Wash and cut the lettuce leaves, cut into pieces the tomatoes, drain and rinse the chickpeas and tuna. **3)** Take a hand blender and mix together 6 tbsp. of olive oil, cashew, lemon juice, vinegar and a bit of salt. **4)** Take a large bowl and add all the ingredients. Season with a bit of oil, vinegar, rosmary and herbs mix and garnish with the cashew dressing.

Nutrition Facts:

Cal. 1480	**Carbs**: 90 g	**Fat**: 123 g	Sat.Fat 22 g	Cholest. -
Protein 54 g	Diet. Fiber 20 g		Mon.Fat 76 g	Sodium 670 mg
	Tot. Sugars 28 g		Poly.Fat 18 g	Salt 1 g

189) *Easy vegan nuggets* 👤 4   ⏰ 80 Min.

Ingredients:

650 g. Potatoes

350 g. Broccoli

150 ml. Oat milk

110 ml. Rice oil

2 tsp. Honey, apple cider vinegar

Paprika powder, turmeric, thyme powder (to taste)

Instructions:

1) Firstly, preheat the oven to 400 °F (200 °C). **2)** Secondly, peel the potatoes into small cubes and put them into a pot. Cover with water. Season with a bit of salt and let them simmer for approx. 30 minutes. **3)** Thirdly, cut the broccoli in small pieces and blend them with a mixer. Put them on a plate. **4)** Add the milk, garlic, paprika powder, honey and vinegar to the mixer and blend everything. **5)** Now, take the potatoes and use a mixer to blend them too. Add the broccoli and mix well together. Season a bit according to your taste and form the nuggets from the mixture. **6)** Take a sheet and place the nuggets. Cook on middle rack for approx. 30 minutes. Check the cooking process and turn the nuggets after appros.15-20 minutes. Serve with the dressing.

Nutrition Facts:

Cal. 1700   **Carbs**: 130 g   **Fat**: 111 g   Sat.Fat   10.5 g   Cholest. 10 mg
Protein 34 g   Diet. Fiber 19 g   Mon.Fat   53.2 g   Sodium 314 mg
               Tot. Sugars 25 g   Poly.Fat 27.3 g   Salt   -

☯

190) *Creamy greens roll-up* 👤 4   ⏰ 30 Min.

Ingredients:

2 Zucchini

1 tbsp. Olive oil

2 Tomatoes

40 g. creamy goat cheese (low fat, low sodium)

Oregano, basil (to taste)

Instructions:

1) First of all prepare the zucchini. Cut the ends and make thin strips. **2)** Secondly, mix all the herbs (add a few if you like) and mix them with the oil. Brush this mixture on the zucchini. **3)** Take a pan and sautée the zucchini on both sides for a few minutes and let them cool down. (approx. 3 min. overall). **4)** Wash and prepare the tomatoes into very small pieces. The same with basil. Mix together and add the oregano in order to season the tomatoes and mix well. **5)** Spread the creamy cheese on the zucchini and add a spoon of the tomatoes pieces. **6)** From one side to the other, roll the strips up. Use a toothpick to secure each of them.

Nutrition Facts:

Cal. 120   **Carbs**: 5 g   **Fat**: 9 g   Sat.Fat   4 g   Cholest. 20 mg
Protein 4 g   Diet. Fiber 1.4 g   Mon.Fat   4.2 g   Sodium   65 mg
               Tot. Sugars 4.6 g   Poly.Fat   0.7 g   Salt   -

191) *Easy roasted potatoes dish* 👤 4   ⏰ 40 Min.

Ingredients:

1 kg. Potatoes

4 Bell peppers

600 g. Zucchini

800 g. Tomatoes

3 Garlic cloves

Olive oil, basil, rosmary powder (to taste)

Instructions:

1) First of all, prepare the potatoes. Peel and cut them into pieces. Take a pot, add the potatoes and fill with cold water until it's covered. Bring to boil. After that low the heat and cook the potatoes for approx. 20 minutes. **2)** Secondly, wash and cut the peppers, zucchini, garlic cloves. Sear the vegetables and the potatoes (after the 20 minutes) in a second pot with a bit of oil for approx. 5 minutes. **3)** Deglaze the vegetables with the peeled and diced tomatoes. Season with a bit of olive oil, rosmary and a bit of salt for 5 minutes. **4)** Garnish with a few fresh basil leaves and serve.

Nutrition Facts:

Cal. 1450	**Carbs**: 217 g	**Fat**: 34 g	Sat.Fat 5 g	Cholest. -
Protein 58 g	Diet. Fiber 54 g		Mon.Fat 20 g	Sodium 2080 mg
	Tot. Sugars 65 g		Poly.Fat 6.2 g	Salt 2 g

☼☼

192) *Cheesy potato soup* 👤 4   ⏰ 20 Min.

Ingredients:

2 Shallots

1 kg. Potatoes

800 ml. Oat milk (low fat)

50 g. Ricotta cheese

30 g. Bacon (sliced)

40 g. Leek

Olive oil, celery (to taste)

Instructions:

1) Firstly, take a pot and cook the bacon until it's crispy (no oil needed). **2)** Secondly, prepare and slice the shallots. Set most of them aside and add 1/5 of them to the bacon. **3)** Prepare the potatoes. Peel and cut them into thick pieces, as well as the leek. **4)** Add them and the milk to the pot and let simmer for approx. 10 minutes. **5)** Take a blender and and purée the potatoes. Split the soup into four bowl and garnish each of them with the crispy bacon and ricotta.

Nutrition Facts:

Cal. 1450	**Carbs**: 207 g	**Fat**: 35 g	Sat.Fat 20.2 g	Cholest. 58 mg
Protein 70 g	Diet. Fiber 13.4 g		Mon.Fat 8 g	Sodium 755 mg
	Tot. Sugars 56.5 g		Poly.Fat 1 g	Salt 1.3 g

193) *Chicken mix soup* 👤 4   ⏰ 15 Min.

Ingredients:

1 L. Meat broth

300 g. Chicken breast fillet (boneless, skinless)

50 g. Leek

150 g. Pasta (the smallest size)

280 g. Mirepoix (frozen)

2 Garlic cloves

Instructions:

1) Firstly, take a pot and pour the chicken broth. Bring to boil. **2)** Secondly, cut the chicken into thin slices. **3)** Add the pasta and meat to the broth and let simmer for 5 minutes. **4)** Crush the garlic and add it with the mirepoix to the pot. Cook for other 5 minutes. **5)** Season with a bit of salt, turmeric and pepper and serve.

Nutrition Facts:

Cal. 1460	**Carbs**: 86 g	**Fat**: 64.6 g	Sat.Fat 20.3 g	Cholest. 555 mg
Protein 134 g	Diet. Fiber 16 g		Mon.Fat 20.2 g	Sodium 1234 mg
	Tot. Sugars 15 g		Poly.Fat 18.3 g	Salt 3 g

☯☪

194) *Yellow greens soup* 👤 4   ⏰ 40 Min.

Ingredients:

4 tbsp. Olive oil

3 tsp. Turmeric

150 g. Lentils

1 L. Water

1 Lime

1 kg. Cauliflower

Instructions:

1) Firstly, preheat the oven to 320 °F (160 °C). Prepare the cauliflower and separate it into florets. **2)** Take a casserole and mix together 2 tbsp. of oil with 250 g. of cauliflower. Cook on a medium rack for approx. 25 minutes and season with oregano, a bit of salt and pepper. **3)** Take another pot and add the rest of the cauliflower and the lentils. Add the water and the turmeric into the pot and simmer over medium heat for 20 minutes. **4)** Squeeze the lime. Take a blender and purée everything and add the lime juice. Blend very well. **5)** Serve the soup with the roasted cauliflowers.

Nutrition Facts:

Cal. 1030	**Carbs**: 112 g	**Fat**: 30.8 g	Sat.Fat 5 g	Cholest. -
Protein 62 g	Diet. Fiber 45.2 g		Mon.Fat 20 g	Sodium 1490 mg
	Tot. Sugars 24.8 g		Poly.Fat 5 g	Salt 3.2 g

195) *Peppers creamy soup* 👤 4   ⏰ 30 Min.

Ingredients:

800 g. Bell peppers

1 L. Vegetable broth

3 Potatoes

100 g. Ricotta cheese

1 tsp. Chili powder

1 Shallot

30 g. Anchovy

Instructions:

1) First of all, wash, peel and remove the seeds from the peppers. Cut them into pieces. **2)** Take a pan, bring the vegetable broth to boil and let simmer for approx. 10 minutes. Then mix with a hand blender. **3)** Peel and grate the potatoes and add them to the pot. **4)** Add the ricotta cheese, chili powder and shallot too. Blend very well again. **5)** Slice the anchovy filets and gernish the soup. Serve.

Nutrition Facts:

Cal. 550	**Carbs**: 88.2 g	**Fat**: 7.2 g	Sat.Fat 1.2 g	Cholest. -
Protein 17.3 g	Diet. Fiber 30.2 g		Mon.Fat 2.3 g	Sodium 2890 mg
	Tot. Sugars 58.9 g		Poly.Fat 2.6 g	Salt 6.2 g

ঔঙ

196) *Julienne zucchini soup* 👤 4   ⏰ 20 Min.

Ingredients:

1 Shallot

40 g. Leek

4 Carrots

5 Zucchini

2 L. Vegetable broth

Olive oil, herbs mix, parmesan (to taste)

Instructions:

1) Very quick soup. Start by cutting joulienne the vegetables, leek and shallot. **2)** Take a pot and heat the broth on medium heat. **3)** Season with a bit of olive oil and herbs mix and simmer for approx. 8 minutes. Serve and garnish with parmesan.

Nutrition Facts:

Cal. 380	**Carbs**: 54.2 g	**Fat**: 3.3 g	Sat.Fat 1 g	Cholest. -
Protein 19.2 g	Diet. Fiber 23.2 g		Mon.Fat 0.5 g	Sodium 5670 mg
	Tot. Sugars 49 g		Poly.Fat 1.3 g	Salt 15 g

197) *Green soup* 👤 4   ⏰ 20 Min.

Ingredients:

- 70 ml. Olive oil
- 150 g. Spinach (fresh)
- 150 g. Kale
- ½ Lemon
- 1 tsp. Garlic powder, turmeric, thyme
- 60 g. Ricotta cheese
- 280 ml. Vegetable broth
- Whole grain bread (to taste)

Instructions:

1) First of all, take a pot, heat a bit of oil and lightly cook the spinach for a few minutes until it wilts. Put in a bowl and let cool down. **2)** Take a second pot, add the broth, ricotta and use a hand blender to mix until creamy. Add the lemon juice and the spices powders and mix again well. **3)** Simmer the soup over medium heat. In a different pan, cook together the kale and spinach for approx. 5-8 minutes. Add to the soup and serve.

!! Warm up a few bread slices until they turn crispy and serve together.

Nutrition Facts:

Cal. 1430	**Carbs**: 24.2 g	**Fat**: 142.3 g	Sat.Fat 105 g	Cholest. -
Protein 17.3 g	Diet. Fiber 21.4 g		Mon.Fat 21 g	Sodium 190 mg
	Tot. Sugars 19.2 g		Poly.Fat 6.3 g	Salt -

☼☼

198) *Pumpkin stew* 👤 4   ⏰ 30 Min.

Ingredients:

- 1 kg. Pumpkin
- 600 g. Potatoes
- 1 Shallot
- 1 L. Vegetable broth
- Thyme, oregano, rosmary powder (to taste)
- 50 g. Leek
- 5 slices. Bacon

Instructions:

1) First of all, remove the seeds from the pumpkin and cut into cubes. Peel and cut the potatoes into very small pieces, slice the shallot. **2)** Sautée the shallot and the bacon slices for 3 minutes with a bit of olive oil. Add the pumpkin, the spices powders and the potatoes. **3)** Deglaze with the broth and let simmer over medium heat for approx. 15-20 minutes. **4)** Garnish with the crispy bacon and serve.

Nutrition Facts:

Cal. 1040	**Carbs**: 158 g	**Fat**: 31.7 g	Sat.Fat 7.5 g	Cholest. 61 mg
Protein 37.4 g	Diet. Fiber 37.2 g		Mon.Fat 16.9 g	Sodium 4490 mg
	Tot. Sugars 54.8 g		Poly.Fat 4.1 g	Salt 11.2 g

199) *Creamy curry-cumin soup* 👤 4   ⏰ 55 Min.

Ingredients:

1 Cauliflower

2 tbsp. Seeds oil

2 tsp. Curry powder, cumin, lime juice

1 Shallot

650 ml. Vegetable broth

150 g. Beans, diced tomatoes (both in water canned)

Basil, oregano, rosmary (to taste)

Instructions:

1) First of all, preheat the oven to 395 °F (200 °C). **2)** Secondly, prepare the cauliflower separating the florets. Take a baking sheet and spread half of them onto it, season with 1 tbsp. of seeds oil and half of the curry powder. **3)** Place the sheet on the middle rack and cook for approx. 12 minutes. **4)** Slice the shallot and sautée it with the remaining seeds oil and curry powder in a pot for approx. 2-4 minutes. **5)** Add the rest of the cauliflower and use the broth to deglaze the ingredients, cover the pot and simmer over medium heat for approx. 20 minutes. **6)** Take a blender and purée everything. Add the beans and the tomatoes and season with a bit of spices. Simmer for others 10 minutes. **7)** As the ingredients are almost ready, add the lime juice, the roasted cauliflower and basil. Simmer for 4 more min. and serve.

Nutrition Facts:

Cal. 655   **Carbs**: 42.3 g   **Fat**: 31.2 g   Sat.Fat 3.2 g   Cholest. -
Protein 32.2 g   Diet. Fiber 35 g   Mon.Fat 13.4 g   Sodium 2240 mg
Tot. Sugars 33.4 g   Poly.Fat 8.2 g   Salt 5.3 g

---

200) *Cold greens & fish soup* 👤 4   ⏰ 10 Min.

Ingredients:

4 Cucumbers

2 Shallots

300 g. Plain yoghurt (low-fat)

20 g. Chives

1 Lemon juice

250 g. Shrimps (cooked)

40 g. Celery

Instructions:

1) First of all, wash and cut the cucumbers and cut them into big pieces. (If you want you can set aside a few of them as garnish) **2)** Cut and prepare the shallots, finely cut them. **3)** Take a hand blender, add all the ingredients except the shrimps and celery. Blend everything until it turns smooth. **4)** Cut the celery into small pieces. Divide the mixture into four bowls and garnish with the shrimps and celery.

Nutrition Facts:

Cal. 750   **Carbs**: 44.2 g   **Fat**: 33.5 g   Sat.Fat 18.7 g   Cholest. 415 mg
Protein 58.2 g   Diet. Fiber 12.3 g   Mon.Fat 6.5 g   Sodium 489 mg
Tot. Sugars 37.4 g   Poly.Fat 3.3 g   Salt 1.2 g

201) *Old west soup* 👤 4 ⏰ 45 Min.

Ingredients:

1 kg. Tomatoes

4 Bell peppers

4 tbsp. Olive oil, fresh basil, parmesan, tomato paste

1,2 L. water

600 g. Beans (in water, canned)

Oregano, rosmary, herbs mix, garlic powder (to taste)

Instructions:

1) First of all, preheat the oven to 360 °F (180 °C). **2)** Secondly, prepare the tomatoes and the peppers. Remove the seeds from the bell peppers and cut the tomatoes in pieces. **3)** Put the tomatoes and peppers into a bowl and add the olive oil, oregano, rosmary and garlic powder. Distribute them over the baking sheet and roast on th emiddle rack for approx. 30 minutes. **4)** In the meantime, drain and rinse the beans. Add them to a pot, add the tomato paste, water and basil. **5)** As the vegetables are cooked, add them with the beans and purèe everything with a blender until it's creamy. **6)** Let the soup boil and then simmer for 5-7 minutes and serve.

Nutrition Facts:

Cal. 1380	**Carbs**: 126 g	**Fat**: 62 g	Sat.Fat 9 g	Cholest. -
Protein 51 g	Diet. Fiber 48.2 g		Mon.Fat 39.1 g	Sodium 1320 mg
	Tot. Sugars 70 g		Poly.Fat 9.1 g	Salt 3.2 g

෴

202) *Spanish gazpacho* 👤 4 ⏰ 15 Min.

Ingredients:

1 kg. Tomatoes

2 Shallots

1 Cucumber, bell pepper (red)

30 ml. Olive oil

15 ml. White wine vinegar

2 tsp. Lemon juice

Instructions:

1) Firstly, wash and quarter the tomatoes. Cut each of them into small pieces and set one of them aside. Put the other three into a large bowl. 2) Slice the shallots and add them to the bowl. 3) Peel and slice the cucumbers into small pieces, leave one of them aside and add the others to the bowl. The same with the bell peppers. 4) Add the lemon juice, olive oil, vinegar, salt and peppers and a few leaves of basil and blend everything very well with a blender until it's creamy. 5) Transfer the gazpacho into four bowls and garnish everything with the chopped vegetables.

Nutrition Facts:

Cal. 839	**Carbs**: 50 g	**Fat**: 58 g	Sat.Fat 8.6 g	Cholest. -
Protein 15.2 g	Diet. Fiber 23 g		Mon.Fat 39 g	Sodium 58 mg
	Tot. Sugars 48 g		Poly.Fat 6.2 g	Salt -

203) *Fresh cucumber finger food*   👤 4   ⏰ 20 Min.

Ingredients:

5 ml. Olive oil

15 ml. Water

½ tsp. Tomato paste, lemon juice

50 g. Cucumber

30 g. Beans (in water canned)

Basil, olives (pitted), oregano powder (to taste)

Instructions:

1) First of all, drain and rinse the beans. Slice the cucumber in thick slices and set aside. **2)** Now, take a bowl and pour into all the ingredients except the cucumber. Take a blender and purée everything into a creamy sauce. **3)** Garnish the cucumber slices with the cream and serve.

Nutrition Facts:

Cal. 110	**Carbs**: 8.2 g	**Fat**: 6.7 g	Sat.Fat 1 g	Cholest. -
Protein 3 g	Diet. Fiber 2.3 g		Mon.Fat 4.2 g	Sodium 120 mg
	Tot. Sugars 1.3 g		Poly.Fat 1 g	Salt -

---

204) *Red skewers*   👤 4   ⏰ 20 Min.

Ingredients:

150 g. Beets (precooked)

200 g. Ricotta cheese

Baby onions and artichokes (as required for the skewers)

Instructions:

1) First of all, cut the cheese and the beets into small pieces. More or less of the same size. **2)** Cut the onions and artichokes lenghtwise. **3)** To create the skewers, alternate the ingredients and serve.

Nutrition Facts:

Cal. 820	**Carbs**: 11.3 g	**Fat**: 68.2 g	Sat.Fat 36 g	Cholest. 150 mg
Protein 40 g	Diet. Fiber 4 g		Mon.Fat 18 g	Sodium 2467 mg
	Tot. Sugars 11.2 g		Poly.Fat 9.2 g	Salt 6.3 g

205) *Quick avocado-mustard rolls* 👤 4 ⏰ 15 Min.

Ingredients:

600 g. Smoked chicken breast

500 g. Lettuce

3 tsp. Mustard, olive oil

1 Avocado

2 Cucumbers

500 g. Tomatoes

100 g. Rice paper

Instructions:

1) First of all, prepare the rice paper to fold the rolls. Quick soak the paper in the water and place it on a towel. **2)** Prepare the chicken breasts, tomatoes and cucumbers. Cut them into strips / small pieces. **3)** Now, prepare the avocado. Mash it's pulp and add the oil and mustard. Blend well together. **4)** Open the rice paper to spread the ingredients and than create the rolls. **5)** Lay the lettuce on the rice paper and than add the chicken breast, cucumber, tomatoes and avocado mix. **6)** As you're done, roll everything and serve.

Nutrition Facts:

Cal. 1780 **Carbs**: 152 g **Fat**: 58.4 g Sat.Fat 11.3 g Cholest. -
Protein 147 g Diet. Fiber 40 g   Mon.Fat 28.6 g Sodium 800 mg
              Tot. Sugars 68.4 g   Poly.Fat 6.8 g Salt   2 g

ഃഃ

206) *Healthy tostones* 👤 4 ⏰ 40 Min.

Ingredients:

1 Onion

300 g. Tomatoes

4 tbsp. Seeds oil

50 ml. Water

4 Shallots

300 g. Plantains

Herbs mix, chili powder, cilantro (to taste)

Instructions:

1) First of all prepare the onion. Cut the tomatoes and cut them into small pieces. **2)** Briefly sautée the onion with a bit of oil (more or less 3 minutes). **3)** Now, add the water and the tomatoes and let everything simmer for approx. 10 minutes. Stir when necessary. **4)** Finely chop the shallots and cut the plantains into finger-thick slices. Take a second pan and fry the plantains with a bit of oil for approx. 2 minutes on each side. Use high heat. **5)** Add the shallots to the tomatoes, season with herbs mix, chili powder and cilantro according to your taste and simmer over medium heat until it's ready. **6)** When ready, carefully transfer the plantains to a plate and serve them with the tomato sauce.

Nutrition Facts:

Cal. 920   **Carbs**: 97.3 g **Fat**: 55.3 g Sat.Fat 47 g Cholest. -
Protein 7 g Diet. Fiber 9.4 g   Mon.Fat 1.2 g Sodium 25 mg
            Tot. Sugars 13.4 g   Poly.Fat 1.5 g Salt   -

207) *Italian ravioli pan* 👤 4   ⏰ 40 Min.

Ingredients:

300 g. Ravoli (choose your favourite filling)

200 g. Ricotta

300 g. Spinach

500 g. Diced tomatoes (in water canned)

Basil, oregano (to taste)

Instructions:

1) First of all, preheat the oven to 325 °F (170 °C). **2)** Take a casserole and lay down all the ingrediets. **3)** Drain the tomatoes and lay them on the bottom of the casserole dish. Than add the ravioli and lastly the baby spinach. **4)** Sprinkle the ricotta on top of the spinach and create other layers with the remaining ingredients. **5)** Cook on th emiddle rack for approx. 30 minutes and serve.

Nutrition Facts:

Cal. 1343	**Carbs**: 70 g	**Fat**: 60 g	Sat.Fat	34 g	Cholest.	-
Protein 114 g	Diet. Fiber 23.5 g		Mon.Fat	4 g	Sodium	2467 mg
	Tot. Sugars 19 g		Poly.Fat	3.3 g	Salt	6.4 g

ଽଓଃ

208) *Lentil dahl* 👤 4   ⏰ 45 Min.

Ingredients:

2 Shallots, carrots, garlic cloves

1 tsp. Cumin, curry powder, turmeric

2 tbsp. Ginger (fresh), rice oil

200 g. Lentils

450 ml. Vegetable broth

160 g. Basmati rice

100 g. Baby spinach

250 ml. Rice milk

Instructions:

1) First of all, peel the shallots and ginger. Slice them as well as the carrots. **2)** Take a pot, heat the oil and add the shallots and ginger. **3)** Peel and crush the garlic clove into the pot and add the cumin, turmeric, carrots and curry. Mix very well and cook for approx. 3 minutes. **4)** Add the lentils and deglaze with the rice milk and broth. Let everything simmer for approx. 15-20 minutes. **5)** Meanwhile, prepare the rice according to the package instructions. **6)** Wash the baby spinach and add it to the lentils when the cooking time has passed. Simmer for approx. 5 minutes and finely chop the cilantro. **7)** Serve the lentils with the rice and garnish this dish with the cilantro.

Nutrition Facts:

Cal. 1902	**Carbs**: 265 g	**Fat**: 50.2 g	Sat.Fat	38.5 g	Cholest.	-
Protein 74.3 g	Diet. Fiber 40 g		Mon.Fat	4.5 g	Sodium	1654 mg
	Tot. Sugars 38 g		Poly.Fat	3.6 g	Salt	3 g

209) *Classic gnocchi with sauce* 👤 4 ⏰ 1 hour

Ingredients:

450 g. Potatoes

3 Garlic cloves

450 g. Tomato purée

150 g. Wheat flour

2 Eggs

½ tsp. Salt

Basil (fresh), olive oil (to taste)

Instructions:

1) First of all, prepare the potatoes. Peel and cut them in half. Take a pot and add the potatoes. Cover with water. Bring them to boil, cover and cook at medium heat for approx. 15 minutes. **2)** Now, take the garlic cloves and crush them, slice the basil and add them to the pot. Season with olive oil. **3)** Add the oil, tomato to the pot and season a bit with oregano. Mix very well and simmer over low heat. **4)** Take a bowl, drain the potatoes and mash them with a fork. Combine the flour, potatoes, salt and eggs. **5)** Divide the dough creating many gnocchi and roll them onto a floured surface. Make sure they're a bit thick. **6)** Take a large pot and bring it to boil and let the gnocchi cook for 2 minutes. (*!! They float to the top when ready*). Serve with the sauce.

Nutrition Facts:

Cal. 1598	**Carbs**: 190 g	**Fat**: 70 g	Sat.Fat 12 g	Cholest. 550 mg
Protein 44.2 g	Diet. Fiber 13 g		Mon.Fat 44 g	Sodium 245 mg
	Tot. Sugars 22 g		Poly.Fat 8.2 g	Salt 1 g

☙☰

210) *Chestnut gnocchi with champignons* 👤 4 ⏰ 50 Min.

Ingredients:

250 g. Chestnut flour

100 g. Wheat flour

150 g. Ricotta

A bit of salt

150 g. Champignons (in water canned)

Parsley, olive oil, parmesan (to taste)

Instructions:

1) Firstly, prepare the gnocchi. Take a bowl and pour both flour types and stir. Create a hole in the middle and add the ricotta and salt. Mix very well until you have a smooth dough and put aside for 30 minutes. **2)** Spread a bit of flour on the shelf and put the dough. Create the small gnocchi. **3)** Put them on a floured sheet and they are ready to be cooked. **4)** Cook them for 2 minutes (see point 6. Rec. 209). **5)** In the meantime, drain, rinse and cook the champignons according to the package directions. **6)** As ready, serve the gnocchi with the champignons and season them with oil, parmesan and pieces of parsley.

Nutrition Facts:

Cal. 1620	**Carbs**: 210 g	**Fat**: 72 g	Sat.Fat 13 g	Cholest. 580 mg
Protein 46 g	Diet. Fiber 14 g		Mon.Fat 45 g	Sodium 347 mg
	Tot. Sugars 24 g		Poly.Fat 9.2 g	Salt 2 g

211) *Lemon tagliatelle* 👤 4   ⏰ 25 Min.

Ingredients:

300 g. Whole grain tagliatelle

2 Lemons (organic)

1 lime

2 Garlic cloves

2 tbsp. Olive oil

200 ml. Ricotta cheese

Basil (fresh, to taste)

Instructions:

1) First of all, take a large pot and bring to boil. Add a bit of salt and prepare the tagliatelle according to the package instructions. **2)** Squeeze the lemons and lime and peel a bit of the skin and slice it. **3)** Peel and slice the garlic and sautée the cloves for 1-2 minutes with a bit of oil. **4)** Add the skin pieces, the lemon and lime juices and the ricotta, season with your favourite herbs mix and simmer for approx. 5 minutes. **5)** As the pasta is ready, drain and add the tagliatelle to the sauce. Mix well and serve.

Nutrition Facts:

Cal. 1850	**Carbs**: 193 g	**Fat**: 104 g	Sat.Fat 44.5 g	Cholest. 378 mg
Protein 44.2 g	Diet. Fiber 33 g		Mon.Fat 42.3 g	Sodium 93.8 mg
	Tot. Sugars 14.3 g		Poly.Fat 8.3 g	Salt -

☼☽

212) *Whole grain rigatoni with pesto* 👤 4   ⏰ 20 Min.

Ingredients:

250 g. Whole grain rigatoni

3 Garlic cloves

3 tsp. Chia seeds

2 tbsp. Sunflower seeds

2 tbsp. Sunflower sseeds

140 ml. Olive oil

100 g. Cherry tomatoes

Parmesan, oregano, basil (to taste)

Instructions:

1) First of all, prepare the pasta according to the package instructions. **2)** Secondly, peel and chop the garlic and cut the basil leaves. **3)** Set a few seeds aside as garnish at the end. Take a blender and mix all three types of seeds with oil, garlic, parmesan and basil leaves. Season with a bit of salt and pepper. Blend very well. **4)** As the pasta is almost ready, drain and put them again in the pot with the pesto and mix together. **5)** Chop the tomatoes and add them to the pasta. Serve.

Nutrition Facts:

Cal. 3170	**Carbs**: 188 g	**Fat**: 224 g	Sat.Fat 53 g	Cholest. 260 mg
Protein 105 g	Diet. Fiber 31.4 g		Mon.Fat 117 g	Sodium 1020 mg
	Tot. Sugars 9 g		Poly.Fat 45 g	Salt -

213) *Noodle soup with kale* 👤 4   ⏰ 30 Min.

Ingredients:

100 g. Ramen noodles, natural tofu

60 g. Kale

2 tbsp. Olive oil, sesame seeds

1 tbsp. Curry powder

1 Shallot

400 ml. Rice milk

Instructions:

1) Firstly, preheat the oven to 395 °F (200 °C). Take a large pot, fill of water and bring to boil. Prepare the noodles according to the directions. When ready, drain them. **2)** Cut the tofu into small pieces and slice the kale. Mix very well the kale with ¼ of olive oil and spread it onto the baking sheet. **3)** Mix together ½ turmeric and half of the remaining oil. Garnish with a bit of salt and spread it onto a second baking sheet. Cook the tofu for 20 min. **4)** When 15 have passed, add the kale baking sheet. Peel and slice the shallot. **5)** Sautée the shallot with the remaining olive oil for a few minutes. Add the remaining turmeric and curry powder. **6)** Deglaze with the milk and let everything simmer for 10 more minutes. **7)** Add the noodles and garnish with kale and sesame seeds. Serve.

Nutrition Facts:

Cal. 1870	**Carbs**: 92 g	**Fat**: 150 g	Sat.Fat 93 g	Cholest. -
Protein 40 g	Diet. Fiber 15 g		Mon.Fat 36 g	Sodium 980 mg
	Tot. Sugars 26.2 g		Poly.Fat 10.5 g	Salt 1.5 g

☼☯

214) *Gado-gado Asian salad* 👤 4   ⏰ 45 Min.

Ingredients:

250 g. Potatoes, napa cabbage

4 Eggs

150 g. Beans, natural tofu

4 tsp. Olive oil + 2 tsp. Honey

1 Cucumber, carrot, garlic clove

30 ml. Balsamic vinegar

100 g. Bean sprout

Cilantro (to taste)

Instructions:

1) First of all, wash and peel the potatoes. Take a large pot and fill it with water in order to cover the potatoes. **2)** Bring to boil and simmer over medium heat for approx. 20 minutes. **3)** Take another pot and boil the eggs for approx. 10 minutes. Use a third pot, add the beans with a bit of salt and let them boil for approx. 15 minutes. **4)** Now, cut the tofu into small pieces and fry them in a pan with a bit of olive oil until it's golden-brown and set aside. **5)** Prepare the veggies. Grate the cabbage, cucumber and carrot. Peel and slice the shallot and combine it with vinegar and honey. **6)** Drain the potatoes, let them cool and cut them into pieces. **7)** Add the potatoes and the oil to the pan and fry for approx. 10 min. **8)** Quarter the eggs and remove the stems of the cilantro. **9)** Serve in a bowl mixing the ingredients and garnish with the dressing.

Nutrition Facts:

Cal. 1570	**Carbs**: 100 g	**Fat**: 91.3 g	Sat.Fat 18.2 g	Cholest. 1080 mg
Protein 97 g	Diet. Fiber 25 g		Mon.Fat 45 g	Sodium 2247 mg
	Tot. Sugars 46 g		Poly.Fat 21.5 g	Salt 2.3 g

215) *Asian spring rolls* 👤 4   ⏰ 25 Min.

Ingredients:

200 g. Basmati rice

450 g. Cabbage, ground beef

2 Carrots, garlic cloves

2 tbsp. Seeds oil, ginger (grated)

4 tbsp. Balsamic vinegar, lemon juice, sweet chili sauce (low-sodium)

200 g. Peas (frozen)

Instructions:

1) Firstly, prepare the rice according to the instructions. In the meantime, peel the carrots and remove the stem from the cabbage. Cut both of them into thin slices. The same with the garlic cloves. **2)** Take a large pan and heat half of the oil to lightly cook the beef for approx. 5-8 minutes until golden-brown. **3)** Now, take a bowl and combine together the garlic with oil, chili sauce, ginger and vinegar. **4)** Now add to the pan the rice, cabbage and carrots and fry for approx. 5 minutes. **5)** Add the peas and sauce and fry for 5-6 more minutes. (*It's ready when the cabbage softens*). **6)** Drizzle with the lemon juice and you favorite harbs mix and serve.

Nutrition Facts:

Cal. 2570 **Carbs**: 300 g **Fat**: 85 g Sat.Fat 28.7 g Cholest. 240 mg
Protein 130 g Diet. Fiber 118 g Mon.Fat 38.3 g Sodium 4580 mg
Tot. Sugars 117 g Poly.Fat 16 g Salt 7 g

༄༅

216) *Cilantro -shrimps rice* 👤 4   ⏰ 20 Min.

Ingredients:

250 g. Basmati rice

3 Garlic cloves

30 g. Cilantro (fresh)

1 Lemon

100 g. Shrimps (cleaned)

2 tbsp. Olive oil, white wine

Oregano, parsley (to taste)

Instructions:

1) First of all, prepare the rice according to the instructions. 2) Peel and slice the garlic. **2)** Finely chop the cilantro and squeeze the lemon. **3)** Sautée the garlic with a bit of oil and add the shrimps. Cook for 2 minutes. **4)** As the rice is almost ready, add the rice and the white wine to the pan with the shrimps and cook for 2 more minutes. **5)** Add the parsley (cut it into pieces), olive oil and stir well. Serve.

Nutrition Facts:

Cal. 1140 **Carbs**: 192 g **Fat**: 28.5 g Sat.Fat 10 g Cholest. 40 mg
Protein 23.5 g Diet. Fiber 7 g Mon.Fat 9.2 g Sodium 130 mg
Tot. Sugars 3 g Poly.Fat 7.5 g Salt -

217) *Thai curry chicken* 👤 4 ⏰ 120 Min.

Ingredients:

3 Garlic cloves

3 tbsp. Curry paste (sugar-free, low sodium)

5 tsp. Lime juice + 2 lime

2 tsp. Ginger and seeds oil

12 Chicken tights

2 tbsp. Sesame seeds

Cilantro (fresh, to taste)

140 ml. Rice milk (unsweetened)

Instructions:

1) First of all, prepare the marinade. Peel and finely chop the garlic. Take a bag and add the curry paste, the milk, lime juice, seeds oil and ginger. **2)** Add the chicken inside, shake well and put in the fridge for 60 minutes. **3)** Once the 60 minutes passed, remove from the fridge and cook on the middle rack for approx. 30 minutes. **4)** Brush the thighs with a bit of oil and cook for 15 more minutes. **5)** Divide the lime into eights and remove the cilantro leaves from the stems. **6)** Garnish the chicken with cilantro and sprinkle a bit of sesame seeds onto them.

Nutrition Facts:

Cal. 2980	**Carbs**: 16.2 g	**Fat**: 236 g	Sat.Fat 86 g	Cholest. 1160 mg
Protein 250 g	Diet. Fiber 5 g		Mon.Fat 78.3 g	Sodium 1270 mg
	Tot. Sugars 8.9 g		Poly.Fat 45.3 g	Salt 3.2 g

218) *Healthy thai salad* 👤 4 ⏰ 15 Min.

Ingredients:

2 Zucchini, carrots, bell peppers

200 g. Red Cabbage, edamame (cooked)

2 Shallots

4 tbsp. Lime juice, balsamic vinegar, water

2 tsp. Ginger, sesame seeds

1 tbsp. Olive oil

100 g. Ricotta

Instructions:

1) First of all, create noodles from the zucchini and carrots using a spiralizer. Remove the seeds from the peppers and cut them into pieces. **2)** Slice the shallots and the cabbage after having removed the stalk. **3)** Prepare the dressing: take a bowl and use half of the shallot, add the ginger powder, lime juice, ricotta, water and oil. Mix very well. **4)** Take a large bowl and combine the vegetables with the edamame. **5)** Serve with the dressing and sesame seeds.

Nutrition Facts:

Cal. 1480	**Carbs**: 132 g	**Fat**: 87.2 g	Sat.Fat 9.3 g	Cholest. -
Protein 78 g	Diet. Fiber 57 g		Mon.Fat 35.2 g	Sodium 2984 mg
	Tot. Sugars 104 g		Poly.Fat 24.4 g	Salt 3 g

219) *Asian quinoa salad* 👤 4   ⏰ 30 Min.

Ingredients:

200 g. Quinoa, red cabbage

500 ml. Vegetable broth

1 Bell peppers + 2 Carrots

1 Shallot, lemon

60 g. Ricotta, cashews

1 tbsp. Sesame seeds, pumpkin seeds, balsamic vinegar

1 tsp. Ginger powder

Instructions:

1) Firstly, prepare the quinoa using the broth according to the package instructions. **2)** Now, prepare the peppers removing the seeds, cut the carrots into pieces and slice the shallot and the cabbage. **3)** Dressing: combine the vinegar, water, lemon juice and ginger powder. **4)** Combine well with the quinoa, add the ricotta and garnish with both types of seeds and cashews.

Nutrition Facts:

Cal. 1580	**Carbs**: 180 g	**Fat**: 87 g	Sat.Fat 14.2 g	Cholest. -
Protein 65 g	Diet. Fiber 39 g		Mon.Fat 40 g	Sodium 1580 mg
	Tot. Sugars 54 g		Poly.Fat 27.2 g	Salt 1.4 g

ಬಿಂಛ

220) *Spicy shrimps salad* 👤 4   ⏰ 15 Min.

Ingredients:

400 g. Shrimps (cleaned)

2 Carrots, onions, garlic cloves

800 g. Cabbage

20 ml. Olive oil, white wine

4 tbsp. Balsamic vinegar

150 g. Tomatoes

Chili powder, herbs mix (to taste)

Instructions:

1) First of all, prepare the cabbage and slice it into thin pieces. Cut the carrots, wash, peel and cut the tomatoes too. **2)** Slice the onion and garlic cloves. Take a pan heat a bit of olive oil and add the onions, shrimps, garlic cloves and tomatoes. Add the shrimps, a bit of chili powder and white wine. Sautée everything for 2-4 minutes. **3)** Take a bowl and add the vegetables and the sautéed shrimps with its spicy sauce. **4)** Season with a bit of herbs mix and serve.

Nutrition Facts:

Cal. 680	**Carbs**: 52 g	**Fat**: 31.3 g	Sat.Fat 4.7 g	Cholest. 270 mg
Protein 46 g	Diet. Fiber 18 g		Mon.Fat 20 g	Sodium 1580 mg
	Tot. Sugars 47.3 g		Poly.Fat 4.4 g	Salt 3.4 g

221) *Healthy peanut bowl* 👤 4   ⏰ 40 Min.

Ingredients:

400 g. Brown rice, natural tofu

3 Garlic cloves

4 tbsp. Olive oil, lemon juice

2 tbsp. Peanut butter, pumpkin seeds + 2 tsp. chia seeds

15 Cherry tomatoes

3 Bell peppers

200 g. Chickpeas, peas (both in water canned)

Vinegar, herbs mix (to taste)

Instructions:

1) First of all, preheat the oven to 360 °F (180 °C). Take a pot and prepare the rice according to the directions. **2)** Dab the tofu dry and cut it into cubes. **3)** Take a bowl and crush the garlic cloves. Add the butter, lemon juice, 2 tbsp. of olive oil and pumpkin seeds. Put the tofu in a casserole dish and cook for approx. 15-20 minutes. **4)** In the meantime prepare the other vegetables, tomatoes and peppers. Take a bowl, cut them into small pieces and add them to the bowl. Add the chickpeas and peas. Season with the remaining oil, a bit of vinegar and your favorite herbs mix. **5)** As the rice and tofu are ready, take more bowls and divide the ingredients. Serve.

Nutrition Facts:

Cal. 2790   **Carbs**: 370 g   **Fat**: 115 g   Sat.Fat 16.2 g   Cholest. -
Protein 142 g   Diet. Fiber 36 g   Mon.Fat 37.8 g   Sodium 3560 mg
Tot. Sugars 58 g   Poly.Fat 47.6 g   Salt -

☙☧

222) *Vegan avocado sushi* 👤 4   ⏰ 30 Min.

Ingredients:

300 g. Sushi rice

300 g. Tomatoes

1 Avocado

15 Nori sheets

Wasabi (to taste)

Instructions:

1) First of all, prepare the sushi rice according to the package instructions. **2)** Prepare the vegetables. Cut in thin strips the peppers and the cherry tomatoes in small pieces. **3)** Prepare the nori sheets. Moisten your hands and and evenly spread the rice onto the sheets. Be careful to leave a small space at the top and bottom of the sheet. **4)** Spread the vegetables pieces lenghtwise in a line in the centre of the rice. Repeat. **5)** Using the bamboo mat, press and roll the ingredients together. Wet a bit the free space you left on the edges and finish rolling up the. **6)** Cut each roll in several pieces and serve with the sauce.

Nutrition Facts:

Cal. 1650   **Carbs**: 289 g   **Fat**: 38.4 g   Sat.Fat 7 g   Cholest. -
Protein 28 g   Diet. Fiber 31.2 g   Mon.Fat 18.3 g   Sodium 2470 mg
Tot. Sugars 52.4 g   Poly.Fat 4.5 g   Salt 2.3 g

223) *Sweet walnuts casserole* 👤 4 ⏰ 50 Min.

Ingredients:

1 Kg. Sweet potatoes

3 Egg whites

90 g. Walnuts

200 g. Plain yoghurt

30 g. Agave nectar

3 tbsp. Olive oil

Cinnamon (to taste)

Instructions:

1) First of all, preheat the oven to 390 °F (200°C). Prepare the potatoes. Peel and cut them into small pieces. **2)** Take a pot, add the potatoes and cover them with water. Bring to boil. Cook them for approx. 5-7 minutes until the potatoes soften but yet firm to bite. **3)** Beat the egg whites until stiff. As the potatoes are ready, use a blender and purée everything. **4)** Season them with the agave, yoghurt and cinnamon. **5)** Now add the egg whites. **6)** Brush the casserole with a bit of olive oil and add the potatoes mix. **7)** Mash the walnuts into small pieces, mix them with the remaining oil and agave nectar and sprinkle them on top of the casserole. **8)** Cook the casserole on the middle rack for approx. 35 minutes. Serve.

Nutrition Facts:

Cal. 1870	**Carbs**: 239.7 g	**Fat**: 116.3 g	Sat.Fat 48 g	Cholest. 70 mg
Protein 42.2 g	Diet. Fiber 32 g		Mon.Fat 16.2 g	Sodium 290 mg
	Tot. Sugars 71 g		Poly.Fat 46.2 g	Salt -

ಬಂಜ

224) *Healthy veg. Mac & Cheese* 👤 4 ⏰ 40 Min.

Ingredients:

1 Potato, carrot

400 g. Macaroni

2 tbsp. Lemon juice

150 g. Cashew butter

50 ml. Oat milk (unsweetened)

Paprika powder, parsley (fresh), herbs mix (to taste)

Instructions:

1) First of all prepare the potatoe and carrot. Peel and cut them into pieces. Take a pot, add the greens and bring to boil. Le them simmer for approx. 18-20 minutes. **2)** Take a second pot and prepare the macaroni according to the package instructions. **3)** Meanwhile, peel the garlic clove, slice it into small pieces and combine it with the milk, lemon juice, paprika powder, butter and chopped vegetables. **4)** Take an immersion blender and purée everything into a creamy sauce. *!! When necessary, remember you can add a bit of the macaroni cooking water.*

5) Drain the pasta and mix very well with the sauce. Serve.

Nutrition Facts:

Cal. 2135	**Carbs**: 338 g	**Fat**: 75 g	Sat.Fat 16.1 g	Cholest. -
Protein 75 g	Diet. Fiber 25 g		Mon.Fat 46 g	Sodium 62 mg
	Tot. Sugars 26 g		Poly.Fat 7.9 g	Salt -

225) *Brussels sprouts spaghetti* 👤 4   ⏰ 30 Min.

Ingredients:

2 Garlic cloves

3 tbsp. Olive oil

280 g. Rye spaghetti

200 g. Brussels sprouts

350 g. Diced tomatoes (in water canned)

Parmesan, basil (fresh), oregano, herbs mix (to taste)

Instructions:

1) First of all, prepare the spaghetti accoring to the package instructions. 2) Drain the tomatoes, prepare the brussels sprouts cutting them into pieces. 3) Mash the garlic cloves and add them to a pot. Add the tomatoes and brussels sprouts too. 4) Add a bit of olive oil and briefly cook them. 5) As the pasta is almost ready, drain it and put it back again in the pot. 6) Add the garlic and vegetable sauce and mix it well together. 7) Cook for 2 more minutes and add the parmesan, oregano, basil and serve.

Nutrition Facts:

Cal. 1650	**Carbs**: 211 g	**Fat**: 58 g	Sat.Fat 13.4 g	Cholest. 218 mg
Protein 60 g	Diet. Fiber 57 g		Mon.Fat 30 g	Sodium 1389 mg
	Tot. Sugars 49 g		Poly.Fat 8.3 g	Salt 2.6 g

☙☜

226) *Shepherd's Pie* 👤 4   ⏰ 70 Min.

Ingredients:

450 g. Potatoes + 300 g. Beef

3 Garlic cloves + 1 carrot

60 g. Peas, corn (both frozen, in water canned)

140 g. Vegetable broth

1 tbsp. Whole grain flour, tomato paste, veg. Butter

50 ml. Oat milk

Nutmeg, parsley, herbs mix (to taste)

Instructions:

1) First of all, preheat the oven to 360 °F (180 °C) and prepare the potatoes. Take a potand peel them. Add enough water to cover the potatoes. Bring them to boil and then simmer for approx. 20 minutes. 2) Finely chop the garlic cloves, carrot and the parsley. Briefly sautée the garlic with a bit of oil and add the beef. Cok for 3 more minutes. 3) Season with the herbs mix and add the flour and tomato paste. 4) Mix well and simmer for 5 more minutes. 5) Deglaze with the broth and add the peas, carrot and corn. Simmer for 5 more minutes. 6) Drain the potatoes and blend them with a mixer. Add the butter, nutmeg and milk until it's creamy. 7) Add this mixture to a pan and top with the potatoes. Cook on middle rack for approx. 25 minutes. Sprinkle a bit of parsley and serve.

Nutrition Facts:

Cal. 1490	**Carbs**: 125 g	**Fat**: 68.5 g	Sat.Fat 26 g	Cholest. 196 mg
Protein 83.4 g	Diet. Fiber 18 g		Mon.Fat 34.4 g	Sodium 807 mg
	Tot. Sugars 26.7 g		Poly.Fat 4.3 g	Salt 1.5 g

227) *Healthy burger plate* 👤 4   ⏰ 30 Min.

Ingredients:

600 g. Ground Beef

500 g. Spinach (fresh)

2 Shallots

5 Tomatoes

150 g. Asparagus

1 Lemon

Olive oil, salt, rosmary, oregano, pepper (to taste)

Instructions:

1) Firstly, peel and chop the shallots. Mix the beef with the shallots, season with a bit of salt and herbs mix and creates small burger patties. **2)** Take a pan, heat the oil and fry the patties. Take advantage of the heated pan and warm up the spinach and asparagus. **3)** Mix the garlic together with the spinach. **4)** Cut the tomatoes into small pieces and put aside. **5)** Serve the patties with the greens and the tomatoes. Sprinkle the lemon juice on top of them. Serve.

Nutrition Facts:

Cal. 1980	**Carbs**: 23.3 g	**Fat**: 140 g	Sat.Fat 50 g	Cholest. 1439 mg
Protein 176 g	Diet. Fiber 16 g		Mon.Fat 69 g	Sodium 1060 mg
	Tot. Sugars 20.6 g		Poly.Fat 11.3 g	Salt 2 g

℘☙

228) *Salmon burger* 👤 4   ⏰ 15 Min.

Ingredients:

900 g. Salmon

1 Lemon

250 g. Plain yoghurt

2 tsp. Coarse-grain mustard

4 Burger buns

100 g. Asparagus

Olive oil, herbs mix (to taste)

Instructions:

1) Preheat the oven to 395 °F (200 °C). Take a baking sheet, brush the fillets with a bit of olive oil and ¼ of the lemon juice and cook them on middle rack for approx. 12 minutes. **2)** Use the rest of the lemon to mix it with the yoghurt and mustard. **3)** More or less 2-3 minutes before the salmon is ready, add the bread and the asparagus to the baking sheet. **4)** As the time has passed, cut the fillets and season them a bit as you prefer and open the burger buns and brush them with the sauce. **5)** Cut the asparagus and add them to the bread. Garnish wth the salmon, sauce and lemon juice. Cover the bun and serve.

Nutrition Facts:

Cal. 2459	**Carbs**: 131 g	**Fat**: 140 g	Sat.Fat 40 g	Cholest. 630 mg
Protein 202 g	Diet. Fiber 3.2 g		Mon.Fat 42 g	Sodium 467 mg
	Tot. Sugars 17.2 g		Poly.Fat 30.5 g	Salt 1 g

229) *Green steak* 👤 4 ⏰ 40 Min.

Ingredients:

- 1 Cauliflower
- 50 g. Spinach (fresh)
- 120 g. Parmesan
- 2 Bell pepper
- 40 g. Whole grain bread crumbs
- 250 g. Tomatoes
- 150 g. Asparagus

Instructions:

1) First of all, preheat the oven to 395 °F (200 °C). prepare a baking sheet and peel 2 leaves from the cauliflower. **2)** Brush them with olive oil and and roast them for approx. 15-18 minutes. **3)** Prepare the other rvegetables. Chop the cauliflower, spinach and parsley. Add these ingredients and the parmesan to a big bowl and mix well. **4)** As the cauliflower leaves are ready, remove them from the oven, season a bit and press them. Garnish them with the mixture and cook them for 15 more min. **5)** Prepare the tomatoes and the asparagus. Lightly cook them for a few minutes and serve with the cauliflower steaks.

Nutrition Facts:

Cal. 1187	**Carbs**: 56 g	**Fat**: 69 g	Sat.Fat 29.3 g	Cholest. 100 mg
Protein 68 g	Diet. Fiber 37 g		Mon.Fat 27.8 g	Sodium 1289 mg
	Tot. Sugars 32.4 g		Poly.Fat 6 g	Salt 1.7 g

⊱⊰

230) *Easy and quick bagel* 👤 4 ⏰ 60 Min.

Ingredients:

- 300 g. Tomatoes
- 1 Avocado
- 150 g. Tuna (in water canned)
- 4 (at least) Whole grain bagel
- 100 g. Lattuce
- Olive oil, herbs mix (to serve)

Instructions:

1) First of all, divide the bread and lightly cook them until warm and crispy. **2)** Peel the avocado and mash the pulp. **3)** Cut into small pieces the lettuce and tomatoes. **4)** Drain the tuna. **5)** As the bread is ready, open the bagel and spread firstly the avocado, the lettuce and than the tuna and tomatos. **6)** Season with a bit of herbs mix and cover. Serve.

Nutrition Facts:

Cal. 870	**Carbs**: 19 g	**Fat**: 21 g	Sat.Fat 5.1 g	Cholest. -
Protein 51 g	Diet. Fiber 10 g		Mon.Fat 8.2 g	Sodium 120 mg
	Tot. Sugars 6.7 g		Poly.Fat 9.1 g	Salt -

231) *Caesar summer Pasta* 👤 4   ⏰ 30 Min.

Ingredients:

180 g. Whole grain pasta (your favourite)

4 tbsp. Olive oil, plain yoghurt

300 g. Chicken breast (boneless, skinless)

300 g. Cherry tomatoes

1 Lemon

Garlic powder, chives, rosmary (to taste)

Instructions:

1) First of all prepare the pasta according to the directions. When it's ready, drain the pasta and add to a large bowl. **2)** Take a pan and heat 1 tbsp. of the oil over medium heat. Add the chicken and season with a bit of salt and pepper. Cook until it's golden-brown on both sides. **3)** Slice into small pieces the chicken breasts and add them to the bowl with the pasta. **4)** Now prepare the vegetables. Chop the tomatoes and the lettuce and add them to the bowl. **5)** For the seasoning: combine well together the remaining oil with the yoghurt, garlic powder, chives and lemon juice. **6)** Divide the salad into four plates and sprinkle the dressing. Serve.

Nutrition Facts:

Cal. 1756	**Carbs**: 132 g	**Fat**: 80.4 g	Sat.Fat 21.8 g	Cholest. 240 mg
Protein 115 g	Diet. Fiber 19 g		Mon.Fat 44.2 g	Sodium 798 mg
	Tot. Sugars 18 g		Poly.Fat 8.3 g	Salt 1 g

☼☾

232) *Mixed jalapeño toasts* 👤 4   ⏰ 40 Min.

Ingredients:

½ Lemon (or lime), avocado

3 Bell peppers,

1 Shallot

300 g. Chickpeas, tomatoes, tuna (in water canned)

2 greens jalapeño

4 slices (at least). Whole grain bread

Olive oil, basil, tahini (to taste)

Instructions:

1) First of all, prepare all the vegetables. Slice the bell peppers, jalapeños, shallot and tomatoes. Drain and rinse the chickpeas. **2)** Take a large bowl and add all the ingredients. **3)** Add the tuna and peel the avocado. Mash the pulp and set aside. **4)** Cook the bread until it's crispy. **5)** Spread the avocado on one side of the bread slice and garnish with all the ingredients. **6)** Add a bit of olive oil and tahini (to taste) and serve.

Nutrition Facts:

Cal. 820	**Carbs**: 82.3 g	**Fat**: 18.3 g	Sat.Fat 6.2 g	Cholest. -
Protein 25.3 g	Diet. Fiber 27.8 g		Mon.Fat 5.8 g	Sodium 760 mg
	Tot. Sugars 27.4 g		Poly.Fat 3.4 g	Salt -

233) *Parmesan crackers* 👤 4   ⏰ 25 Min.

Ingredients:

80 g. Kale

60 g. Parmesan (grated)

½ tsp. Garlic powder

¼ tsp. Chili powder

Instructions:

1) First of all, preheat the oven to 395 °F (200 °C). Wash the kale, remove the ends and cut the kale leaves into pieces. **2)** Secondly, take a food processor and purèe the leaves. **3)** Put them in a bowl with the parmesan, garlic and chili powder. **4)** Take a tablespoon and create the crackers with a bit of mixture. **5)** Bake for approx. 5 minutes. 6) Let them cool down and serve.

Nutrition Facts:

Cal. 105	**Carbs**: -	**Fat**: 7.5 g	Sat.Fat 6 g	Cholest. 25 mg
Protein 8 g	Diet. Fiber -		Mon.Fat 2 g	Sodium 240 mg
	Tot. Sugars -		Poly.Fat -	Salt -

---

234) *Savory snacks* 👤 4   ⏰ 40 Min.

Ingredients:

15 g. Baked ham

½ Shallot

20 g. Ricotta

15 g. Rye flour

½ tsp. Baking powder

56 g. Eggs

Instructions:

1) First of all, preheat the oven to 360 °F (180°C). **2)** Secondly, prepare the ham and finely slice the shallot. **3)** Use a hand mixer and pour together the eggs, ricotta, flour, baking powder and mix well. **4)** Add the ham and shallot pieces, use a spoon to create small balls and place them onto a baking paper. **5)** Place in the middle rack and cook for approx. 30 minutes. Serve.

Nutrition Facts:

Cal. 305	**Carbs**: 2.5 g	**Fat**: 25.3 g	Sat.Fat 10.4 g	Cholest. 280 mg
Protein 16 g	Diet. Fiber 0.5 g		Mon.Fat 10.2 g	Sodium 600 mg
	Tot. Sugars 1 g		Poly.Fat 4 g	Salt 1 g

235) *Shrimps couscous*   👤 4   ⏰ 15 Min.

Ingredients:

200 g. Couscous

4 Tomatoes

150 g. Tuna

3 Garlic cloves

300 g. Shrimps (cleaned)

Olives (pitted)

Parsley, walnuts (crushed), olive oil, vinegar, lemon juice (to taste)

Instructions:

1) First of all, prepare the couscous according to the package instructions. **2)** Cut the tomatoes, drain the tuna and slice the parsley. **3)** Wash the shrimps and take a pan. Lightly cook them for a few minutes with a bit of olive oil, crushed garlic cloves and lemon juice. **4)** Take a big bowl and add the tuna, couscous, shrimps, olives, sliced parsley, walnuts, oil, vinegar an sprinkle the remaning lemon juice. **5)** Serve.

Nutrition Facts:

Cal. 1345	**Carbs**: 132 g	**Fat**: 56 g	Sat.Fat	17 g	Cholest.	280 mg
Protein 83 g	Diet. Fiber 18 g		Mon.Fat	12 g	Sodium	1540 mg
	Tot. Sugars 12 g		Poly.Fat	7 g	Salt	5 g

---

236) *Burger mixed salad*   👤 4   ⏰ 15 Min.

Ingredients:

500 g. Ground beef

250 g. Lettuce

4 Tomatoes

180 g. Corn (in water canned)

4 Bell peppers

Pickles, olives (pitted), vinegar, olive oil, lemon juice (to taste)

Instructions:

1) Firstly, take a pan, cut the beef into small pieces and lightly cook them for approx. 10 minutes. Garnish with a bit of olive oil and herbs mix. **2)** Wash and cut the lettuce, as well as the tomatoes. **3)** Drain and rinse the corn. **4)** Take a big bowl and layer the lettuce, corn, tomatoes, and beef. Add the olives, pickles and sprinkle the lemon juice, oil and vinegar. Serve.

Nutrition Facts:

Cal. 1280	**Carbs**: 17 g	**Fat**: 72 g	Sat.Fat	31 g	Cholest.	430 mg
Protein 97 g	Diet. Fiber 7 g		Mon.Fat	24 g	Sodium	1280 mg
	Tot. Sugars 14 g		Poly.Fat	17 g	Salt	3 g

237) *Flatbread* 👤 4 ⏰ 110 Min.

Ingredients:

- 100 g. Ricotta
- 4 g. Dry yeast
- 90 ml. Lukewarm water
- 3 Garlic cloves
- 150 g. Smoked salmon
- 1 tsp. Sea salt
- Parsely, olive oil, arugola, olives (pitted) (to taste)

Instructions:

1) First of all, take a bowl and combine the flour, sea salt and yeast. Secondly, add the warm water and half tsp. of olive oil. 2) Knead with your hands the dough until it's smooth. Keep in a warm place for 1 hour and let rise. 3) Preheat the oven to 395 °F (200 °C) and prepare a baking sheet. Flour a surface and roll out the dough. 4) Cut rectangle pieces and bake them for 20 minutes (*see when they're golden brown*). 5) Finely peel the garlic cloves and mix them together with the ricotta, olive oil, olives and parsley. 6) Spread this sauce over the bread and serve with the smoked salmon.

Nutrition Facts:

Cal. 910	**Carbs**: 121 g	**Fat**: 28 g	Sat.Fat 13.5 g	Cholest. 60 mg
Protein 38 g	Diet. Fiber 5.6 g		Mon.Fat 8 g	Sodium 980 mg
	Tot. Sugars 12.5 g		Poly.Fat 3.5 g	Salt 3 g

---

238) *Classic focaccia* 👤 4 ⏰ 60 Min.

Ingredients:

- 10 g. Dried yeast
- 80 ml. Warm water
- 250 g. Rye flour
- 3 tbsp. Olive oil
- Herbs mix, fresh basil (to taste)
- 250 g. Tomatoes

Instructions:

1) First of all, take a bowl and combine together the yeast and 10 ml. of warm water. 2) Secondly, add the rye flour and mix well. 3) Add gradually the rest of the water and knead the dough. 4) Moisture your hands with a bit of olive oil and rub the ball, place it in a bowl and leave in a warm place for 40 minutes (until the size double). 5) Preheat the oven to 465 °F (240 °C), spread a bit of flour on the baking sheet. 6) Finely cut the basil and the tomatoes. 7) Divide the dough in 4 pieces, rub them with a bit of oil and press the basil and tomatoes pieces into the dough. 8) Bake the focaccia on the middle rack for approx. 20 minutes. Serve.

Nutrition Facts:

Cal. 1080	**Carbs**: 160 g	**Fat**: 21 g	Sat.Fat 3 g	Cholest. -
Protein 34 g	Diet. Fiber 31 g		Mon.Fat 11 g	Sodium 22 mg
	Tot. Sugars 11 g		Poly.Fat 4.5 g	Salt -

239) *Chicken quesadillas* 👤 4   ⏰ 15 Min.

Ingredients:

2 tbsp. Seeds oil

2 Chicken breast fillets

2 Limes

100 g. Ricotta

2 Bell peppers

4 Whole grain tortillas

Olive oil, rosemary and garlic powder (to taste)

Instructions:

1) First of all, take a pan and heat the seeds oil to breast the chicken fillets for 5 minutes on each side. Season with a bit of rosemary and garlic powder. **2)** In the meantime, remove the seeds from the peppers and and cut into small pieces. **3)** As the fillets are ready, remove them from the heat and slice them. **4)** Spread the ricotta on the tortillas and add the peppers and chicken breasts. **5)** Sprinkle the limes juice on top of them and serve.

Nutrition Facts:

Cal. 1760	**Carbs**: 162 g	**Fat**: 83 g	Sat.Fat 37 g	Cholest. 297 mg
Protein 134 g	Diet. Fiber 22 g		Mon.Fat 22.7 g	Sodium 1987 mg
	Tot. Sugars 7 g		Poly.Fat 10 g	Salt -

☙☸

240) *Sweet potato quesadillas* 👤 4   ⏰ 30 Min.

Ingredients:

1 Sweet potato

2 tbsp. Olive oil

150 g. Black beans (in water canned)

50 g. Baby spinach (fresh)

2 tsp. Paprika powder

4 Whole grain tortillas

150 g. Cherry tomatoes

Instructions:

1) First of all, take a pan, peel and grate the potato and drain the black beans. **2)** Wash and cut the tomatoes and put them into a bowl. **3)** Heat a bit of oil and lightly cook the grated potato into the pan for a couple of minutes. **4)** Add 10 ml. of water to the pan and add the black beans and baby spinach. Cook for 2-4 more minutes. **5)** Add the potatoes, spinach and black beans to the tortillas and fry them for 3-5 minutes on each side. **6)** Garnish with the tomatoes and serve.

Nutrition Facts:

Cal. 1240	**Carbs**: 180 g	**Fat**: 48.2 g	Sat.Fat 4 g	Cholest. -
Protein 26 g	Diet. Fiber 31 g		Mon.Fat 14 g	Sodium 870 mg
	Tot. Sugars 15 g		Poly.Fat 5 g	Salt -

241) *Horseradish shrimps* 👤 4   ⏰ 15 Min.

Ingredients:

300 g. Shrimps (cleaned)

3 Cucumber (middle size)

2 tsp. Horseradish (grated)

30 g. Ricotta

2 Garlic cloves

1 Lemon

Olive oil, parsley (to taste)

Instructions:

1) First of all, wash and cut the cucumber into small pieces. **2)** Secondly, take a pan and lightly cook the shrimps with a bit of oil and lemon juice. **3)** Mix the horseradish with olive oil and ricotta and blend well together. **4)** Serve together the shrimps and cucumbers and garnish them with this cream. Enjoy!

Nutrition Facts:

Cal. 980	**Carbs**: 30 g	**Fat**: 71 g	Sat.Fat 34 g	Cholest. 745 mg
Protein 92 g	Diet. Fiber 5.2 g		Mon.Fat 22.8 g	Sodium 1043 mg
	Tot. Sugars 12.5 g		Poly.Fat 7.2 g	Salt -

☙☙

242) *Hash muffins* 👤 4   ⏰ 50 Min.

Ingredients:

150 g. Potatoes

150 g. Broccoli

50 g. Egg

3 tbsp. Rice oil

1 Lemon

Parmesan, rosmary (to taste)

Instructions:

1) Firstly, preheat the oven to 360 °F (180 °C). Secondly, take a bowl and peel and then grate the potatoes and broccoli. Add them to the bowl. **2)** Season the vegetables with olive oil, eggs, rosmary and lemon juice. **3)** Take a muffin molds and pour the mixture into the molds. **4)** Bake these greens muffins on the middle rack for 40 minutes. Serve.

Nutrition Facts:

Cal. 435	**Carbs**: 24 g	**Fat**: 25.3 g	Sat.Fat 12 g	Cholest. 230 mg
Protein 24.5 g	Diet. Fiber 4.5 g		Mon.Fat 9.3 g	Sodium 430 mg
	Tot. Sugars 4.5 g		Poly.Fat 1.7 g	Salt 1 g

243) *Creamy dip* 👤 4   ⏰ 20 Min.

Ingredients:

80 g. Kale (fresh)

150 g. Artichokes hearts

1 Avocado, lime

2 Garlic cloves

1 Cucumber

Olive oil (to taste)

Instructions:

1) Firstly, take a large pan and heat a bit the oil iver medium heat. Secondly, wash and prepare the kale and cook it for more or less 5-7 minutes. Remove from the heat when yousee it's wilted. **2)** Prepare the artichokes and quarter them. Set them aside. **3)** Squeeze the lime and cut the pulp of the avocado into pieces. Take a hand blender and add the pulp, the lime juice and the crushed garlic cloves. Blend everything until it's creamy and smooth. **4)** Put this cream into a large bowl and use it to fill the artichokes and crispy kale. **5)** Serve the remaining dip with whole grain bread.

Nutrition Facts:

Cal. 980   **Carbs**: 94 g   **Fat**: 46.8 g   Sat.Fat   9 g   Cholest. -
Protein 26 g   Diet. Fiber 35 g   Mon.Fat 27.8 g   Sodium 1103 mg
    Tot. Sugars 23 g   Poly.Fat 6.3 g   Salt 3 g

☼☾

244) *Corn salad* 👤 4   ⏰ 15 Min.

Ingredients:

450 g. Roasted corn (frozen)

600 g. Tomatoes

2 Avocados

2 Shallots

2 Lemons

Basil and parsley (fresh), olive oil, herbs mix (to taste)

Instructions:

1) First of all, heat a pan and add a bit of olive oil. Lightly cook the corn for 5-7 minutes. **2)** Wash and cut the tomatoes into quarters. Take a large bowl and add them. **3)** Prepare the avocados, peel them and chop the pulp in pieces. Peel and chop the shallots and add both of these ingredients to the bowl. **4)** Add the roasted corn to the bowl as ready. **5)** Squeeze the lemons and sprinkle the juice over the bowl with all the ingredients. Season a bit more with a bit of olive oil, parsley (cut it), basil and herbs mix.

Nutrition Facts:

Cal. 1280   **Carbs**: 88 g   **Fat**: 91 g   Sat.Fat   17.8 g   Cholest. -
Protein 26 g   Diet. Fiber 40 g   Mon.Fat 57 g   Sodium 915 mg
    Tot. Sugars 48 g   Poly.Fat 14 g   Salt -

245) *Lemon cream*

👤 4   ⏰ 40 Min.

Ingredients:

1 ½ Lemons

40 g. Ricotta

1 Egg

7 g. Egg yolk

Erythritol (to taste)

Instructions:

1) First of all, grate the lemon and squeeze it. Take a bowl and mix well the ricotta, lemon juice and erythritol. Put them in a water bath. **2)** Take a second bowla nd mix together the egg yolk and and eggs with a mixer. **3)** Put the eggs in the water bath and, with the help of a whisk, blend everything very well. **4)** Simmer all the ingredients for 15 more minutes and stir frequently. **5)** Keep the cream in a jar and place in the fridge. You can use it to garnish other vegetable dishes or whole grain bread slices.

Nutrition Facts:

Cal. 410	**Carbs**: 4.8 g	**Fat**: 37 g	Sat.Fat 21 g	Cholest. 435 mg
Protein 10 g	Diet. Fiber 1.5 g		Mon.Fat 11.2 g	Sodium 110 mg
	Tot. Sugars 4.8 g		Poly.Fat 2.5 g	Salt -

๛Ƈ

246) *Mexican casserole*

👤 4   ⏰ 45 Min.

Ingredients:

2 Shallots

350 g. Ground beef

300 g. Tomatoes

300 g. Black beans (in water canned)

220 g. Corn (in water canned)

4 Jalapeños

3 Corn tortillas

Parsley, cilantro (to taste)

Instructions:

1) First of all, preheat the oven to 325 °F (180°C). Take a pan and chop the shallots. Take a pan, heat some oil and lightly cook both the shallots and the beef. **2)** Take a pan and add the tomatoes, jalapeños, corn and beans. Simmer everything for 5 minutes. **3)** Take a casserole dish and cover the bottom with the tortillas. Add the beef and vegetables on top of the tortillas and cook for 20-30 minutes. Low the heat as the time passes. **4)** Garnish the casserole with fresh cilantro and parsley. Serve.

Nutrition Facts:

Cal. 1560	**Carbs**: 140 g	**Fat**: 87 g	Sat.Fat 41 g	Cholest. 270 mg
Protein 138 g	Diet. Fiber 38 g		Mon.Fat 34 g	Sodium 1890 mg
	Tot. Sugars 22 g		Poly.Fat 6.5 g	Salt 3 g

247) *Vegan gratin* 👤 4   ⏰ 70 Min.

Ingredients:

500 g. Potatoes

180 g. Zucchini, asparagus

1 Shallot

100 g. Walnuts (crushed)

160 ml. Rice milk (unsweetened),

160 ml. Vegetable broth

11 g. Nutritional yeast flakes

Parsley (to taste)

Instructions:

1) First of all, preheat the oven to 360 °F (180 °C). Peel the potatoes, zucchini and asparagus and slice them. **2)** Peel and chop the shallot too. **3)** Take a pan and heat the olive oil. Add the shallot and lightly cook the zucchini and asparagus. **4)** Take a bowl and combine the broth, milk, yeast and herbs mix and purée into a smooth sauce. **5)** Take a casserole dish and lay down half of the zucchini, potatoes and asparagus and half of the sauce. Repeat with the remaining ingredients. **6)** Bake on middle rack for 55 minutes. **7)** Garnish with a bit of parsley and serve.

Nutrition Facts:

Cal. 1150	**Carbs**: 119 g	**Fat**: 64 g	Sat.Fat 10 g	Cholest. -
Protein 45 g	Diet. Fiber 15.3 g		Mon.Fat 34 g	Sodium 505 mg
	Tot. Sugars 17.6 g		Poly.Fat 10.5 g	Salt -

---

248) *Delicious turkey treats* 👤 4   ⏰ 40 Min.

Ingredients:

80 g. Ground turkey

30 g. Hummus

20 g. Sliced bacon

1 tsp. Garlic powder

25 g. Egg

Vinegar, herbs mix, parsley, olive oil (to taste)

Instructions:

1) First of all, preheat the oven to 250 °F (150 °C). **2)** Take a pan and fry a bit the bacon until crispy. Then remove it from the heat and chop it. **3)** Finely cut the parsley too. **4)** Take a bowl and combine together the eggs, a bit of garlic powder, bacon, herbs mix, vinegar. **5)** Form small round treats and place them on the baking sheet. **6)** Cook on the middle rack for approx. 25 minutes. **7)** Mix together the hummus with the remaining parsley, garlic powder and a bit of olive oil. Stri well together and serve with the turkey treats.

Nutrition Facts:

Cal. 400	**Carbs**: 1.6 g	**Fat**: 34 g	Sat.Fat 14.5 g	Cholest. 215 mg
Protein 22 g	Diet. Fiber -		Mon.Fat 12.8 g	Sodium 230 mg
	Tot. Sugars 1 g		Poly.Fat 5 g	Salt -

249) *Cauliflower healthy gnocchi* 👤 4   ⏰ 1 Hour

Ingredients:

1,5 Kg. Cauliflower

150 g. Whole grain flour

3 tbsp. Seeds oil

2 tbsp. Pine nuts

250 g. Tomatoes

Basil (fresh), parmesan (to taste)

Instructions:

1) Firstly, take a pot and fill it with water, wash the cauliflower, separate into florets and bring to boil the pot. Cook the cauliflowers on lower heat until it softnes. (Approx. 30 min.) 2) Drain the cauliflower and let cool. Remove the excess of water with a clean towel. 3) Take a big bowl, add the cauliflower and mash it. Add the flour and a pinch of salt and knead into an elastic dough. If necessary (*the dough is too moist*) add flour. 4) Roll the dough and cut into pieces. They should be 3 cm. thick. 5) Take a pan and fry on each side until they're golden-brown. 6) Wash and cut the tomatoes and the pine nuts. 7) Combine the gnocchi with the pine nuts and tomatoes and garnish with a bit of olive oil, parmesan and fresh basil. Serve.

Nutrition Facts:

Cal. 1480	**Carbs**: 193 g	**Fat**: 44 g	Sat.Fat 5 g	Cholest. -
Protein 50 g	Diet. Fiber 52 g		Mon.Fat 11 g	Sodium 870 mg
	Tot. Sugars 61 g		Poly.Fat 21g	Salt 2 g

---

250) *Arrowroot -apple fritters* 👤 4   ⏰ 20 Min.

Ingredients:

300 g. Apples

100 g. Arrowroot flour

3 tsp. Baking soda

180 g. Agave nectar

2 Eggs

1 tbsp. Olive oil

4 tbsp. Oat milk

Instructions:

1) Firstly, preheat the oven to 360 °F (180 °C). Secondly, peel and cut the apples into small pieces. 2) Take a large bowl and stir well together the flour, 130 g. of agave nectar, the eggs, the baking soda and oat milk. Mix well until the mixture is smooth. 3) Add the apple pieces and mix very well. 4) Prepare a baking sheet. 5) With a tablespoon create the fritters and place them on the baking sheet. Brush them with a bit of oil. 6) Bake them for 15 minutes until gold-brown. Before serving, garnish them with the remaining agave nectar.

Nutrition Facts:

Cal. 1490	**Carbs**: 236 g	**Fat**: 49 g	Sat.Fat 35 g	Cholest. 560 mg
Protein 31 g	Diet. Fiber 26 g		Mon.Fat 6.2 g	Sodium 540 mg
	Tot. Sugars 198 g		Poly.Fat 3 g	Salt -

251) *Corn fritters with ricotta* 👤 4   ⏰ 30 Min.

Ingredients:

750 g. Corn (in water canned)

200 g. Ricotta

150 g. Rye flour

2 Shallots + 6 tbsp. Cornmeal

250 ml. Water

1 Lemon

1 tbsp. Baking powder

Olive oil, parsley, salt (to taste)

Instructions:

1) First of all, peel and slice the shallots into thin slices and drain the corn using a sieve. 2) Secondly, take a big bowl and mix together the rye flour, cornmeal, lemon juice and baking powder. 3) Add the water and stir until the batter is smooth and thick. 4) Take a non-stick pan to cook the fritters. Heat the oil over medium heat and add a spoon of batter to the pan. Fry for 2-3 minutes on each side. 5) Take the ricotta, add the lemon juice and parsley. Serve.

Nutrition Facts:

Cal. 2200	**Carbs**: 268 g	**Fat**: 98 g	Sat.Fat 60 g	Cholest. -
Protein 45 g	Diet. Fiber 30 g		Mon.Fat 22 g	Sodium 2060 mg
	Tot. Sugars 28 g		Poly.Fat 7 g	Salt 3.2 g

※

252) *Kale tortillas* 👤 4   ⏰ 20 Min.

Ingredients:

200 g. Kale (fresh)

200 g. Chickpeas (in water canned)

150 g. Tuna (in water canned)

2 Garlic cloves + 4 Tortillas

200 g. Tomatoes

70 g. Olives (pitted)

Olive oil, herbs mix, lemon juice, water (to taste)

Instructions:

1) First of all, drain and rinse chickpeas. Peel and slice the garlic cloves. 2) Secondly, take a blender and purée the chickpeas. Add the lemon juice and 3 tbsp of water and blend well. 3) Wash and slice the tomatoes in chunks. Drain and rinse the olives and set aside. 4) Take a pot, wash the kale, cut the ends and cook them over medium heat for 5-8 minutes. Season with a bit of olive oil, crushed garlic cloves and herbs mix to add flavour. 5) Drain the tuna and in a bowl add all the ingredients. Mix well and prepare the tortillas. 6) Divide the ingredients and add the right amount of them on each tortillas. Serve.

Nutrition Facts:

Cal. 1690	**Carbs**: 198 g	**Fat**: 80 g	Sat.Fat 20 g	Cholest. 890 mg
Protein 87 g	Diet. Fiber 27 g		Mon.Fat 33 g	Sodium 1350 mg
	Tot. Sugars 25.5 g		Poly.Fat 18 g	Salt 1 g

253) *Whole-grain salmon pasta* 👤 4   ⏰ 20 Min.

Ingredients:

200 g. Whol grain pasta (pick your favourite)

200 g. Smoked salmon

1 Lemon

150 g. Tomatoes

Olives (pitted), olive oil, fresh basil (to taste)

Instructions:

1) First of all, prepare the pasta according to the package instructions. **2)** Cut the tomatoes and the smoked salmon into small pieces and set aside. **3)** As the pasta is almost ready, drain it and put it back into the pot together with the tomatoes and the salmon. **4)** Season with the lemon juice, olives, olive oil and fresh basil. Mix well together and let cook for 2 more minutes. Serve.

Nutrition Facts:

Cal. 1140	**Carbs**: 144 g	**Fat**: 68 g	Sat.Fat 22 g	Cholest. 350 mg
Protein 95 g	Diet. Fiber 25 g		Mon.Fat 24.4 g	Sodium 596 mg
	Tot. Sugars 5.4 g		Poly.Fat 13 g	Salt -

೸೦ೞ

254) *Choco-chickpeas* 👤 4   ⏰ 60 Min.

Ingredients:

40 g. Dark chocolate

60 g. Cjickpeas (in water canned)

½ tsp. Rice oil

Instructions:

1) First of all, preheat the oven to 395 °F (200 °C). **2)** Drain and rinse the chickpeas. Use a towel to dry them. **3)** Prepare a baking sheet and mix the chickpeas with the oil. **4)** Roast on the middle rack for approx. 30 minutes. **5)** Remove the chickpeas from the heat and let cool. **6)** Melt the chocolate with a water bath. **7)** Mix together the chickpeas with the chocolate. **8)** Use a baking paper and with spoon create small cookies with the chickpeas. **9)** Place in the fridge for a couple of hours and serve.

Nutrition Facts:

Cal. 275	**Carbs**: 16.2 g	**Fat**: 14.8 g	Sat.Fat 9 g	Cholest. -
Protein 6.8 g	Diet. Fiber 6 g		Mon.Fat 4 g	Sodium 160 mg
	Tot. Sugars 18 g		Poly.Fat 1 g	Salt -

255) *Eggplant-shrimps skewers* 👤 4   ⏰ 40 Min.

Ingredients:

2 Eggplants

250 g. Shrimps (cleaned)

1 Lemon

3 Garlic cloves

Skewers

Parsley, basil, olive oil (to taste)

Instructions:

1) First of all, wash and slice in thick slices the eggplants. Heat the griddle and griddle the eggplants slices more or less 2 minutes on each side. **2)** The same thing with the shrimps. Briefly cook them and set aside. **3)** Season both ingredients with lemon juice, parsley and olive oil. **4)** Alternate the eggplants and shrimps and compose the skewers. Serve.

Nutrition Facts:

Cal. 680	**Carbs**: 45 g	**Fat**: 48.2 g	Sat.Fat 7 g	Cholest. -
Protein 12 g	Diet. Fiber 12.7 g		Mon.Fat 33 g	Sodium 1560 mg
	Tot. Sugars 40 g		Poly.Fat 5.2 g	Salt -

---

256) *Grapefruit salmon* 👤 4   ⏰ 25 Min.

Ingredients:

4 Salmon fillets

2 Grapefruit

1 Shallot

250 g. Asparagus

100 g. Cherry tomatoes

Herbs mix, olive oil (to taste)

Instructions:

1) First of all, prepare the grill with medium heat. **2)** Brush the fillets with a bit of olive oil and grill them on each side for more or less 5 minutes. *(You see when they're golden brown)* **3)** Slice one grapefruits in small pieces and squeeze the second one. Set aside. **4)** Wash and chop the tomatoes and sautée the asparagus with a bit of oil and the sliced shallot. **5)** Garnish the fillets with the asparagus, tomatoes, the grapefruit pieces and sprinkle the juice of the second pomegranate. Serve.

Nutrition Facts:

Cal. 2400	**Carbs**: 48 g	**Fat**: 180 g	Sat.Fat 26 g	Cholest. 350 mg
Protein 140 g	Diet. Fiber 14 g		Mon.Fat 60 g	Sodium 740 mg
	Tot. Sugars 45 g		Poly.Fat 68 g	Salt 1 g

257) *Herbs chicken* 👤 4   ⏰ 30 Min.

Ingredients:

- 4 Chicken breast fillets
- 3 Zucchini
- 100 g Cherry tomatoes
- 40 ml. Olive oil
- 3 tsp. Paprika powder
- 40 g. Parmesan
- Oregano, basil, parsley, herbs mix (to taste)

Instructions:

1) Firstly, preheat the oven to 395 °F (200 °C). **2)** Secondly, prepare a sheets of foil for each fillets. **3)** Prepare the vegetables. Cut the tomatoes, zucchini and parsly into small pieces and add them to the fillets. **4)** Season the fillets with olive oil, herbs mix, basil, oregano and paprika powder. **5)** Close the foil and fold the fillets. Cook for approx. 25-30 minutes. Serve.

Nutrition Facts:

Cal. 1230	**Carbs:** 17 g	**Fat:** 51 g	Sat.Fat 15 g	Cholest. 380 mg
Protein 162 g	Diet. Fiber 8 g		Mon.Fat 24.3 g	Sodium 825 mg
	Tot. Sugars 17 g		Poly.Fat 6.3 g	Salt -

---

258) *Grilled chicken & green sauce* 👤 4   ⏰ 30 Min.

Ingredients:

- 4 Chicken breasts fillets
- 2 tbsp. Seeds oil + 160 ml. Olive oil
- 3 Garlic cloves
- 20 g. Parsley, cilantro (fresh)
- 5 tbsp. Vinegar
- 150 g. Cherry tomatoes
- Thyme, herbs mix (to taste)

Instructions:

1) Firstly, prepare the grill with medium heat. Brush the fillets with a bit of seeds oil and season with a bit of herbs mix. **2)** Grill the chicken for approx. 10 minutes on each side. **3)** Prepare the sauce: peel and chop the garlic cloves, the parsley, cilantro, vinegar and thyme. Take an immersion blender and purée everything. **4)** Add the olive oil gradually until you obtain a smooth mixture. **5)** Wash and slice the cherry tomatoes and the fillets and serve with the sauce.

Nutrition Facts:

Cal. 2280	**Carbs:** 9.7 g	**Fat:** 185 g	Sat.Fat 26.7 g	Cholest. 350 mg
Protein 143 g	Diet. Fiber 5 g		Mon.Fat 115 g	Sodium 424 mg
	Tot. Sugars 5 g		Poly.Fat 30 g	Salt -

259) *Summer greens spaghetti* 👤 4   ⏰ 10 Min.

Ingredients:

5 Cucumbers

1 Shallot

3 Bell peppers

4 Tomatoes + 1 Lemon

Basil (fresh), olive oil (to taste)

4 tbsp. Walnuts

Instructions:

1) First of all, use a spiralizer to create the vegetable noodles from the cucumbers. Dry them a little bit with a towel. **2)** Secondly, wash and cut into small pieces the peppers and the tomatoes. Add them to a bowl. **3)** Slice the shallot and add it to the bowl. **4)** Crush the walnuts and add them to the bowl. Add the cucumber spaghetti and crush the walnuts. **5)** Use them to garnish the bowl and season a bit with the lemon juice, olive oil and vinegar. Serve.

Nutrition Facts:

Cal. 1280	**Carbs**: 75.3 g	**Fat**: 93 g	Sat.Fat 19 g	Cholest. -
Protein 46 g	Diet. Fiber 20 g		Mon.Fat 53 g	Sodium 70 mg
	Tot. Sugars 52 g		Poly.Fat 16 g	Salt -

☙☸

260) *Hazelnuts salad* 👤 4   ⏰ 10 Min.

Ingredients:

70 g. Hazelnuts

2 1/2 tbsp. Olive oil

250 g. Tomatoes

4 Bell peppers

50 g. Celery

100 g. Olives

Vinegar (to taste)

Instructions:

1) Take a big bowl and start adding the ingredients as long as you prepare them. **2)** Wash, peel and cut the tomatoes the bell peppers and the celery. Add them to the bowl. **3)** Cut the celery into pieces and add them; the same with the olives. **4)** Chop the hazelnuts and briefly roast them in a pan for approx. 5 minutes. **5)** Add them to the salad and garnish with a bit of vinegar.

Nutrition Facts:

Cal. 850	**Carbs**: 48 g	**Fat**: 52 g	Sat.Fat 5.1 g	Cholest. -
Protein 38 g	Diet. Fiber 35 g		Mon.Fat 30 g	Sodium 120 mg
	Tot. Sugars 46 g		Poly.Fat 12 g	Salt -

261) *Summer mango snacks* 👤 4   ⏰ 80 Min.

Ingredients:

30 g. Mango

40 g. Ricotta

20 g. Chocolate scales

Instructions:

1) First of all, take a mixer and purée the mango. **2)** Take a bowl and mix together the ricotta and mango. **3)** Create small balls with the help of a spoon and sprinkle the chocolate scales. **4)** Put in the fridge for 2 hours and serve.

Nutrition Facts:

Cal. 600	**Carbs**: 28 g	**Fat**: 45.6 g	Sat.Fat 26.9 g	Cholest. -	
Protein 12.8 g	Diet. Fiber 9.2 g		Mon.Fat 13.7 g	Sodium 15 mg	
	Tot. Sugars 20 g		Poly.Fat 4.5 g	Salt -	

---

262) *Pomegranate pralines* 👤 4   ⏰ 45 Min.

Ingredients:

60 g. Dark chocolate

100 g. Pomegranate seeds

½ tbsp. Agave nectar

Instructions:

1) Firstly, melt the chocolate with a water bath and add the agave nectar. **2)** Take the silicone muffin pan and add 1 tsp of pomegranate seeds. Adjust the quantities of the seeds and the amount of the chocolate according to the size of the muffin pan. **3)** Add a layer of chocolate to each well. **4)** Repeat the layers. **5)** Place the pralines in the freezer for 40 minutes.

Nutrition Facts:

Cal. 340	**Carbs**: 28 g	**Fat**: 16 g	Sat.Fat 10 g	Cholest. -	
Protein 5 g	Diet. Fiber 7.2 g		Mon.Fat 5.2 g	Sodium 50 mg	
	Tot. Sugars 41 g		Poly.Fat 0.5 g	Salt -	

263) *Crunchy cookies* 👤 4   ⏰ 30 Min.

Ingredients:

2 tbsp. Agave nectar

1 tbsp. Rice oil

½ tbsp. Peanut butter

15 g. Puffed rice

10 g. Dark cocoa

Instructions:

1) Firstly, take a pan and heat the cocoa powder, butter, oil and agave nectar. Stir and mix until homogenous. **2)** Combine this mixture with the puffed rice and mix well with a spoon. **3)** Use a sheet of foil and two spoons as help to create the cookies from the mixture onto the foil. **4)** Place the crunchy cookies in the fridge for approx. 30 minutes and serve.

Nutrition Facts:

Cal. 310	**Carbs**: 24.8 g	**Fat**: 20 g	Sat.Fat 13.2 g	Cholest. -
Protein 5 g	Diet. Fiber 3.5 g		Mon.Fat 3.8 g	Sodium 25 mg
	Tot. Sugars 18 g		Poly.Fat 1.8 g	Salt -

---

264) *Delicious pecan bars* 👤 4   ⏰ 50 Min.

Ingredients:

50 g. Rye flour

5 tbsp. Agave nectar

2 tbsp. Brown sugar

30 ml. Olive oil

40 g. Eggs

60 g. Pecans

1 tbsp. Rice milk

Instructions:

1) First of all, preheat the oven to 360 °F (180°C) and prepare a casserole dish covered with baking paper. **2)** Secondly, prepare the crust: take a bowl and mix together the flour, 1 tbsp. agave nectar, 1 tbsp of oil and the eggs. **3)** Press the dough on the bottom of the dish. **4)** Bake on the middle rack for 10 min. **5)** Take a pan and combine together the remaining honey, oil and sugar. Heat until the sugar becomes liquid. Stir often. As liquid, increase the heat and bring to boil for 2 minutes. **6)** Remove fromt he heat and add the milk. **7)** Crush the pecans and mix until they're coated. **8)** Spread the mixture over the crust and bake for approx. 30 minutes. **9)** Let cool down and cut into bars.

Nutrition Facts:

Cal. 1040	**Carbs**: 50 g	**Fat**: 78 g	Sat.Fat 33 g	Cholest. 140 mg
Protein 30 g	Diet. Fiber 6.2 g		Mon.Fat 25 g	Sodium 120 mg
	Tot. Sugars 46 g		Poly.Fat 10 g	Salt -

265) *Classic roasted almond* 👤 4   ⏰ 10 Min.

Ingredients:

100 ml. Water

4 tbsp. Agave nectar

140 g. Almonds

Instructions:

1) First of all, take a pot, fill it with water and agave nectar and bring to boil. 2) Secondly, add the almonds to the pot and let everything simmer until most of the water has evaporated and turns light brown. 3) Remove the almonds from the heat and let cool down on a baking sheet covered with baking paper. Serve.

Nutrition Facts:

Cal. 810	**Carbs**: 7.4 g	**Fat**: 71 g	Sat.Fat 5.3 g	Cholest. -
Protein 32 g	Diet. Fiber 15 g		Mon.Fat 41 g	Sodium -
	Tot. Sugars 4.5 g		Poly.Fat 14 g	Salt -

☼☼

266) *Choco-banana ice cream* 👤 4   ⏰ 2 Hours

Ingredients:

3 tbsp. Peanut butter

2 tsp. Coconut oil

900 g. Bananas (slice, ripe, frozen)

2 tsp. Dark Cocoa powder

Walnuts (to taste)

Instructions:

1) First of all, if the bananas are not frozen, slice them and put them in the fridge for at least 3 hours. 2) Take a hand blender, add some water and purée the bananas. Add them to a bowl. 3) Mix the ice cream with the peanut butter and crush the walnuts. Add some of them to the ice cream. 4) Take a small pot and let the cocoa powder and oil to melt and blend them together. 5) Spread them over the ice cream and it should harden. 6) Sprinkle the remaining walnuts on the ice cream and serve.

Nutrition Facts:

Cal. 1300	**Carbs**: 190 g	**Fat**: 40 g	Sat.Fat 19 g	Cholest. -
Protein 25.2 g	Diet. Fiber 24 g		Mon.Fat 12.4 g	Sodium 70 mg
	Tot. Sugars 160 g		Poly.Fat 7 g	Salt -

267) *Choco-pumpkin cookies* 👤 4   ⏰ 20 Min.

Ingredients:

- 2 tbsp. Olive oil
- 10 g. Agave nectar
- 20 g. Rolled oats, quick cooking rolled oats
- 2 tbsp. Dark cocoa powder
- 3 tsp. Pumpkin seeds
- 15 g. Apple sauce
- 30 g. Eggs

Instructions:

1) First of all, preheat the oven to 320 °F (160 °C). **2)** Secondly, take a bowl and mix well together the oats, cocoa powder, apple sauce, pumpkin seeds. Take a mixer and blend together. **3)** Add the oil and agave nectar and mix again very well. **4)** Prepare a baking sheet and with a spoon place heaps of dough on top of it and then flatten slightly. **5)** Bake the cookies on the middle rack for 10-15 minutes. Serve.

Nutrition Facts:

Cal. 460	**Carbs**: 40 g **Fat**: 25 g	Sat.Fat 11.6 g	Cholest. 110 mg
Protein 15 g	Diet. Fiber 7.2 g	Mon.Fat 5.1 g	Sodium 70 mg
	Tot. Sugars 18.3 g	Poly.Fat 6.2 g	Salt -

ಸಂಛ

268) *Healthy granola bars* 👤 4   ⏰ 50 Min.

Ingredients:

- 20 g. Hazelnuts
- 35 g. Rolled oats
- 70 g. Dates (pitted)
- 3 tsp. Chia seeds
- 2 tsp. Olive oil
- 15 g. Penut butter

Instructions:

1) Firstly, preheat the oven to 360 °F (180 °C) and finely cut the hazelnuts. **2)** Secondly, combine the hazelnuts with the rolled oats and put them into a baking sheet and roast them on the middle rack for 10 minutes. **3)** Prepare the dates. Chop them and take a blender. Add the dates and a bit of water and purée them. **4)** Take a bowl and combine the dates with the seeds. **5)** Take a pot and add the olive oil and butter. Heat them up and mix well. **6)** Add the rolled oats, hazelnuts and butter and mix well. **7)** Take a casserole dish and add the mixture evenly. Put in the fridge for approx. 30 minutes. **8)** As the time has passed, cut the granola into bars and conserve in the fridge.

Nutrition Facts:

Cal. 700	**Carbs**: 84 g **Fat**: 27.3 g	Sat.Fat 3.4 g	Cholest. -
Protein 19 g	Diet. Fiber 16.4 g	Mon.Fat 12.1 g	Sodium 10 mg
	Tot. Sugars 59 g	Poly.Fat 9 g	Salt -

269) *Mulberries cup*

👤 4   ⏰ 20 Min.

Ingredients:

200 g. Mulberries

100 g. Rolled oats

2 tsp. Chia seeds, linseeds

3 tbsp. Buckwheat

30 g. Puffed oat

900 g. Bananas (peeled, frozen)

Instructions:

1) First of all, let the bananas thaw for 5-8 minutes and prepare the mulberries. Remove the stems from the berries. **2)** Secondly, combine together the oats with the seeds, buckwheat and puffed oat. **3)** Take a hand blender and blend well together the bananas and mulberries until it's creamy. *(When necessary add a bit of water to dilute)*. **4)** Take a glass and start layering the berries nice cream and the oat-seeds mix. Serve.

Nutrition Facts:

Cal. 1900	**Carbs**: 340 g	**Fat**: 30 g	Sat.Fat 4 g	Cholest. -
Protein 47.2 g	Diet. Fiber 53.2 g		Mon.Fat 5.3 g	Sodium 20 mg
	Tot. Sugars 186 g		Poly.Fat 17 g	Salt -

☙☉☋

270) *Healthy blueberry pie*

👤 4   ⏰ 4,5 Hours

Ingredients:

40 g. Eggs + 100 g. walnuts

20 g. Vegetable butter

2 tbsp. Agave nectar

250 g. Blueberries

30 ml. Water + 1 Lemon

9 leaves Gelatine

400 g. Vanilla yoghurt (low-fat)

130 g. Plain greek yoghurt

Instructions:

1) Firstly, preheat the oven to 360 °F (180°C). Cover the baking paper and cover the botton of the pan. **2)** Secondly, combine together 1 tbsp of agave nectar, eggs, butter and the crushed walnuts. Bake the mixture for approx. 20 minutes. **3)** Take a pot, add the blueberries with the agave nectar and water and bake for 5 min. and blend with a mixer. **4)** Add and mix 6 gelatine according to the package instructions. **5)** Pour the berries mix onto the cooled crust and let cool down. **6)** Take a pot and heat the 3 remaining gelatines and the lemon juice. **7)** Add the yoghurt and mix well. **8)** Add this mixture to the blueberries layer and let solidify in the fridge for at least 4 hours. Serve.

Nutrition Facts:

Cal. 1680	**Carbs**: 113 g	**Fat**: 128 g	Sat.Fat 43.5 g	Cholest. 270 mg
Protein 65 g	Diet. Fiber 12.8 g		Mon.Fat 70 g	Sodium 300 mg
	Tot. Sugars 43 g		Poly.Fat 10 g	Salt 1 g

271) *Classic berries cake* 👤 4 ⏰ 1,5 Hours

Ingredients:

100 g. Strawberries (fresh)

100 g. Mulberries

10 g. Vanilla bean

60 g. Vegetable butter

70 g Eggs + Agave nectar (to taste)

95 g. Whole grain flour

3 g. Baking powder

40 g. Vanilla yoghurt (unsweetened)

Instructions:

1) First of all, preheat the oven 320 °F (160 °C). **2)** Secondly, prepare the strwaberries and mulberries. Wash them and remove the stems, cut the strawberries into pieces. **3)** Take the vanilla bean and cut open it lenghtwise. With the help of the knife scrape out the pulp. **4)** Use a mixer to combine together the butter, agave nectar and vanilla pulp. **5)** Mix the eggs and in a bowl mix together the baking powder and the flour. **6)** Combine together alternating them the flour and yoghurt with the egg-butter mixture. Stir and mix until it's creamy. **7)** Prepare a springform pan with baking paper and add the mixture. **8)** Garnish the batter with the berries and press them a bit into the batter. Bake them for approx. 60 minutes, low a bit the heat as 45 minutes have passed. Test the cake with a toothpick. Serve.

Nutrition Facts:

Cal. 920 **Carbs:** 79 g **Fat:** 57 g Sat.Fat 34 g Cholest. 410 mg
Protein 20.3 g Diet. Fiber 5.4 g Mon.Fat 16.5 g Sodium 420 mg
 Tot. Sugars 12 g Poly.Fat 3 g Salt -

272) *Berries tostadas* 👤 4 ⏰ 15 Min.

Ingredients:

4 Whole grain tortillas

2 tbsp. Rice oil

100 g. Ricotta

1 Lemon

100 g Strawberries

2 Apples

100 g. Mulberries

Instructions:

1) First of all, preheat the oven to 360 °F (180 °C). Brush the tortillas with oil and bake them 5 minutes on both sides. **2)** Mix together the ricotta with the lemon juice. **3)** Preprare the fruits. Peel the apples and slice them. Same thing with the strawberries, remove the stems and cut them into pieces. **4)** Spread the tortillas with the ricotta cream and top with berries.

Nutrition Facts:

Cal. 780 **Carbs:** 86 g **Fat:** 40 g Sat.Fat 9 g Cholest. 4 mg
Protein 19 g Diet. Fiber 16.4 g Mon.Fat 8.2 g Sodium 115 mg
 Tot. Sugars 15.3 g Poly.Fat 15.8 g Salt -

273) *Berry sherbet* 👤 4 ⏰ 5 Hours

Ingredients:

250 g. Strawberries

100 g. Raspberry

150 ml. Water

1 tbsp. Agave nectar

2 Lemons

Mint (fresh, to taste)

Instructions:

1) Firstly, prepare the fruits. Remove the leaves and stems from the strawberries and raspberries. **2)** Secondly, take a blender, add the water, agave, lemon juice and berries and purée all the ingredients until it's creamy. **3)** Take fill a form with the berries cream and place in the fridge for at least 5 hours. Serve.

Nutrition Facts:

Cal. 200	**Carbs**: 36 g	**Fat**: 1.3 g	Sat.Fat -	Cholest. -
Protein 3.2 g	Diet. Fiber 7 g	Mon.Fat 0.2 g	Sodium 5 mg
	Tot. Sugars 34.2 g	Poly.Fat 1 g	Salt -

༄༅

274) *Strawberries pie* 👤 4 ⏰ 1 Hour

Ingredients:

50 g. Rye flour

1 Egg

3 g. Baking powder

130 g. Strawberries

8 g. Clear glaze

60 g. Greek yoghurt

Instructions:

1) First of all, preheat the oven to 360 °F (180 °C). **2)** Secondly, beat the egg whites until stiff. **3)** Use a hand blender and mix together the yolks, flour, baking powder and greek yoghurt until the the mixture is smooth. **4)** Take a springform pan, fold th egg whites into the batter and pour into the form. **5)** Place in the oven and bake for 20 minutes. **6)** Prepare the strawberries and cut them into pieces. As the cake has cooled garnish with the berries and prepare the glaze following the package instructions. **7)** Spread the glaze over the cake and let in the fridge for at least 30 minutes. Serve.

Nutrition Facts:

Cal. 345	**Carbs**: 50 g	**Fat**: 7.3 g	Sat.Fat 2 g	Cholest. 280 mg
Protein 14 g	Diet. Fiber 5 g	Mon.Fat 3 g	Sodium 400 mg
	Tot. Sugars 15 g	Poly.Fat 2.3 g	Salt -

275) *French brioche*

👤 4   ⏰ 2,5 Hours

Ingredients:

- 80 ml. Milk
- 60 g. Ricotta
- 20 g. Fresh yeast
- 200 g. Whole grain flour
- ½ tbsp. Erythritol
- 25 g. Butter
- 10 g. Egg yolk

Instructions:

1) First of all, set aside 3 tbsp. of milk and mix the remaining milk with ricotta and yeast. **2)** Combine the yeast mixture with the egg, erythritol, flour and mix into a smooth dough. **3)** Cut the butter and add it to the bowl. Stir and mix well. **4)** Cover with a towel and let rise in a warm place for 1 hour. **5)** Knead the dough over a floured surface and create 4-6 balls. Cover and let rise in a warm place for 30 more min. **6)** Take a bread tin and cover with baking paper. **7)** Combine the yolk with the rest of the milk and preheat the oven to 400 °F (200 °C). **8)** Cover the dough with the milk mixture and bake for aprox. 40 minutes. **9)** Taste if the bread is ready with a toothpaste.

Nutrition Facts:

Cal. 1250	**Carbs**: 157 g	**Fat**: 42.8 g	Sat.Fat 25 g	Cholest. 310 mg
Protein 31 g	Diet. Fiber 7 g		Mon.Fat 13.2 g	Sodium 110 mg
	Tot. Sugars 14 g		Poly.Fat 3 g	Salt -

☼☼

276) *Salty French croissants*

👤 4   ⏰ 110 Min.

Ingredients:

- 150 g. Whole grain flour
- 15 g. Fresh yeast
- 30 ml. Lukewarm water
- 80 g. Plain yoghurt (low-fat)
- 40 g. Egg
- 1 tbsp. Coconut oil
- 1 tsp. Pumpkin seeds, chia seeds, poppy seeds
- Salt (to taste)

Instructions:

1) First of all, preheat the oven to 395 °F (200 °C). Take two bowls. One large for the flour and one smaller to combine the water with the yeast to dissolve. **2)** Mix the flour and yeast to dissolve and mix very well. **3)** Add the yoghurt, olive oil, egg and salt and knead into a smooth dough. **4)** Cover the dough and let rise in a warm place for 50 minutes. **5)** Then knead again the dough and split into two parts. Roll them onto a floured surface. **6)** Cut them into 8 wedges and from the wider start to roll each wedge up. **7)** Prepare a baking sheet and place them onto it. Leave enough space between the croissants. **8)** Beat the egg and brush the croissants with it. **9)** Sprinkle the seeds over them and bake. Serve.

Nutrition Facts:

Cal. 735	**Carbs**: 100 g	**Fat**: 21 g	Sat.Fat 4 g	Cholest. 145 mg
Protein 30 g	Diet. Fiber 14 g		Mon.Fat 10 g	Sodium 590 mg
	Tot. Sugars 10 g		Poly.Fat 4.3 g	Salt 2 g

277) *Choco mousse* 👤 4   ⏰ 80 Min.

Ingredients:

170 g. Vegan Chocolate

2 tbsp. Honey

500 g. Chickpeas (in water canned)

Instructions:

1) First fo all, melt the chocolate in a water bath. Add the honey and set aside to cool down. 2) Drain and rinse the chickpeas but keep the aquafaba (their liquid) and beat it until its foamy. 3) Place the chickpeas in the fridge to use another time. 4) Combine the foamy liquid of the chickpeas with the choco mixture and let it rest in the fridge for 70 minutes at least. 5) Serve.

Nutrition Facts:

Cal. 1650	**Carbs**: 179.9 g	**Fat**: 67.8 g	Sat.Fat 37 g	Cholest. -
Protein 42 g	Diet. Fiber 23.6 g		Mon.Fat -	Sodium 1278 mg
	Tot. Sugars 99 g		Poly.Fat 7.6 g	Salt 2.4 g

---

278) *Dipped pineapple with ricotta* 👤 4   ⏰ 15 Min.

Ingredients:

1 Pineapple

150 g. Ricotta

200 g. Plain yoghurt (low-fat)

3 tbsp. Olive oil

100 g. Walnuts (crushed)

Instructions:

1) First of all, peel and cut into small cubes the pineapple. 2) Mix the ricotta with the yoghurt and mix well. 3) Take a pan, heat a bit of the olive oil and warm the pineapple slices until they're almost light brown. (Or you can eat them fresh) 4) Take a plate and put the yoghurt in the middle and serve with the pineapple slices.

Nutrition Facts:

Cal. 1245	**Carbs**: 89 g	**Fat**: 100 g	Sat.Fat 31.3 g	Cholest. 34 mg
Protein 52 g	Diet. Fiber 13 g		Mon.Fat 54.8 g	Sodium 122 mg
	Tot. Sugars 89 g		Poly.Fat 7.9 g	Salt -

279) *Easy dipped apples*

👤 4　　⏰ 5 Min.

Ingredients:

160 g. Vanilla yoghurt (unsweetened)

2 tbsp. Honey

3 Apples

1 Lemon

Instructions:

1) First of all, peel and slice the apples. **2)** Combine the yoghurt with the honey. **3)** Take a bowl and put the yoghurt mixture in the middle. Place the apple slices all around the bowl. Serve.

Nutrition Facts:

Cal. 760	**Carbs**: 83.4 g　**Fat**: 40 g	Sat.Fat 14 g	Cholest. 48 mg
Protein 18 g	Diet. Fiber 12 g	Mon.Fat 16.8 g	Sodium 80 mg
	Tot. Sugars 77 g	Poly.Fat 7.9 g	Salt -

☙☗

280) *Quick blackberry smoothie*

👤 4　　⏰ 5 Min.

Ingredients:

650 g. Blackberries

250 ml. Vanilla milk

400 g. Vanilla yoghurt

Agave nectar, coconut flakes (to taste)

Instructions:

1) Take a big bowl and mix together the blackberries, yoghurt and the vanilla milk. Blend them with a mixer until it's smooth. **2)** Add the agave nectar and mix well. **3)** Sprinkle the coconut flakes on top of the smoothie and serve.

Nutrition Facts:

Cal. 980	**Carbs**: 78 g　**Fat**: 18.3 g	Sat.Fat 12.4 g	Cholest. 25 mg
Protein 130 g	Diet. Fiber 27.4 g	Mon.Fat 4.5 g	Sodium 650 mg
	Tot. Sugars 87 g	Poly.Fat 2.3 g	Salt 1.3 g

281) *Caribbean skewers* 👤 4   ⏰ 15 Min.

Ingredients:

- 1 Mango
- 1 Papaya
- 4 Kiwi
- 2 Bananas
- 20 Grapes
- Skewers

Instructions:

1) In this Caribbean version you have to peel, cut and slice the mango, papaya, bananas and kiwi. 2) Prepare the skewers and add the fruit pieces as you prefer. 3) You should be able to to at least 8-10 skewers. *If you want more duplicate the quantities.* 4) Serve.

Nutrition Facts:

Cal. 320	**Carbs**: 61.3 g	**Fat**: 2 g	Sat.Fat 0.4 g	Cholest. -
Protein 4.6 g	Diet. Fiber 13.2 g		Mon.Fat 0.5 g	Sodium 10 mg
	Tot. Sugars 61.3 g		Poly.Fat 0.9 g	Salt -

☼☽

282) *Mixed fruits skewers* 👤 4   ⏰ 15 Min.

Ingredients:

- 350 g. Melon
- 1 Banana
- 20 Cranberries / Blueberries (pick your favourite)
- Skewers

(!!! You can use a cookie cutter to give the fruits a particular form)

Instructions:

1) Firstly, prepare the melon. Remove the seeds and cut the pulp into slabs. 2) Peel and slice the banana too. 3) Drizzle the fruits with the lemon juice. 4) Alternate the fruit pieces to fill the skewers and serve.

Nutrition Facts:

Cal. 340	**Carbs**: 71 g	**Fat**: 1 g	Sat.Fat 0.4 g	Cholest. -
Protein 4.3 g	Diet. Fiber 6.3 g		Mon.Fat -	Sodium 5 mg
	Tot. Sugars 65 g		Poly.Fat 0.6 g	Salt -

283) *Choco-dipped apples* 👤 4 ⏰ 40 Min.

Ingredients:

80 g. Chocolate

2 Apples

Instructions:

1) First of all, bring a pot of water to boil. Use a bowl to place in the pot and melt the chocolate in it. **2)** Secondly, peel the apples and slice them. **3)** As the chocolate is melted, dunk one side of each apple slice into the chocolate. Let dry. Serve.

Nutrition Facts:

Cal. 610	**Carbs**: 77.3 g **Fat**: 24 g	Sat.Fat 13.5 g	Cholest. -
Protein 8.6 g	Diet. Fiber 14.2 g	Mon.Fat 5.4 g	Sodium 78 mg
	Tot. Sugars 73.5 g	Poly.Fat 1 g	Salt -

ఌఆ

284) *Summer popsicles* 👤 4 ⏰ 4 Hours

Ingredients:

130 g. Strawberries

180 g. Watermelon

½ Lemon

Instructions:

1) Simple staps for this tasteful recipe. First of all, cut the watermelon into big pieces. **2)** Squeeze the lemon and take a bowl to blend together strawberries, lemon juice and watermelon. **3)** Fill at least 8 popsicle molds withe the juice and place in the freezer for 4 hours. Serve.

Nutrition Facts:

Cal. 130	**Carbs**: 20 g **Fat**: 1.4 g	Sat.Fat -	Cholest. -
Protein 2 g	Diet. Fiber 3.1 g	Mon.Fat -	Sodium 4 mg
	Tot. Sugars 22 g	Poly.Fat 0.8 g	Salt -

285) *Apple-cinnamon crumble*   👤 4   ⏰ 50 Min.

Ingredients:

5 Apples

100 g. Rolled oats

40 g. Walnuts (crushed)

2 tbsp. Olive oil

100 ml. Apple juice

Dark chocolate (scales), erythritol, cinnamon (to taste)

Instructions:

1) First of all, preheat the oven to 320 °F (180 °C). Secondly, peel the apples and cut them into pieces. **2)** Take a pot and combine the apples with the apple juice and half of the cinnamon. Simmer on medium heat for more or less 15 minute. **3)** Take a food blender and finely grind the walnuts and oats. **4)** Add the chocolate scales, olive oil and a bit of cinnamon. Add erythritol to taste. Mix well. **5)** Remove the apple slices from the heat and place them in a casserole. Drain the remaining juice. **6)** Now, crumble the oat mixture over the apples and bake for 30 minutes. Serve.

Nutrition Facts:

Cal. 1480 **Carbs**: 176 g **Fat**: 72 g Sat.Fat 41.2 g Cholest. -
Protein 23.4 g Diet. Fiber 30 g   Mon.Fat 7.3 g   Sodium 20 mg
            Tot. Sugars 107 g   Poly.Fat 20 g   Salt   -

꧁꧂

286) *Oatmeal little sweets*   👤 4   ⏰ 15 Min.

Ingredients:

15 g. Rolled oats

10 g. Peanuts

50 g. Dates

5 g. Vegetable butter (or peanut butter)

½ tsp. Olive oil

Instructions:

1) First of all, take a food processor and add the oat flakes and the butter you prefer. Mix everything into flour. **2)** Wash and cut the dates into small pieces, remove the pit. **3)** Add the dates into the food processor with some water and blend everything into a creamy consistency. **4)** Mix together the date mixture with the butter and olive oil. Blend well togheter. **5)** Add the other dry ingredients and mix them well together until the dough is smooth. **6)** Moisture your hand a little bit and create little balls. **7)** If you prefer, put them in the fridge or serve immediately.

Nutrition Facts:

Cal. 250   **Carbs**: 33 g   **Fat**: 8.7 g Sat.Fat 2.7 g Cholest. -
Protein 6 g Diet. Fiber 6 g   Mon.Fat 3.6 g Sodium 4 mg
            Tot. Sugars 26.7 g   Poly.Fat 2.4 g Salt   -

287) *Orange sauce pancakes* 👤 4 ⏰ 15 Min.

Ingredients:

250 g. Yoghurt (low-fat, unsweetened)

5 tsp. Olive oil + 40 g. Cashew butter

4 Eggs + 2 ripe Bananas

2 Oranges (or 4 tangerines)

5 tsp. Agave nectar (or erythritol)

100 g. Quick cooking rolling oats

Cinnamon (to taste)

Instructions:

1) First of all, take a bowl and peel the bananas, mash them with a fork. Add the oat flakes, yoghurt, and the eggs and mix very well together. **2)** Take a pan and heat a bit of olive oil. Add a spoon of the mixture and bake the pancakes on both sides until golden-brown. **3)** Create the cashew sauce: squeeze the oranges (or the tangerines) and add the juice in a bowl. **4)** Add the cashew butter, agave nectar and (if you like it) the cinnamon. Heat the sauce and stir well until it's creamy. **5)** Pour the sauce over the pancakes and serve.

Nutrition Facts:

Cal. 1980	**Carbs**: 237 g	**Fat**: 83.5 g	Sat.Fat 39.5 g	Cholest. 1100 mg
Protein 68.5 g	Diet. Fiber 24 g		Mon.Fat 26.6 g	Sodium 560 mg
	Tot. Sugars 163 g		Poly.Fat 9 g	Salt 1 g

༺༻

288) *Healthy pink ice cream* 👤 4 ⏰ 5 Min.

Ingredients:

250 g. Ricotta

1 Lemon

250 g. Strawberries

Agave nectar or honey (to taste)

(Try different versions with different fruit !)

Instructions:

1) First of all, take a hand blender and purée together the strawberries (clean and cut them into small pieces) and the ricotta. Blend well until the mixture is creamy. **2)** Squeeze the lemon and add the juice to the mixture. Mix well. **3)** Add the sweetener too and mix well. **4)** Place in the freezer and serve.

Nutrition Facts:

Cal. 568	**Carbs**: 14 g	**Fat**: 40 g	Sat.Fat 24 g	Cholest. 100 mg
Protein 27.4 g	Diet. Fiber 12.3 g		Mon.Fat 11.2 g	Sodium 230 mg
	Tot. Sugars 14 g		Poly.Fat 2.5 g	Salt -

289) *Healthy lemon cake* 👤 4   ⏰ 30 Min.

Ingredients:

3 g. Baking powder

30 ml. Lemon juice

100 ml. Water

2 g. Salt

100 g. Whole grain flour

2 tbsp. Olive oil

Erythritol or agave nectar (to taste)

Instructions:

1) First of all, preheat th eoven to 350 °F (180 °C). **2)** Secondly, take a bowl and whisk together the whole grain flour, baking powder, a bit of salt and the erythritol (or other sweetener you like). Blend well. **3)** Now, squeeze the lemon and add the juice, olive oil and water and stir very well until it turns creamy. **4)** Take a springform pan and grease it a little bit with oil. Add the batter. **5)** Bake for more or less 20 minutes. Serve.

Nutrition Facts:

Cal. 450	**Carbs**: 60 g	**Fat**: 16.4 g	Sat.Fat 12.2 g	Cholest. -
Protein 12 g	Diet. Fiber 10 g		Mon.Fat -	Sodium 300 mg
	Tot. Sugars 1 g		Poly.Fat 1 g	Salt 2 g.

✿

290) *Coconut little sweets* 👤 4   ⏰ 10 Min.

Ingredients:

20 g. Peanut butter

6 g. Dark chocolate (scale)

15 g. Cocoa powder (unsweetened)

10 g. Coconut flakes

Agave nectar (to taste)

Instructions:

1) First of all, take a food processor and put all the ingredients together except the coconut flakes. Purée the ingredients until you have a creamy mixture. **2)** From that, create small little balls. **3)** Roll them into the coconut flakes. **4)** Put them in the fridge and serve.

Nutrition Facts:

Cal. 225	**Carbs**: 6.3 g	**Fat**: 17.4 g	Sat.Fat 8.2 g	Cholest. -
Protein 8.3 g	Diet. Fiber 5.8 g		Mon.Fat 6.2 g	Sodium 55 mg
	Tot. Sugars 2.6 g		Poly.Fat 2.4 g	Salt -

291) *Coco-choco cupcakes*

👤 4   ⏰ 70 Min.

Ingredients:

35 ml. Coconut oil

70 g. Ricotta

70 g. Coconut flakes

20 g. Dark cocoa powder

Erythritol (to taste)

Instructions:

1) First of all, heat and mix 20 ml of oil with the ricotta and sweetener until the oil is liquid. Stir frequently. **2)** Now, add the flakes and keep on stirring. **3)** Take a muffin tin and grease with the coconut oil. With a spoon press the mixture on the bottom of the molds. **4)** In a second pot heat the remaining oil, add the cocoa powder and your favourite sweetener and stir until the oil dissolve. **5)** Brush this second mixture on the top of the cupcakes. **6)** Put the tin in the fridge for 1 hour until the chocolate is thick. Serve.

Nutrition Facts:

Cal. 890   **Carbs**: 16.5 g   **Fat**: 88.1 g   Sat.Fat 79 g   Cholest. -
Protein 7.5 g   Diet. Fiber 14.5 g   Mon.Fat 3.8 g   Sodium 60 mg
            Tot. Sugars 13.2 g   Poly.Fat -   Salt   -

೫೦೦೩

292) *Little blue cake*

👤 4   ⏰ 3.4 Hours

Ingredients:

70 g. Rolled oats

150 g. Dates (pitted)

130 g. Vegetable butter

120 ml. Oat milk (unsweetened)

50 g. Blueberries (or other berries, frozen)

Instructions:

1) First of all, cut the dates into small pieces and combine half of them with the rolled oats. Take a hand blender and purèe. **2)** Fill the molds of a muffin form, but stop before the top. **3)** Press well down and put in the freezer for more or less 30 minutes. **4)** Now, combine the other dates with the butter and with a blender mix until it's creamy. **5)** Now, add this second mixture to top the muffin molds and garnish with the berries. **6)** Put in the freezer for 3 more hours (better overnight). **7)** Remove from the freezer approx. 20 minutes before serving, so that they thaw a little.

Nutrition Facts:

Cal. 1379   **Carbs**: 158 g   **Fat**: 70 g   Sat.Fat 15 g   Cholest. -
Protein 35 g   Diet. Fiber 23 g   Mon.Fat 43.4 g   Sodium 28 mg
              Tot. Sugars 120 g   Poly.Fat 7.4 g   Salt   -

293) *Fresh roll-ups*

👤 4   ⏰ 6 Hours

Ingredients:

130 g. Blueberries (or other berries)

½ tbsp. Lemon juice

½ tbsp. Honey (organic)

Instructions:

1) First of all, preheat the oven to 140 °F (60 °C). **2)** Secondly, prepare the berries. In this case we use the blueberries so take a hand blender add the fruits, the lemon juice and honey and blend well. **3)** Prepare a baking sheet with the baking paper and spread a thin layer of the ourée. **4)** Bake in the oven for 5-6 hours. **5)** Once cooked, make sure the roll ups don't stick together by cutting the baking paper into strips and roll them up. Serve.

Nutrition Facts:

Cal. 55	**Carbs**: 10 g	**Fat**: 0.5 g	Sat.Fat -	Cholest. -
Protein 1.4 g	Diet. Fiber 2.5 g		Mon.Fat -	Sodium -
	Tot. Sugars 9 g		Poly.Fat -	Salt -

---

294) *Easy chip cookies*

👤 4   ⏰ 25 Min.

Ingredients:

10 g. Dark chocolate

20 g. Vegetable batter

10 g. Erythritol

10 g. Egg

30 g. Rice flour

0.5 g. Baking powder

Instructions:

1) First of all, preheat the oven to 360 °F (180 °C). **2)** Secondly, cut the dark chocolate into small pieces. **3)** Take a pot and melt the butter. Add the erythritol and blend well with the hand blender. **4)** Now, add the egg and continue to blend. **5)** Add the flour, chocolate pieces and baking powder. Blend very well using the mixer. **6)** Take a baking sheet and place small spoon-size dough on the sheet. **7)** Bake for more or less 10 minutes. Serve.

Nutrition Facts:

Cal. 1489	**Carbs**: 20 g	**Fat**: 119 g	Sat.Fat 42.3 g	Cholest. 260 mg
Protein 82.2 g	Diet. Fiber 9.2 g		Mon.Fat 38.1 g	Sodium 1769 mg
	Tot. Sugars 29.2 g		Poly.Fat 25 g	Salt 4.2 g

295) *Cranberry muffins* 👤 4   ⏰ 20 Min.

Ingredients:

115 g. Rolled oats

½ tsp. Baking powder

160 ml. Oat milk

40 g. Cranberrie (dried)

20 g. Walnuts (crushed)

Cinnamon, Agave nectar (to taste)

Instructions:

1) Firstly, preheat the oven to 375 °F (190 °C). **2)** Secondly, take a large bowl and combine all the ingredients together except the walnuts. **3)** Take the muffin molds and fill them with the mixture, top them with the walnuts and cook them for approx. 15-18 minutes until they turn golden -brown and serve.

Nutrition Facts:

Cal. 658	**Carbs**: 97 g	**Fat**: 22 g	Sat.Fat 2.6 g	Cholest. -
Protein 19 g	Diet. Fiber 14 g		Mon.Fat 5 g	Sodium 207 mg
	Tot. Sugars 26.4 g		Poly.Fat 11.7 g	Salt -

꧁꧂

296) *Little cheesecake* 👤 4   ⏰ 90 Min.

Ingredients:

1 ½ tbsp. Butter

40 g. Ground almond

150 g. Ricotta

1 Egg

Agave nectar, blueberries (to taste)

Instructions:

1) First of all, preheat the oven to 360 °F (180 °C). **2)** Take a pot and melt the butter using a spoon. After that, take a bowl and combine the butter with the ground almonds. **3)** Use a silicone muffin pan and pour into each well a spoon of the batter. **4)** Cook it for approx. 5 minutes until the crust is golden-brown. **5)** Blend the ricotta with a hand mixer until creamy and add the egg and agave nectar (or other sweetener). Mix very well. **6)** Use this mixture to spread it over the baked crusts and bake for more or less 20 minutes. **7)** Store the sweets in the fridge, sprinkle with a few blueberries and serve.

Nutrition Facts:

Cal. 1000	**Carbs**: 9.2 g	**Fat**: 101 g	Sat.Fat 53 g	Cholest. 534 mg
Protein 39 g	Diet. Fiber 5 g		Mon.Fat 35 g	Sodium 680 mg
	Tot. Sugars 8 g		Poly.Fat 7.3 g	Salt 1 g

297) *Classic choco berries*

👤 4   ⏰ 30 Min.

Ingredients:

350 g. Strawberries

170 g. Dark chocolate

20 g. Walnuts

Instructions:

1) First of all, wash the strawberries and let them dry. **2)** Secondly, finely chop the chocolate and let it melt in a water bath. (*Dark chocolate is healthier but you can try different versions!*) **3)** Soak the strawberries in the chocolate and finely chop the walnuts. **4)** Sprinkle the walnuts on top of the strawberries and let them dry.

Nutrition Facts:

Cal. 980	**Carbs**: 51.7 g	**Fat**: 62 g	Sat.Fat 33 g	Cholest. 2 mg
Protein 16.7 g	Diet. Fiber 23.1 g		Mon.Fat 24 g	Sodium 165 mg
	Tot. Sugars 93.7 g		Poly.Fat 2.6 g	Salt -

☙☓

298) *Berries summer shortcake*

👤 4   ⏰ 30 Min.

Ingredients:

150 g. Vanilla yoghurt (unsweetened)

2 tbsp. Olive oil, agave nectar

½ tsp. Vanilla extract

½ tsp. Baking powder

70 ml. Vanilla milk (unsweetened)

140 g. Whole flour

140 g. Blackberries

Instructions:

1) First of all, preheat the oven to 350 °F (175 °C). Secondly, prepare an 8-inch round pan with baking paper. **2)** Take a bowl and combine together the agave nectar, milk, whisked eggs, vanilla extract and the olive oil. Blend well together. **3)** Take a second bowl and stir together the flour and baking powder. **4)** Combine the two bowl and form a smooth batter. **5)** Put the batter into a pan and bake for approx. 20 minutes. (*!!! It's ready when the cake starts to brown on top and it's firm*). **6)** In the meantime prepare the berries. Wash and dry the blackberries. **7)** Remove the cake from the pan only **after** that it's competely cooled. **8)** Garnish with the yoghurt on top and sprinkle the blackberries.

Nutrition Facts:

Cal. 980	**Carbs**: 39 g	**Fat**: 69 g	Sat.Fat 38.5 g	Cholest. 340 mg
Protein 69 g	Diet. Fiber 5.7 g		Mon.Fat 8 g	Sodium 650 mg
	Tot. Sugars 22 g		Poly.Fat 5.8 g	Salt -

299) *Berries chia pudding*

👤 4   ⏰ 3,5 hours

Ingredients:

- 250 ml. Oat milk
- 800 g. Vanilla yoghurt (low-fat, unsweetened)
- 100 g. Chia seeds
- 250 g. Raspberries (frozen)
- 250 g. Blackberries
- 4 tbsp. Agave nectar

Instructions:

1) First of all, take a large jar and add the milk and yoghurt. Add the chia seeds and mix well. **2)** Cover and let cool in the fridge for at least 3 hours, better if you leave them overnight. **3)** Take a pan and add the raspberries. Heat them over medium heat until they completely thawed. Mash and cook them for approx. 10 minutes until they thicken. Remove from the heat and let cool down. **4)** Stir the chia pudding and start to compose the treat. Add a layer on the bottom of a small glass, add a layer of the raspberry mixture and again, a pudding layer. **5)** Sprinkle the blackberries on top and serve.

Nutrition Facts:

Cal. 1769   **Carbs**: 148.5 g   **Fat**: 84.7 g   Sat.Fat 35.6 g   Cholest. -
Protein 32 g   Diet. Fiber 64.3 g   Mon.Fat 3.6 g   Sodium 250 mg
              Tot. Sugars 74.6 g   Poly.Fat 23.4 g Salt -

---

300) *Red skewers with choco drizzle*

👤 4   ⏰ 15 Min.

Ingredients:

- 120 g. Blueberries
- 120 g. Blackberries
- 150 g. Raspberries
- 150 g. Strawberries
- 10 (or more) Skewers
- 80 g. Dark chocolate

Instructions:

1) First of all, prepare the fruits and slice the strawberries in big pieces. **2)** Use a baking paper to lay the skewers and thread the fruits. **3)** Melt the chocolate in a water bath and stir until it's completely smooth. **4)** Drizzle the chocolate over the skewers and let cool in the fridge. Serve.

Nutrition Facts:

Cal. 580   **Carbs**: 56 g   **Fat**: 31.1 g   Sat.Fat 17 g   Cholest. -
Protein 5.3 g Diet. Fiber 15.3 g   Mon.Fat -   Sodium 4 mg
              Tot. Sugars 47.2 g   Poly.Fat -   Salt -

4-Weeks-Meal-Plan

1 Week

	Breakfast	Lunch	Dinner
Monday	n.1 Banana oat muffins	n.73 Stuffed peppers	n.219 Asian quinoa salad
Tuesday	n.18 Melon salad with berries	n.125 Asian spicy chicken	n.228 Salmon burger
Wednesday	n.22 Granola with cranberries	n.161 Lemon pasta	n.237 Flatbread
Thursday	n.50 Caramel overnight oats	n.102 Greens chicken quinoa	n.252 Kale tortillas
Friday	n.72 Ginger muffins	n.172 Greens quick fritters	n.245 Lemon cream
Saturday	n.71 Tumeric latte with honey	n.88 Chicken veggie mix	n.255 Eggplant-shrimps skewers
Sunday	n.30 Oatmeal blackberry waffle	n.82 Tacos mix	n.216 Cilantro -shrimps rice

2 Week

	Breakfast	Lunch	Dinner
Monday	n.5 Dark chocolate cookies	n.86 Cauliflower rice with salmon	n.183 Fresh shrimps - cuttlefish soup
Tuesday	n.21 Raisins couscous	n.99 Vegetable chili	n.192 Cheesy potato soup
Wednesday	n.45 Tomato bread	n.108 Spinach pizza	n.196 Julienne zucchini soup
Thursday	n.19 Fruit tortillas	n.115 Fish & chips with greens	n.202 Spanish gazpacho
Friday	n.66 Kale smoothie	n.165 Thyme pasta with walnuts	n.206 Healthy tostones
Saturday	n.54 Strawberry smoothie	n.174 Italian classic rice	n.213 Noodle soup with kale
Sunday	n.44 Sourdough Bread	n.119 Melon-chicken salad	n.217 Thai curry chicken

3 Week

	Breakfast	Lunch	Dinner
Monday	n.9 Blackberries pancakes	n.103 Crispy nuggets with greens	n.243 Creamy dip
Tuesday	n.41 Rice pudding	n.112 Rice with beets	n.239 Chicken quesadillas
Wednesday	n.57 Coconut shake	n.147 Creamy mushrooms	n.213 Noodle soup with kale
Thursday	n.34 Yoghurt and apricots pancakes	n.122 Lentil Sloppy Joe	n.226 Shepherd's Pie
Friday	n.65 Summer smoothie	n.129 Black beans burger	n.222 Vegan avocado sushi
Saturday	n.62 Dates smoothie	n.159 Spinach quesadilla	n.184 Green broccoli pureed soup
Sunday	n.35 Pumpkin pancakes	n.128 Colorful Thanksgiving	n.195 Peppers creamy soup

4 Week

	Breakfast	Lunch	Dinner
Monday	n.13 Berries cake	n.118 Cod salad	n.214 Gado-gado Asian salad
Tuesday	n.48 Gluten-free buns	n.120 Roasted greens risotto	n.258 Grilled chicken & green sauce
Wednesday	n.56 Yellow smoothie	n.150 Leek with eggplants	n.203 Fresh cucumber finger food
Thursday	n.50 Caramel overnight oats	n.134 Rye pasta with spinach	n.216 Cilantro-shrimps rice
Friday	n.63 Peach smoothie	n.152 Honey walnut shrimps mix	n.176 Mediterranean red soup
Saturday	n.68 Sweet potatoes fries	n.123 Turmeric chicken risotto	n.227 Healthy burger plate
Sunday	n.40 Vanilla soufflé	n.131 Orange salad	n.232 Mixed jalapeño toasts

References

Photo page 33: https://pixabay.com/it/photos/lamponi-fresco-ciotola-portafrutta-2023404/ Creative Common

Photo page 70: https://pxhere.com/en/photo/1537931 Creative Common

Photo page 122: https://www.maxpixel.net/Beer-Celebration-Cheese-Delicious-Dinner-Dining-2178693 Creative Common

Printed in Great Britain
by Amazon